DOUBLE DOLL

Turning Myself Upside Down

Sharleen Daugherty

abbott press®
A DIVISION OF WRITER'S DIGEST

Abbott Press books may be ordered through booksellers or by contacting:

Abbott Press
1663 Liberty Drive
Bloomington, IN 47403
www.abbottpress.com
Phone: 1-866-697-5310

ISBN: 978-1-4582-1480-5 (sc)
ISBN: 978-1-4582-1481-2 (hc)
ISBN: 978-1-4582-1482-9 (e)

Library of Congress Control Number: 2014904370

Printed in the United States of America.

Abbott Press rev. date: 03/14/2014

Dedicated

To the memory of the women known in this book as Anna Mae Hoskie and Grace Yazzie

Contents

PART THREE

Foreword

Instead of asking her Navajo subjects to shape-shift to conform to preconceived Anglo ideas about them, Sharleen Daugherty shape-shifts herself like the double doll of her childhood, becoming a person of entirely rehabilitated values with their mediation. Immersing herself in Navajo culture, Daugherty learns from them with humility, and feels through their dilemmas with compassion. She is trustworthy and respectful, a reliable guide to a world outside the American mainstream, as well as a fine story-catcher. This book represents her lifework, for which I have great respect.

—Diana Hume George,
Author of *The Lonely Other: A Woman Watching America*

Acknowledgments

Over the years my story has taken many forms before it became the book you hold in your hand. I come from a mathematics and computer background; I never planned to be a writer. And then, through circumstances that you will read about, my life was changed.

I owe thanks to many people who encouraged me along the way. My husband, Len, has supported me in every step as I made this life-changing transition. Michael Thunder, a writer's coach and friend from Durango, Colorado, was the first person to promote my ideas and guide me in this new endeavor. Michael is the one who knew when I was merely glossing over emotional trauma and needed to dig deeper. Under his tutelage, I was emboldened to enroll in Goucher College's Master of Fine Arts in Creative Nonfiction Writing program. During my MFA studies, I was fortunate to be mentored by Philip Gerard, Diana Hume George and Lisa Knopp. Each brought with them the experience and guidance I needed to continue in my path as an author. The Summer Writer's Workshop in Taos, New Mexico was an enriching experience. Many thanks go to Rob Wilder, facilitator for a Master Class on Memoir, and the other participants in our small group: Kathy Berg, Frances Burke, Julie Ort, Herb Silverman, and Annie Ward. Their contributions to my final manuscript were significant.

During these writing experiences my longtime friends, Ann Crouch and Carol Schmudde, were always there and ready to help correct my mathematician's punctuation and grammar. Most recently, my thanks go to Marcia Rosen, Literary Agent and Publicist extraordinaire, and Terry Lucas. Marcia keeps my spirits, motivation and expectations in check, while Terry does the final content-copy editing.

But most of all, my thanks go to all the beautiful Navajo men and women who changed my life and gave me a story to tell.

Introduction

The title, ***Double Doll: Turning Myself Upside Down***, comes from a pivotal experience in my life. I was only eight-years-old when I received a rag doll with a Navajo face and body on one end, an Anglo body on the other. The doll became a symbol for my journey into the world of the Navajo and the manifestation of a childhood prayer, *Please God, turn me upside down and make me an Indian.*

My story is divided into three parts. The first two chronicle the early years that led to a life-changing event and the formation of a new business with a mission to "Promote American Arts through the Sale of Amish Quilts and Navajo Weavings." The last section tells of a learning time for me—lifelong customs and habits had to be replaced with the mores of a new culture. I share with you experiences that tested and, in some cases, shattered the core belief systems that had been my foundation for more than fifty years. Through intimate relationships built among the Navajo, I was forced to examine my own "world order" only to find those guiding principles were flawed. My journey started on the Navajo Reservation at the age of eight. Along the way my life was turned upside-down multiple times.

She Faces Her Enemy: The Journey Continues, the second book in the trilogy follows the Durango Trading Company and two Navajo women as they travel to Germany for the Domotex International Trade Fair. The business story intertwines among my personal involvement with Crystal Redshirt, the woman who through a Navajo adoption ceremony became my niece. I not only had to face my own enemies, but was called upon to become an advocate for her.

The 3rd book in the trilogy, *Lives Turned Upside Down: The Journey Comes Full Circle* tells of my path as I followed a Navajo Medicine Man's prophecy to "Be the eyes and ears to keep us in touch with the rest of the world." My turned-upside-down life once again took a new direction.

In all three of these books many names have been changed to protect the identity of the characters. I invite you to come along on what has been, and continues to be, an extraordinary journey.

Sharleen Daugherty

Map of the Navajo Reservation

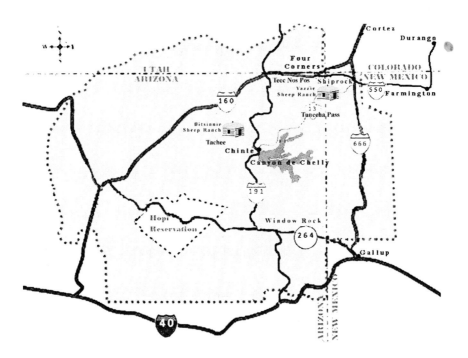

The Navajo (*Diné*) are the largest federally recognized tribe of the United States, with 300,048 enrolled tribal members. They have an independent governmental body, the Navajo Nation, which manages the Navajo Indian Reservation—territory that covers 27,425 square miles located in portions of northeastern Arizona, southeastern Utah, and northwestern New Mexico. The 2011 census shows the states with the largest Navajo populations to be Arizona with 140,263 and New Mexico with 108,306. Over three-quarters of the Navajo population reside in these states.

Alphabetical Listing Navajo Names & Roles

The Navajo Indians are a very private people; names and places have been changed to protect the identity of those who appear in these writings. This listing is intended to assist in identifying the roles of the primary Navajo characters that appear in the first book of the trilogy.

Jessie Begay – Weaving instructor at Crow Canyon from Teec Nos Pos

Bertha Benally – Weaver from Teec Nos Pos and daughter of Anna Mae Yazzie

Sonya Bitsinnie – Weaver from Tachee

Tyler Bitsinnie – Sonya's husband and Traditional Navajo Medicine Man

Anna Mae & Roy Hoskie – Parents of Bertha Benally, Lewis McGuire and Grace Yazzie from Red Valley

Lucy Joe – Weaver from Beclabito

Lewis McGuire – Biological father of Crystal Redshirt

Crystal Redshirt – Adopted daughter of Grace and Thomas Yazzie

Naalzheí & Little Eagle Redshirt – Sons of Crystal Redshirt

Lola Tsosie – Weaving instructor at Crow Canyon from Teec Nos Pos

Grace Yazzie – Weaver from Red Valley

PART ONE

New York City—1992

The shrill screech of a diving hawk jarred me from the dream-filled sleep of early morning. I was back on the Navajo reservation, and Nanabah was there. We ran through the canyon, climbed up to the cave and exchanged gifts. I could feel the cool breeze against my face and smell the smoke of burning sage. And then I became my double doll—a brown-faced girl on one end and white-faced on the other—held in the arms of grandmothers who spun me like a pinwheel: Indian ... Anglo ... Indian ... Anglo.

I searched for elusive images, but as I groped to turn off the alarm clock the scenes began to fade. The dream put me on edge; I felt unsettled and disoriented. I showered and dressed hurriedly—the dream soon forgotten. A quick glance at the phrase taped to my vanity mirror from Christopher Matthews' book <u>The Power Game</u>—*The key is to be a porcupine ... Have a reputation for being difficult*—reinforced the importance of everything being perfect for today's meeting. Clothes selected precisely in a Sunday night ritual lay waiting: a cream-colored raw silk suit, a burnt-orange blouse and brown lizard-skin shoes. The only decision was the scarf—swirls of green and tan paisley that perfectly complemented the ensemble. *Was it too much?*

Parking spaces at the train station were difficult to find, and the coffee vending machine took my dollar bill, giving nothing in return. I ran down

1

the platform, passed through the train's sliding doors, and collapsed into a seat. At precisely 6:13 AM the conductor called his last "All Aboard." As the train left the urban sprawl of Lancaster and snaked its way through the rolling hills of Pennsylvania farm country, I leaned my forehead against the window and watched the silhouette of a young Amish boy on a horse-drawn plow move slowly across the horizon. Behind him the rising sun streaked the sky crimson and gold.

"Pa-ooo-li." The conductor put an exaggerated drawl on the name of the Philadelphia mainline suburb. "Next station stop is Paoli." He moved through the car, stopping momentarily at my seat. "That's your cue, Missus."

Most of the conductors knew this was the point in the trip when I transformed from a suburban housewife/mother to a steel-armored consultant who could withstand the slings and arrows of New York City's corporate world. I owned half of a company that provided computer-consulting services for human resource management systems—a lucrative but competitive business that required a lot of travel and many hours of stress-inducing meetings. I loved the surge of power that came over me when a successful executive asked for my help; I loved that my business partner and I were females on a male-dominated playing field; and I loved that my company was in such demand that customers were willing to pay premium prices for our assistance.

Paoli was forty minutes into the three-plus hour trip, the place where I began to prepare for the day. I pulled a document from my briefcase, scanned through pages of a carefully crafted presentation, and then replayed in my mind the marketing proposal.

"Got a big one today, have you?" the conductor asked when he stopped a second time.

"Sure do. I've been after this one for months."

Typically my customers were Fortune 100 companies, but today I was pitching to get a contract for consulting services with the New York

Stock Exchange. Their prestigious name among the client list would be a real coup, and the account would be worth half-a-million dollars. It was a big contract; all my expertise would be required. Previous meetings confirmed that the financial world was more heavily steeped in male dominance than corporate America, but I was ready. I'd trained for this for a lifetime. I knew how to beat the men at their game.

The train pulled into New York City's Penn Station. Commuters checked their watches and started the daily routine of jockeying for better positions—closer to the exit. I gathered my laptop computer, briefcase, and an overnight bag with enough business suits for a five-day stay. It was rush hour, no chance for a taxi. My only recourse was to make the long trek to the subway through the underground passages.

"What's the hold-up?" A male voice hollered from behind. I struggled to get my baggage through the turnstile entrance.

"So where's your gallantry?" I shot back.

The Wall Street train arrived. I pushed my way into the crowded car, wrapped an arm around an aluminum pole in the center, hugged my shoulder bags, straddled my suitcase between my legs and crouched, then stretched, to see my stop through the train window. When the doors sprang open, crowds elbowed and shoved, sweeping me forward. Throngs of rushing people made their way to the escalator. Another train approached the platform and deposited hundreds more people to the already-crowded space. The body odors came in sickening waves followed by the dampness of my own sweat.

I fought my way to one of several pillars that stood in the middle of the long underground platform and leaned against it to gulp deep breaths of stagnant air. Ten years ago my doctor told me to get a good book on stress management and give up my job. At the time I was a single mother—there soon would be college tuition to pay, as well as my ongoing need to prove I could be financially independent of a man—so he scribbled out a prescription for blood pressure medication. Things got easier a few years later when I remarried, so I took the doctor's advice and bought a book. It suggested using images of a favorite place as a form of stress relief. I drew upon a special summer when I traveled the Navajo Reservation with my father. Remembering that time helped me feel connected to something soothing—as though an inexplicable thread had woven me into the tapestry of a people and a place.

I leaned against the platform pillar and tried to recall reservation images. The roar of the subway trains became a whistling wind that circled through steep canyon walls. *"Sharleen," it whispered, as it brushed against my cheek and engulfed me with the pungent aroma of burning sage. A brown-skinned girl timidly touched my hand, and I heard her giggle as she turned and ran down the trail that led into the canyon.*

"Are you okay, Lady?" The voice was abrupt. My eyes opened to the blue uniform of a security officer. The subway platform was almost empty.

It took a moment or so to bring myself back to reality. The images just past hadn't come from my conscious memory—they were straight out of my dream. "Fine," I said and glanced at my watch. "Thank you. I'm fine."

Outside the subway station sheets of blowing rain assaulted anyone who left the safety of the building. I sprinted into the street, thrust my hand in the air and shouted, "Taxi!" The rear wheels of a speeding cab drenched my feet with sprays of muddy water. I fought the push-button opener on my umbrella. "Damn piece of junk," I murmured. Being late to a meeting of this importance was not an option. Four blocks to go, and I had only ten minutes.

Dozens of umbrellas and dripping raincoats left the marble entryway of the Stock Exchange slippery and difficult to manage. My silk blouse clung wet against my chest, and cold water dripped from my hair down the back of my neck. There was no ladies' room in sight; I used a crumpled tissue from a pocket to wipe muddy water from my shoes and ankles.

My directions told me to go to the third floor and turn right. This led me to an imposing pair of dark mahogany-paneled doors. Many years in business taught me that my entry must be just right: not too timid, not too forceful. Another glance at my watch—fifty-eight minutes past nine. I took a deep breath and pushed open the door.

A young man sat alone at a massive polished-wood table surrounded with high-backed green leather chairs. He glanced up briefly and then returned to his calculator and stack of papers. The room was sedately elegant: a large Grandfather clock stood next to the mahogany doors; a hand-carved oriental credenza, complete with a silver coffee service, was against the long wall; and a large round tapestry—an intricate arrangement of arabesque designs in bold shades of red, gold, purple, blue and green—hung above the wooden chest.

I avoided the visitor chairs lined up against the wall and purposefully walked to the place at the oval table known to be "second in command." The seat at the head of the table, the one with its back to the windows, was saved for the vice president. Today the overcast sky would work to my benefit—on a sunny day, with the backlight, it would be impossible to detect anything more than a shadowy figure of the person who sat there. I learned long ago the key to effective marketing was a combination of good listening and being able to read the body language and facial expressions of your customer.

On the table, in front of each chair, I placed one color-printed and spiral-bound copy of my proposal. The men arrived in groups of two and three—young, late twenties, early thirties; I had at least twenty years on most of them. Some acknowledged my presence with a nod, most merely took a seat. I'd once overheard my salesman father tell a group of friends, *"Envision your customer stark naked, that's the key to my success."* The playing field leveled when I mentally stripped the men of their look-alike pin-striped suits, button-down shirts, and power-red ties.

Five minutes after the appointed hour there were only two empty seats, the vice president's and one other. Cold crept from my feet up to my knees, and I felt tightness as my lizard-skin shoes shrank; wrinkles appeared in the drying fabric of my raw-silk suit, and I discreetly pulled at my clinging blouse. Tick … tick … tick. Each tick of the Grandfather clock cut deeper into my allotted thirty minutes. I focused on the tapestry—stared at the piece until the swirling depths of color calmed me, like the ruby-red marbles I'd carried the day I met Nanabah.

Eighteen minutes after ten, the vice-president stormed through the door. He was my age, perhaps a few years older, and, unlike the rest of his team, his jacket was off, his tie loosened, his shirt collar unbuttoned. He was a large man, balding and with a paunch that made it impossible for him to button the vest of his three-piece suit. No words were spoken as he crossed the room and sat at the head of the table. Eyes looked up; pencils were poised. Everyone was ready for his pronouncements.

He scanned the faces around the table, glanced at the Grandfather clock, and rested his eyes on me. "Okay, Lil' Lady … I am a very busy person. You have ten minutes."

His condescending salutation struck like a kick to my stomach. Images from my dream flashed: *I'd hesitated only a moment … and I ran, deep into the canyon after the laughing girl. A young teenage boy sat astride a roan-colored horse … As the horse and rider passed, the boy glared at me from his lofty position and then spat on the ground.*

Ten minutes. I could have easily boiled my presentation down—directed them to the pages in my proposal that listed the inefficiencies my research on the Exchange's human resource procedures unearthed; presented the six-figure savings of upgrading to new software; and, by the thoroughness and detail in my document, shown why they needed me and my company. My ability to do this, and to do it very well, was the reason my services were in such high demand. I knew how to be a porcupine and how to have a reputation for being both effective and difficult.

It was the "Lil' Lady" and all the connotations that came with those two words that made my decision. Scripted by that day in my dream, I stood slowly, grasped the edge of the table for balance, and stared directly into the vice-president's eyes. "You have no idea what I went through to be here on time. I deserve the same courtesy."

I leaned down, lifted my leather Gucci case to the table and placed the remaining proposals inside. Twenty pair of eyes watched while I gathered my belongings and stared directly into the face of the vice-president. "I'm through playing your game," I said and paused to watch the reaction. His expression was one of total consternation—his eyes narrowed into slits, his brow furrowed, his mouth twisted as though ready to speak, and he rose halfway out of his chair. "What the hell," someone muttered. I turned and calmly walked out the door.

Before the mahogany doors fully closed behind me I could hear the tumult of the conference room. My knees felt weak, so I bent down, pulled off my high heels and stuffed them into a side pocket of my suitcase. The stairwell was my means of exit. Outside, steam rose where patches of sunlight reached the asphalt; horns blared, vendors hawked, cabdrivers shouted. I didn't want to think about what I had just done, nor did I want to make eye contact with the homeless people who sat against the buildings, arms out with tin cans, begging for coins. I stared at the sidewalk, straight ahead, in front of my feet.

In my path a tattered street pigeon, with a wing that jutted awkwardly from its body, circled frantically in an attempt to avoid the crush of oncoming feet. New Yorkers despise the begging birds—think of them as nothing more than gutter-rats—but I dropped to my knees and scooped up the frightened pigeon. More scenes from my dream flashed. *He gently lifted a young bird from the box. Sticks tied with strips of cloth supported a wing that protruded at an angle from the fledgling's body. The bird seemed unbothered as the boy stroked its head and placed it on the dirt floor of the cave.* I stroked the back of the pigeon and mused on the mantra that shaped my business career and much of my life—"Success equates to money and control."

"Pardon, Missy."

My eyes traveled from mud-caked shoes, up a pair of baggy slacks held in place by a piece of rope and, above that, layers of various colored shirts. "Best watch out for these." The man moved my baggage closer to me. "Peoples'll steal 'em."

"The bird …" I looked up into his smiling eyes.

Two large black hands, palms pink and smooth, reached down and took the pigeon. "I kin he'p it. Fixed up lotsa hurt things." The man cradled the bird in the crook of one arm and, with his other hand, rearranged a dirty cloth tote bag with rope handles to make a nest. "It's gonna be jus' fine, Missy."

As quickly as he arrived, he was gone—headed down the street carrying the bulging bag. The man left nothing but a small white feather that clung to my skirt. I don't know how long I knelt on the wet sidewalk with the ebb and flow of rushing people around me. Happenings from that day on the Navajo Reservation, so long ago, were playing out in the events of my current life. The dream was merely my wake-up call.

The Navajo Reservation

It was the summer of 1950, and I was eight years old.

"Today I want you to come with me, Sharleen," my father announced at the breakfast table. "You are a very fortunate little girl. It's time you see for yourself the poverty and despair in which other children have to live."

Daddy worked for the Singer Sewing Machine Company and we had been transferred to Albuquerque, New Mexico. In addition to other duties, his job required him to travel the Navajo Reservation to collect on past-due accounts and to make repairs on the treadle-style machines the women used to stitch their clothing. School started next week, so this would be my last chance this summer to go with him.

We traveled Route 66, headed west from Albuquerque towards Gallup, and then north on a highway that led directly into the Navajo Reservation. I rode in the backseat. "Wives submit yourselves unto your husbands…" Daddy's words sounded far away, "…for the husband is the head of the wife. Chapter and verse, Shawn?"

"I'm Sharleen, not Shawn." My father often forgot and called me the wrong name; he wished I were a boy.

"Well, Sharleen Marie Dickson. You're not listening."

I was examining my collection of marbles. It was the biggest and best in the neighborhood. Brassies, peewees, and cat's-eyes—I had them all.

"Ephesians, Daddy. Someplace in Ephesians."

"Five, twenty-two; the chapter and verse are five, twenty-two."

I stared deeply into the glass globe of my favorite—a ruby-red cleary—and wished for the Bible game to be over. Images would often appear inside the marble; sometimes they even talked to me. My father's sunburned arm rested on the open window of the car, and between his fingers he held a cigarette. I had to keep the window of the backseat closed so the ashes he shook off in the wind wouldn't blow back into the car.

"Damn it, Sharleen." His knuckles turned white from gripping the steering wheel and then, holding the wheel with the cigarette hand, he took a swig from the bottle in the brown paper bag that always traveled with him. "These verses are the best way I know to teach you your place and how to behave. It's a man's world. And you're a girl. It's time you learned to behave like one ... more like your mother. You know, she was standing in line at the registrar's window at San Diego State. I told her that I could never marry a woman who earned more money than me. And all the other men are just like me."

"Daddy, I've heard this story a hundred times."

"You must not have listened very well. I wanted to go to college but couldn't because my parents needed me to work and help support them. I told your mother that I loved her and wanted to marry her, but she had to make a choice. It was either a college education or me. You know, I think she even had a scholarship to go to that school. But after the longest time, and one person away from the window, my little Margie stepped out of that line."

Today Daddy wouldn't be able to finish the story the way he usually did. At home it was: *"Isn't that right, Honey?"* And a teasing slap on Mommy's behind. I had no intention of becoming someone's "little Margie."

"Put the damned marbles away and act like a girl for a change."

We traveled on a stretch of highway dotted with vendors selling jewelry and other Indian trinkets. I was in the midst of gathering the round balls when the car abruptly slowed, pulled to the side of the road, made a U-turn, and came to a stop in front of a makeshift stand. My father didn't even turn off the motor; he shifted into neutral and set the emergency brake. "Stay here," he shouted as he pulled himself out of the car.

He returned moments later, "Play with this," tossing a rag doll into the backseat. The doll had no arms or legs—only a tube-shaped body with a head at each end and ruffled skirts around the middle, a double doll. There was a white face on one end with yellow hair and a skirt made of pink and blue calico; on the other end was a brown-faced girl with black yarn tied in a bun for hair. She had a purple velveteen skirt and a belt of silver buttons. Attached to the chest of the doll with a glued-on safety pin was a pendant made in the shape of a thunderbird decorated with chips of alabaster, coral and turquoise.

The double doll was my first girl-toy in many years. I thought about telling my father I wasn't interested in playing with a doll or acting like a girl. He was the one who said that boys have the run of the world. I wanted that for myself. But Daddy was angry enough already.

It started as a way to pacify my father. I held the Indian version of the double doll to the window and watched the storybook-shaped rock formations move as a backdrop to her antics. But soon my game transported me to a magical place. My Indian girl danced across distant mountains that floated in the clouds, through grazing flocks of sheep, and into a canyon filled with sandstone drip castles and monsters that look as if God formed them by squeezing wet sand through His fingers.

Daddy turned off the dirt road, into the yard of a round mud-covered hut with smoke rising from the roof. "This is a godforsaken place," he muttered as he slid his stout body from behind the steering wheel. He opened the trunk and took out his black case of sewing machine repair tools. I climbed out of the backseat and watched a red cloth pull away from the doorway of the hut to reveal a slender Indian woman. She looked much like my doll: three tiers of red and turquoise paisley ruffles that hung to her ankles; a blood red, long-sleeved blouse fastened at the neck with a large pendant of turquoise chips; and jet-black hair pulled away from her face and tied with white yarn into the shape of a bone at the nape of her neck.

"Yah-ta-hey," my father shouted, in his loud, salesman voice.

I heard a giggle and turned to see a brown-faced girl, eyes hidden by black bangs that hung to the bridge of her nose, peering around the corner of a nearby shed. She watched my father struggle; he had to turn sideways to get the cumbersome case and his bulk through the narrow doorway.

The girl walked toward me. She looked to be my age, but dressed similar to the woman in the hut in a ruffled skirt that hung down to bare feet and a long-sleeved cotton blouse. She wore no jewelry, but at her waist was a pink and purple woven sash belt. As the girl approached, she held out a dirt-encrusted hand and our fingers touched. "Nanabah," she said and pointed to her chest. Then she picked up her skirts, turned and ran. "*Hágo*," she hollered and waved for me to follow.

I could hear my heart beat—it was pounding so fast. Daddy warned me not to wander or get too close to any of the people on the reservation. Something about them having a different sense of values and cleanliness. He would be very angry. But in that brief touch of her fingers, I felt love and friendship. Back home there weren't many girls I wanted to be around— they all played silly games with their dolls—and as for the boys, well it was all about the competition with them. Boys got to do the fun stuff: go fishing, run through the woods, play ball. Girls were supposed to stay at home and learn how to cook and do dishes. I loved playing and beating the boys at their games; that's how I won all the pretty marbles.

I glanced only briefly at the door where my father disappeared and ran after my new friend. She went further into the canyon, on a pathway that narrowed and twisted among huge boulders that hid what lay ahead. I rounded a large group of rocks and saw her; she faced a young teenage boy who sat astride a roan-colored horse. He was barefoot too, and rode without a saddle. The horse's bridle was made of coarse twine. I couldn't see the boy's face clearly; a broad-rimmed cowboy hat set low on his forehead. His shirt was tucked into well-worn Levis with holes in the knees, and around his waist was a leather belt with a large turquoise-embedded silver buckle. He nudged his horse forward, forcing me to step off the path. As the horse and rider passed, the boy glared at me from his lofty position and then spat on the ground.

Nanabah shouted something in foreign-sounding words and stretched out her hand for me to grasp. It felt warm and rough and loving, all at the same time. A stern voice in my head said to turn around, go back to the car, and the voice was reinforced with a twinge of fear. I wasn't adventuresome like my sister, who defiantly rebelled against authority—I always obeyed my parents—until that day. Nanabah and I ran together to the end of the canyon, where the path turned steep. It hugged a ledge that angled up the side of a sheer rock wall. Part way we stopped and she showed me how to hold my face and hands to catch a taste of the cool water that trickled from cracks in the wall. A few feet beyond the spring Nanabah pulled away some underbrush and exposed a dark hole that led inside the mammoth rock.

I could hear a soft chant coming from inside the cave; I bent down and followed my friend into the darkness. Inside a shaft of sunlight from an opening in the back wall made it possible to see the form of a young boy sitting cross-legged beside a small wooden box. He appeared to be younger than the boy on the horse and looked quite different: his trousers were of buckskin, moccasins covered his feet, and he wore a long-sleeved cotton shirt draped with strands of turquoise. Nanabah moved to the back of the cave and collected a cloth bag. She pulled it to her chest and motioned for me to sit with her, facing the boy.

He gently lifted a young bird from the box. Sticks tied with strips of cloth supported a wing that protruded at an angle from the fledgling's body. The bird seemed unbothered as the boy stroked its head and placed it on the dirt floor. He picked up a cigar-shaped bundle of weeds and used a match from his pocket to light one end. The plants didn't blaze; they smoldered, giving off a thick pungent-smelling smoke. His chant resumed as he waved the smoking bundle over the wounded bird. Nanabah reached into the cloth bag and pulled out an object that she cradled in both hands and held in front of her. The boy directed the smoke over the object and then over the heads of Nanabah and me.

"*Awéé',*" she said, and showed it to me. It was a crudely made corncob doll with clothes from scraps of fabric.

The boy spoke to Nanabah. She nodded and handed me the doll. It felt soft and warm as I held it to my cheek. When I tried to give the doll back, Nanabah shook her head. I took off a gold locket from around my neck and showed her how to open the heart that dangled from a delicate chain. I pointed first to the picture inside, then to my chest, and said, "Sharleen." Nanabah giggled when I fastened the gold locket around her neck.

The horn of a car honked, and I heard my father's angry voice call my name. I crawled out of the cave and gingerly slid my body down the ridge to the narrow path. "I'll be back," I shouted to my friends and turned and ran to the car.

When I showed my father the corncob doll he tossed it out the car window. I stared in disbelief at the bush where my precious gift landed and tried unsuccessfully to suppress my tears. Early on I had learned that to cry only brought the taunts, *"Crybaby, crybaby, Sharleen is a crybaby."* I hated my father at that moment. My sister would have screamed at him to turn around and go back for the doll, but all I could do was bury my face in the skirts of my double doll and fight to hold back the convulsive sobs.

"They're nothing but a bunch of heathens," my father ranted. And then he quoted from Ezekiel, Chapter 36—something about "sprinkling me clean from all my filthiness." I looked for Nanabah through tear-filled eyes and the trail of dust left by our car, but in my heart I knew we would never see one another again.

The silence of the drive home was broken with my father's intermittent lectures about not worshipping graven images and believing in the only one true God. I blanked out his words and stayed in my mind with my double doll in the smoke-filled cave sitting next to Nanabah. She was my friend, and the cave was my safe place. It was a new feeling for me having someone accepting me just because. There wasn't a need to act or look any special way. I could be the eight-year-old girl that I was and still be loved. I promised myself to tell no one, not even my mother, about Nanabah or the corncob doll or the cave. I could be the "good" girl for my parents—the girl who got A's in school, said her prayers every night, cleaned her room without being told, and never acted disrespectful—while still holding onto who I was in the cave.

Dad's anger sent me to bed early that night; Mother's hushed voice against my father's boisterous laughter meant he had continued with his drinking. I only pretended to take my bath. I filled the tub with water and sat on the floor and waited the appropriate amount of time. The sweet, pungent smoke from the cave still clung to my hair and skin; I wanted it to last as long as possible. In bed I pulled the covers over my head and curled into a tight ball, hugging my double doll. In my fantasies Nanabah gifted me with her and kept the corncob doll for herself. We held hands and with our dolls ran together through the canyon. We played hide and seek among the strangely shaped rock formations. We crouched by the side of a trickling stream and waded barefoot through the cold water. We stretched out on our backs and pointed and giggled at the funny shapes of the clouds. And we climbed back to the cave to see the baby bird.

The images of the Navajo Reservation became my special place of retreat. When I felt alone or not good enough, I went in my mind to the canyon and listened to the whispering voice of the breeze call my name; I smelled the smoldering sage and ran free with Nanabah along the path. There were no bible verses, no expectations, no name calling, no crybaby taunts—only acceptance and love.

"Please God," I prayed that night and countless more, "turn me upside-down, just like the double doll, and make me an Indian."

The Durango Trading Company

"So, Lady, ya wanna cab or not?" A gruff voice came at me from the window of a taxi. I nodded, gathered my belongings from the sidewalk, and made my way to the waiting cab. "Penn Station, please."

Empty phone booths were plentiful at the train station. I fiddled with the pigeon feather as I punched in the telephone number. I was scheduled for another meeting mid-afternoon. "Hello, John. It's Sharleen. I won't be in as planned today, something's come up."

John was a longtime customer, the director of human resources for one of my major clients, and enough of a friend to question. "Not like you, Sharleen, what's up?"

Images of the double doll, spinning like a pinwheel, played in my thoughts while I talked. "I can't explain it to you right now … you can call it a melt-down."

The board posting Amtrak departures listed a train leaving at two o'clock headed for Philadelphia's 30th Street station. I would have an hour-and-a-half layover until the Keystone departed for Lancaster, but I felt an urgency to get out of New York City. I needed to process all that had happened. I hastily bought a copy of the <u>New York Times</u> and ran to catch the train. My suitcase bumped the legs of people on the escalator, and the conductor on the platform below signaled the engineer to depart. "Wait,"

I shouted and pushed my way down the moving stairs. Moments later I sank into the seat of an almost empty coach car and raised my footrest.

My body fought against efforts to relax. My chest tightened and my throat constricted with the dull ache I felt when trying to hold back tears. I was having a full-blown anxiety attack, which meant my blood pressure was rocketing. The anticipated repercussions of my earlier performance swept over me with a stunning force. *I made a mistake. I acted in haste. Maybe I should go back and apologize.* Thoughts of being obsequious with the arrogant vice-president were what I needed to bring myself under control. I took the newspaper and made my way to the club car for a glass of wine.

A few sips eased the ache in my throat. To calm my anxiety I focused on the message I'd sent to the vice president of the Exchange: *"I'm through playing your game."* Whether he heard or understood what I was saying was irrelevant; I had found my voice. My body relaxed into the knowing. Maybe it was finally time for me to become the person I was meant to be. My voice could articulate who I didn't want to be, but just like when I was in high school, I struggled with thoughts of who I did want to be. If I threw away my definition of success and the game of beating the boys, what was left?

I varied from my habit of reading the business news and opened the New York Times to the Arts and Entertainment section. The headline that topped the page was, "Native American Artifacts Highlight Antiques Show." The New York City spring event ended a ten-day run, and Indian wares were the most visible new category. The last line of the story read, "When a blanket sold for more than $100,000, it brought in a new group of status-conscious collectors." The article was next to a picture of a Navajo sandpainting weaving auctioned off at Sotheby's as part of the Andy Warhol collection.

Somewhere, on the Amtrak train between New York City and Lancaster, Pennsylvania, a plan for the "new me" began to emerge. *"I'll* go back to the reservation," I thought. *"I'll learn how to weave. No, I'll start a new business that buys weavings from the Navajo women and sells them to the discriminating collector. I'll travel the world displaying the rugs. I'll create a global market for Navajo weavings."* It was as if another piece of the seismic puzzle that was turning my world upside down had fallen into place. Little did I realize that day, that I was simply concocting a new means of following the old patterns for success. "Playing the game" could take place on the reservation as easily as on Wall Street.

My first task when I arrived home was to find my double doll. I needed something tangible to carry me through the early stages of my journey. She, along with my father's scribbled-on map of the Navajo Reservation, lay atop diaries and high school scrapbooks in a cardboard box stashed away in the attic. Threads were rotted, the doll's buttons and beads were scattered throughout the box, and mice had chewed through the fabric— only a thunderbird decorated with chips of coral, alabaster and turquoise pinned to the doll's chest appeared unscathed by time.

Our dog, BJ, barked a signal that Len was home from work. He poked his head through the attic door. "I thought you were in New York. What are you doing up here?"

Early in our relationship, I learned that timing was the key with Len. His personality and many years in a management position contributed to his thoughtful, studied approach to decisions or change. He didn't like surprises or what he considered to be impulsive actions. I approached difficult subjects with the "seed planting" method: Tell just enough to plant the idea, and let it germinate before hitting him with the full information.

"Just looking at some old keepsakes … things I brought back after Mom died." I collected the doll and the map and carried them down the stairs.

Len was Director of Corporate Benefits for the Fortune 500 Company that hired me sixteen years ago for their Information Systems department. During the last three years of my time at the company, he was my boss. Len had a special way of pulling qualities from deep inside me. Those were learning years. I learned to stand my ground and face down executive decisions, and to develop proposals and present them in conference rooms filled with arrogant, intimidating men. I learned to view problems in a logical, bottom-line manner and cut straight to the chase to make things happen. Len taught me to refine my business acumen; he fostered in me the ability to think with my head instead of my heart. And he taught me to be prepared. New ideas or concepts were only presented after the homework was done. These traits served me well when I ventured out and started my own consulting business.

As second-timers, Len and I both came into our marriage with a wary sense of how easily the foundations of a relationship can deteriorate and weaken. We were cautious and hesitant about treading on supporting ideologies and egos—I tried not to behave or make decisions spontaneously, and he backed off from giving critical or controlling advice. So, the events of New York City and my ideas for change would be gingerly sprinkled into our discussions. I would tread softly with my planting stick until I could mold my intentions into something cohesive and logical.

Meal preparation started by uncorking a bottle of Chardonnay. I'd replaced Perfect Manhattans with wine. Hard liquor had been a way to dull the pain of my previous unhappy marriage; now I routinely drank one or two glasses of wine as relief to the stress of traveling, business meetings and high blood pressure. One glass for the pot, one glass for the chef—just as my father did when he made the brandy sauce. It wasn't the complexity of the night's meal that caused me to consume an entire bottle of wine before Len came into the kitchen; it was the anticipation of the dinnertime conversation.

"I think it's time we live the good life," I said and turned my attention away from sautéing garlic and onions for stir-fry.

"What does that mean?" Frown lines formed in Len's wrinkle-free face as he struggled to open another bottle of wine. The only thing that hinted of his fifty-nine years was a full head of shocking white hair.

"You want to retire," I said and held out my glass for a refill. "Let's do it."

Three years earlier Len and I purchased two acres of land northeast of Durango, Colorado; we'd been working with an architect on plans to build our dream home. Len had another year before he could retire with full benefits. I'd been the one to resist setting a date. I was almost ten years younger than Len and wasn't willing to give up my career—until now.

"I didn't think you were ready." He filled my glass and poured one for himself.

"I wasn't … until the Stock Exchange presentation." I sipped my wine and took a deep breath. "I think I've retired myself."

"What do you mean, retired yourself? I can't follow when you use metaphors."

I spooned portions of the chicken stir-fry onto plates and motioned for Len to join me at the table. "I walked out on my presentation at the Exchange."

There was a long and pregnant pause.

"You walked out. Is that what you just said?"

So much for seed planting, the words just slipped out. My intentions were to find solid ground on which to stand and a plausible reason for what I'd done before I revealed the happenings of my day. I shouldn't have drunk so much wine.

"I told them I wasn't playing the game any longer. Then I picked up my things and left. I walked out."

"Jesus, Sharleen. What possessed you?"

I'd never heard Len curse—other than under his breath—and certainly never at me.

"I don't know … something just snapped." It was too soon to tell him about the dream. "It was a bad day from the start. The train was late into New York; I got caught in the subway during rush hour; and the rain ruined my new silk suit. To top it off, the vice president, the one I was making the presentation to, showed up twenty minutes late."

Len said nothing—just stared at the amber liquid in his glass. He twirled his wine goblet with long elegant fingers, so different from the massive stubby hands that had cradled the street pigeon. But his quiet demeanor was more reassuring than his previous reaction.

"The VP was a real pig. I'd just plain had it! I was done."

"Sharleen," he said. "You've stood up to countless egomaniacs, chauvinists and pigs." His words came slowly as though talking to a child. "Why this pig?"

I hadn't done my homework and had drunk far too much wine. I wasn't ready for this conversation. I blurted out the first thing that came to mind. "After I left the boardroom there was this pigeon with a broken wing. It was frantic … kept racing around in circles to avoid being stepped on."

Silence.

"What's that got to do with anything?"

"It reminded me of myself. You know … the way I just keep doing the same things over and over." The words tumbled rapidly. "I've spent my whole life working twice as hard, trying to prove I could be as good as the men. It's gotten me nowhere." At the moment, all my accomplishments fell by the wayside. In my mind, the men at the Stock Exchange were just like my father and I would never gain their approval. "I just keep going in circles … like the bird." I paused to catch my breath and looked into Len's quizzical face.

"Some pretty successful circles, if you ask me."

I hadn't given an adequate answer to Len's question: "Why this pig?" The vice-president was nothing more than the means to set my dream in reality; he became the disapproving father who threw the corncob doll out the window. I didn't fully understand, nor was I ready to convey, the significance of my dream. That would come later as the seed germinated and ripened. "We'll retire to Durango, just like you've wanted to do. I'll sell my part of the business and start again in Colorado."

"You may not have a business to sell when the Stock Exchange gets through with you."

Reputation was my company's only real asset, and Len knew how quickly news traveled in the financial and corporate world.

The next morning I cancelled my client appointments for the remainder of the week. Each of the following three days, I pinned the thunderbird to the collar of my blouse, stuffed my father's old map in my briefcase and headed for the library to research Navajo Indians and the different styles of weaving. There wasn't much. The Internet was just emerging as a tool for accessing information, and Pennsylvania was a long way, culturally and in distance, from the Navajo Reservation.

I was able to find one book that stated: "For the traditional Navajo, weaving is much more than an art form; it is a way of life." The magazine Southwest Art had telephone numbers of bookstores where I could order more information. By thumbing through old issues of the magazine I learned that sandpainting weavings, like the one I'd seen pictured in the newspaper article and the old blanket hanging in my parents' living room, were woven reproductions of the images and designs created with colored sand by a medicine man during a healing ceremony. I learned it took a very skilled weaver to manage the intricacies of the detail in this type of tapestry; a person was deemed to be a Master Weaver only after mastering complete control of all aspects of the weaving process from raising the sheep to producing the rug and were capable of creating the gamut of regional designs.

The next few days were spent with my laptop computer developing a business plan:

> Name: Durango Trading Company, Inc.
> Mission: Promoting American Arts through the Sale of
> Amish Quilts and Navajo Weavings

By the end of the week I was ready to approach Len with a formulated plan. "I know what I want to do," I said and handed him the newspaper article from <u>The New York Times</u>. "This really triggered the whole idea." I gave him a moment to read about the popularity and value of Navajo weavings, all along assuring him I was doing additional research at the library.

"I'll buy Amish quilts here in Lancaster and take them west. And buy Navajo rugs and bring them to the East Coast. There's a big market right now. Travel expenses between Pennsylvania and Colorado can be written off to the business."

My plan wasn't fully formulated, but it wasn't the time to sound uncertain. "I'll go to the Navajo Reservation, find some talented weavers and sell their work to collectors."

"You don't know a thing about the collector's market."

"I'll learn."

"And you still haven't explained to me why you walked out of the Stock Exchange."

We ate another meal in silence. Len didn't speak until he was clearing the dishes from the table. "What are you using for money?"

His words thrust me back to the kitchen with my mother—"*Sharleen, money is control ... you don't want to end up like me.*" Len had crossed a line. I retreated into that "somewhere else" of an independent child determined to do this myself.

"That isn't your problem."

Somewhere Else

"**I** am sick and tired of your behavior."

Dad burst into my bedroom. His face was red and puffy and the distinct smell of bourbon emanated from him. "Home is a place for happiness and security," he shouted. "If you have troubles or problems, take them somewhere else." He was almost out the door when his foot caught on a dress my sister had worn that afternoon. "And this place looks like a pig sty. Your mother spends all her time making nice clothes for you girls, and this is how you show your appreciation."

The small bedroom my sister and I shared was barely big enough for the double bed and dresser. I was neat; she was messy. On most days you could look into a room with half the bed made, the other half a tangle of sheets, and a floor strewn with a week's worth of clothes. I'd run a piece of yellow masking tape along the floor to divide our space, but her clutter had a way of encroaching on my territory.

Mom stood in the hallway and only came into the room when Dad stormed out. Her hand pressed against the side of her cheek, pushing so she could bite down on already raw skin inside her mouth. "You know I must agree with your father on this." She bent over scooping up clothes and putting them on hangers in the closet; when she turned to look at me her eyes brimmed with tears. "We have to come first to each other, and you children are second."

"Where is somewhere else? If I can't bring my problems home, where do I take them?"

"It's just that now isn't a good time, with your sister's wedding and all."

Sherry was getting married in two days. She had blossomed early and developed a full figure, stayed out beyond curfew, smoked cigarettes in the secrecy of our shared bedroom, and wore makeup before she was allowed. "You look like a streetwalker," Dad told her. She did all those things that would make any parent crazy, while I, the "goody-two-shoes" of the family, made her crazy. "Tattletale, tattletale," my sister sang to the same tune of my father's "crybaby." Sherry simply argued with my parents and then went her own way, doing whatever she pleased. Saturday afternoon she would dash any hopes of college and marry a high school dropout.

"Mom, Jimmy doesn't want to be my boyfriend anymore," I sobbed. "He wants to be with one of the cheerleaders. Her name is Linda." Three days ago the boy I chose to be my "first love" broke up with me. Since then I'd spent every free moment in my bedroom in lovesick pining.

"We'll talk about this later. You just turned fourteen. You know your dad and I think you're too young to have boyfriends anyway." Eyes that earlier had shown empathy, hardened. "Just come out of your room, Sharleen, before your father gets really angry."

Mom's biggest threat was: "Don't upset your father." I knew she loved me, but just couldn't allow herself to side with me against Dad. Today, like so many other days, her love was cautious; it walked on eggshells. She was the peacemaker in our home, always trying to be the kind of wife she was "supposed to be" and making my sister and me behave like the young girls we were "supposed to be." It was all done to ensure that no one provoked the rage of my father. The "supposed to be" definition came from his strict upbringing as a hard-shelled Southern Baptist.

The endless list of things that needed to be done before the wedding consumed our dinner table discussions, and since Sherry was out with girlfriends celebrating her soon-to-be-cut-short freedom, I would wash and dry the dishes. By the time I finished, Mom was back at her sewing machine putting the final touches on my sister's wedding gown. Dad sat, bourbon in hand, staring at the television.

"I'm sleeping out in the fort tonight," I announced to my mother and gave her a peck on the cheek. "It's not as cold as it has been, and Sherry will be getting home late."

Fort Ticonderoga had come to be two years earlier, about the same time the double doll was exchanged for a diary as a confidante. In history class I'd studied about the place "where American Liberty began" and really liked the sound of the singsong name. When my sister secretly—in-bed-at-night-with-the-door-closed—imitated Dad's chain smoking, I decided to create some "Sharleen Liberty." My private place was the raised four-foot deep plywood shelf along the back wall of our detached, one-car garage. A long extension cord for electricity to a lamp, a sleeping bag for a bed, a stepladder for access, and an old blanket hung from the rafters for privacy—it was all I needed. It was perfect, except in cold weather. It was early April; Albuquerque's winter had sent me back to the house since Thanksgiving.

The garage smelled musty from being closed up for the winter. I climbed the ladder to my safe place with an extra blanket and my diary tucked under one arm. The entry that night started: *Well, dear diary, I guess you and the fort will have to be my "somewhere else."* I raged on, using many more pages than the one day allowed, writing through a gamut of feelings: despair about my boyfriend leaving, anger with my father, betrayal by my mother, and finally, guilt-ridden self-blame. *I hate myself. I'm not enough … not pretty enough, not good enough, not even smart enough. I need to work harder and learn to act more like Mom.*

I prided myself in being like my mother, a real "do-gooder" and "people-pleaser." I always did my homework and never talked on the phone too long. Teachers at school said I was a model student and put me in charge of the classes if they had to step out of the room. Mom was such a kind and good person, it only made sense that I should emulate her. But that was where things got confusing. I wanted to be like her, but I didn't want to be like her. I wanted to be smart and kind and capable and loving; I just didn't want to pretend I wasn't those things to please someone else.

The January 1 diary entry for the next two years started with these words—*Home is a place for happiness and security. You have troubles or problems ... take them somewhere else*—written in red ink to remind me of the scorn with which my father had spoken them.

During my junior year in high school the family relocated within Albuquerque. Distance wise the move wasn't far, but socio-economically it was vast. Fort Ticonderoga was dismantled, and I was forced to find a new "somewhere else." I still had lots of troubles and problems: I was seriously skinny with a condition later diagnosed as an over-active thyroid; my skin was oily, plaguing me with the common teenage scourge of acne; girlfriends told me that I needed to wash my hair more often, but that was not allowed—Mom said I would lose the natural oil if I shampooed more than once a week. Putting all that together meant there were no boyfriends.

Church became my new "somewhere else." Our home was walking distance to a Baptist church. Attending was acceptable to my parents and it was the only activity that got me out of a Sunday morning ritual— listening on the radio to Oral Roberts, Charles E. Fuller or Billy Graham.

"I'm headed off to Sunday School now." I hollered the words over my shoulder as I passed the entry to the living room; Dad had the radio tuned to Oral Robert's Abundant Life Prayer Group.

"Do you want us to pick you up after the service?" Mom asked.

"No need. It's a nice day." I made my trek alone. Our family didn't attend church together; Dad traveled during the week and on the weekends he said that he needed time to relax. Only my diary knew how I relished my "acceptable" alone time.

Today, like every Sunday, I entered the building from the back—down the long corridor that led to the church classrooms. "Sharleen," a high-pitched voice called out. "We haven't seen you in ages. Will you be joining us today?" It was the Sunday school teacher who taught the girls in my age group. She was a classic June Cleaver with the added feature of telling us that being a good mother and wife would result in a special place in heaven for her. She lost any hopes for my adoration with that line.

"Uh, no." I felt my face redden. "I'm sorry, I thought I told you. I'm helping out the teachers in the preschool classes." *Liar, liar … pants on fire.*

"We really have been missing you. But that's a very Christian thing you are doing."

I watched her continue down the hallway. Once she turned the corner, I darted into the darkened rooms at the front of the sanctuary—the rooms where the choir changed clothes and baptismal candidates readied themselves for the full submersion ceremony. Usually I sat in the corner of the sanctuary to be alone with my thoughts, but this morning I made my way to the empty rectangular baptism pool.

A month ago I walked down those concrete steps into waist-high water and leaned into the supporting arms of Pastor Whitfield. "We do this in the name of the Father, the Son and the Holy Spirit," he intoned and lowered me under the water. Symbolically I died and was born again. When I lied to Mom and Dad after returning home with wet hair, I concluded it must not have "taken." Accepting Christ as my Savior and being baptized would have pleased my parents, but I did it for me, not for them. More and more, anything that felt special or important was pushed inside, taken somewhere else along with the troubles and problems.

I sat on the steps and prayed the struggle—balancing what others wanted of me against who I wanted to be—would end. The trouble was I didn't know who I wanted to be; I only knew who I didn't want to be. So I prayed about that, too.

My mother was certainly a better role model than my Sunday school teacher. She grew up as the daughter of a self-taught genius. Granddad played a key position in the design and construction of Hoover Dam, as well as being an accomplished ship builder—all without as much as a high school education. He taught himself the mathematics of angles and stress, those calculations necessary to become a master carpenter. And he instilled his genius in my mother. She competed nationally on the high school debate team and graduated at the top of her class. But, as the story went, she gave it all up to be Dad's "little Margie."

Shooting marbles was just the beginning of many years spent "beating the boys at their game." The classroom was a subtler and more acceptable venue for my battle of the sexes. My achievement in math and science was a godsend—it not only surrounded me with the less popular students, the ones like me who were hiding behind books, but it was my ticket to get away from home and go to college. I told my friends the hard work was a way to prove to my father I was as good as a boy; deep inside, in my own somewhere else, I knew it had a lot more to do with being like my mom, being like her but not following in her footsteps.

"Girls don't need to go to college for an education." My father split his time talking with me between bites of food, glances at the television and sips of his bourbon and water. "Use your time there to find a good Baptist man who can support you."

"I know, Dad." He didn't realize I'd already found that good Christian provider at a summer church camp. Ivan was the most handsome boy I'd ever seen. The only problem was that he was the son of a Methodist minister and not a Southern Baptist. He worked at the camp as part of the staff, and I was in love with him. Unfortunately, Ivan didn't know this.

"That's why I want to go to Hardin-Simmons."

"Not Baylor?"

Ivan attended a Methodist college in Abilene, Texas, the same town of my selected university. It was perfect—we could attend college, date, and eventually fall in love and marry. Of course Mom and Dad would never have allowed me to pick a school just to follow a boy, but they eventually did accept the idea of my school because it was Southern Baptist.

I was the first person on either side of the family to go to college, and this was a bragging point for Dad. When I overheard him tell people I was accepted and enrolled at a university, he qualified it with, "Well, her Mom and I wanted her to go to Baylor … it's bigger and a much better school, you know." Maybe he thought the bigger the school the better my chances of finding a husband. None of that mattered; I'd charted my own course.

"Ivan Hall," I shouted into the pay phone handset. "Does he live in this dorm?" Loud music played in the distance, and it sounded like a tag football game was going on in the hallway.

"Who?" A hand cupped over the receiver and there were shouts to settle down. "I'm sorry. Things are a little noisy here tonight. Now who was it you wanted to talk with?"

"Ivan Hall. I'm trying to speak with Ivan Hall."

There was another pause with a muffled shout, "Quiet," followed by "Hey, guys … anybody know where Ivan is? … Sorry. He transferred to SMU. Didn't leave any phone number." Southern Methodist University was in Dallas, Texas—hundreds of miles away.

My fantasy shattered. But fortunately I'd been lucky and had been assigned a wonderful roommate. Emelda was from Waco, Texas, and a bundle of raw energy. She must have given off a certain vibe; we hadn't been at school long when she was picked by one of the older men on campus to be his girlfriend.

"I think one of the reasons he likes you is because you have so much energy." Emelda and I sat up through the wee hours of the morning talking about her date with Ron.

"I think you're right," she said. "He's headed into the ministry, you know, and needs a wife who can set an example for the other women in the church." I chose not to finish her sentence with my thoughts: "Be duly submissive, love the Lord and do all the 'shit-work' that had to be done in running a church."

Emelda smiled when she added, "You know, the role of a minister's wife is a very important calling."

They married before our freshman year was over. Emelda dropped out of school, and I had to find a new roommate.

I got lucky a second time. Stephanie was a beautiful redhead who lived in Abilene but wanted to move into the dorm for a better college experience. She was very popular, and I could come along for the ride. Early in our sophomore year several girls approached me—they really approached Stephanie but got me in the deal—to form a girl's social club at Hardin-Simmons.

"Well, it can't be a real sorority," the young woman acting as a spokesperson said, "because of the no drinking or dancing rules on campus, but we can have afternoon teas and banquets and all sorts of things." A second girl stepped forward and put a hand on the spokesperson's arm. "There is quite a bit of opposition to this. The school administration, the community churches and the Baptist Student Union … they've all spoken out against us. That's the main reason we can't apply for Greek affiliation."

"Why?" I asked.

"The national groups require the sanctions of the university."

"No, I mean, why is there so much opposition here in Abilene?"

A hush came over the room until the spokesperson came forth. "Like I said, it's all about the drinking and dancing. People think the Greek sororities and fraternities promote improper activities ... that we're all going to be led down the wrong path."

"Some think social clubs are the work of the Devil," the other girl said, "like we are trying to set up our own mini-version of Hell right here on the Hardin-Simmons campus."

Two weeks later, Stephanie bounced into our room, flung her books on the bed and sat cross-legged in the middle. "We both got in," she shrieked. "We're going to be Delta's!" Celebration meant a strawberry float at the corner drugstore. Later that night Stephanie motioned for me to come over to our dorm room window.

"What's happening?" I looked through the darkness of night to a sea of candles.

"It's a prayer vigil," Stephanie said.

Pamphlets proclaiming, "The way to the Lord" and the "cost of living a life of sin" began to appear, shoved under our door. Students were forced to draw lines—either you were for the social clubs or you were against. For the next month, prayer meetings in the lobby of the dorms and candlelight vigils outside room windows were held for the "sinners."

A church would never again be my "somewhere else." I wasn't ready to reject God or most of my childhood teachings, but I was ready to reject the religious institutions that tried to control with such absurd tactics.

My senior year I was elected president of the Delta social club and dated a young man who was a member of the Tau Alpha Phi group. Selecting an on-campus boyfriend or girlfriend was limited for those who were in a social club; I sometimes thought that was the only reason I was dating. There were now six social groups and a new school tradition—the annual Spring Sing. Each organization on campus, including the Baptist Student Union, was invited to put on a mini-musical production, complete with scenery, costuming and either live or mimed music. It was the biggest event of the year and attendance required formal dress.

When I went home to Milwaukee, where my parents had relocated, for the Christmas holiday, I solicited help. "Mom, this is really special. I need a dress that is perfect."

"We'll go into Chicago and walk the Million Dollar Mile," she announced, "and shop the better dress stores to get ideas." Among Mother's many talents was the ability to design and create women's clothing. Money was always sparse in my family, so we often tried on dresses until I found one I liked. Mom would then make a sketch, go home and draw a pattern and create it. She was a great seamstress, able to make beautiful garments that never looked homemade.

"This is the one!" I shouted and danced around the dressing room. In a shop so exclusive you did not search the racks—they brought the garments to you—I found my dream dress. The bodice was cut very low and made from red taffeta covered completely in sequins. The skirt billowed with dozens of yards of gathered red chiffon. I twirled around in a cloud of red as the ugly duckling changed into a graceful swan. The red dress had magically transported me somewhere else.

"We'll take this one," my mother said and pulled a bulging envelope out of her purse.

"Mom … its way more than you can afford."

"I have a little stash here," she said, "for a very special occasion. We just won't tell your father about this, okay?"

"Are you sure you want to do this?"

Tears came; it was the first time ever she had conspired with me against Dad.

That night, my red dress safely hidden in the back of the closet, I stood in the kitchen drying the dishes as my mother washed them. "Have I told you how much I love my new dress? I'm just worried that you shouldn't have spent so much money on it." I gave her a peck on the cheek as I spoke. "But I'm glad you did."

When she turned I saw tears in her eyes. "Sharleen, money is control … you don't want to end up like me." Her eyes pleaded when she looked at me over her shoulder. "Don't ever become dependent on a man for money."

Letter of Intent

T hree weeks had passed since that rainy morning in New York City. My resolve and confidence were like a roller coaster—up one day and down the next. Len and I stepped cautiously around one another.

So, I wrote down my fears: *I don't have enough stick-to-it. People will think I'm a quitter. I'm all 'talk' and no 'do.' Len will lose respect for me. I won't make any money. Nobody will hire me if I need to go back to work.* I posted them in my office and forced myself to laugh at them daily. Then I countered each fear with a plan of attack. The documented strategies always came back to money. Len's question about how I planned to finance these ideas served as a gauntlet, reminding me of my father's words: "You can't do that. You're only a girl," and mother's admonishments to never let a man control my finances.

The time came to take action, and that meant telling my business partner. When I first established my consulting firm I was the sole employee. I built a reputation as a "user guide" to the implementation of a mainframe computer package. The state-of-the-art software answered a large corporation's need to replace manual record-keeping procedures with a computerized human resource management system. The software development company was located near California's Silicon Valley, but the customers were exclusively East Coast based. My consulting firm provided needed support. Travel demands across the continent and up and down the coastline were brutal.

And then, Janice Gamblin joined me. She'd been the user coordinator for the installation of the same human resource software at an international conglomerate headquartered in Cleveland, Ohio. We met several times at conferences held throughout the country—the way company professionals learned to use their HR software. When her implementation project was completed, Janice approached me with the idea of becoming business partners. I was a single mom at the time with two teenage children. She was childless and not married—the answer to reducing my long work and travel hours.

At the onset, our working relationship went well. There was even a time she told me that I was like a sister to her. A year later, when Len and I married, he had reservations. He couldn't quite tell me the problem; it was merely something that nagged at him. He'd been in the management side of personnel for more than thirty years and developed good instincts for people. I passed it off as Janice's attitude toward men: she was attractive, expensively groomed, and a real bitch when she got angry—the kind of woman men called a "ball buster." But she knew the business, and I needed help.

I scripted every detail of the manner in which I would break the news to Janice. Where we met and how I dressed were part of the decision. I booked airline tickets to Cleveland and made reservations at the restaurant where we would meet. I even purchased clothing for my new persona—an ankle-length denim skirt and a pearl-buttoned blouse with the thunderbird pin attached to the collar.

"Will a gentleman be joining you?" The *maître d'* examined me over the rim of his glasses. The upscale restaurant had previously been a men's-only club; it was quite recent that they allowed unaccompanied women.

"Another woman," I replied. "We'd like to sit by the window."

Janice was prompt. She always was. I'd positioned myself to watch her make an entrance. The *maître d'* was all smiles, and at least one head from every table turned to look in the direction of the clicking spike heels as they moved across the tile floor. There was a time I thought it was her perfume. Later, I realized that "attitude" has its own smell.

"So what's this big decision you need to talk about?" She settled into her chair and rearranged items on the table, like a packrat building a nest.

"Will you ladies be having anything to drink with lunch?"

"Two martinis … and make them dry." Janice glanced my way for approval. "You haven't given me any details on your meeting at the Exchange."

"I've decided to quit. Get out of the rat race."

I didn't have to plant seeds with Janice—abrupt and to the point was the way she liked things. I speculated that my announcement would be positively received. Janice didn't like to share. Her reaction came as no surprise. She paused momentarily, leaned forward and lowered her voice. "So what are your plans? I know you're not going to fold up your tent and take an allowance from Len."

"That's what we're here to talk about."

"Cheers." We both savored that first long sip with the thin film of ice on top.

"How is your blood pressure these days?"

"Not good." I picked up my menu. "Are the crab cakes worth having here?"

When the waiter arrived to take our order, Janice was ready for a second martini. A little tipsy was the perfect condition for Janice when talking about money. "What's your definition of success?" I asked, purposely stalling for time.

"Honey, that's easy. It's making so much money the bastards can't help but know who you are." The waiter arrived with her drink.

I nodded. "You know Janice, a while back, I would have agreed. Now ..." I interrupted my sentence when I realized she wasn't listening. Her eyes wandered over the people in the dining room; my sense was that she was scrutinizing their worth.

When her attention turned back to me, Janice asked, "What do you think it is?"

I reached up, unpinned the thunderbird and handed it to her. "I'm not sure yet, but somehow this is part of it." She simply turned it over in her hand to see the glued on safety pin and mumbled something about it being pretty tacky. "It came from the Navajo Reservation." I took the pendant and rubbed my fingers over the rough-cut stones. "What happened at the Stock Exchange reminded me that I want to go back."

"What *did* happen at the Exchange?"

"I walked out. The VP was twenty minutes late, and he called me Lil' Lady."

I had Janice's attention. She leaned back in her chair and gave an uncharacteristic guffaw. "And for this you're giving up a six-figure income?"

"The Exchange was just the start. I'm afraid I'm becoming like all the power-hungry men we work with. I want to go to the Navajo Reservation and start a business selling rugs. You know, a gentler kind of business." And then I threw in the phrase that was becoming a new mantra, "I want to think with my heart instead of my head."

Janice scowled at me. "You sure as hell can't make any money there. I mean, isn't it Third World?" She went back to her martini and study of the other diners. Janice knew money was my most sensitive issue; it was how I defined myself. Money was my cloak of identity, the key to acceptance, the means for independence, and my defense against being controlled. My script for the meeting resulted in her speculation on the enormity of my decision and her understanding that this was not a fleeting idea. Once this sank in, Janice would jump at the opportunity to take all the spoils for herself, and she was smart enough not to hold out.

When our food arrived, we ate in silence until Janice pushed her sparsely eaten salad aside and motioned for the waiter to take her plate. "It will be difficult to determine our company's value," she said.

There were no real business assets. Janice and I, along with four employees, operated from our homes. We did all of the consulting work at the site of the customer or through the mail and telephone. Clients paid travel and business expenses. Janice and I received between one and two hundred dollars for an hour of our time, including travel, and twenty percent of the fees paid to our employees.

"Any ideas?" Janice asked, as the waiter took her plate.

I'd spent a lot of time during the last few days planning an answer to this question. I knew the loss of the Stock Exchange contract wouldn't be that damaging to the company. There were plenty of other buyers in the wings; the software package we worked with was the only one in the marketplace that could meet a large company's requirements and, as far as implementation consulting services, we were the only show in town. I also knew it would take at least five years to establish my new business.

"The VP at the Stock Exchange wants me to come back. His secretary called and said he liked my proposal enough to up the ante from half-a-million. You could woo him … all it would take is a visit. And there's a million-three in my nailed down contracts. Pay me two-hundred thousand now and payments of a hundred thousand each for the next three years."

Janice took a slow, thoughtful sip of her martini and looked at me over the rim of the glass. "Do you know anything about Navajo rugs?"

"A little," I lied. "This fall I'm going to a place called Crow Canyon … it's in Cortez, Colorado. They have some weaving workshops taught by Navajo women."

"Is Len going with you?" Janice didn't wait for an answer. She took the last swallow of her martini and stood to leave. "I'll call our attorney and have him draft a Letter of Intent."

It was close to midnight by the time I flew from Cleveland to Harrisburg and made the drive home, and Len was off to work the next morning before I was out of bed. I spent the day updating my business plan.

Len arrived home early. He looked over my shoulder at the computer screen. "Have you and Janice talked buyout?"

"Five-hundred-thousand. Our attorney is drafting a Letter of Intent."

"That's it?"

I nodded and went back to work. Len closed the lid on my computer. "You don't settle on a payout of half-a-million over a cup of tea and a letter." His hands clenched into fists as he paced. "You know better."

His sharp words put me back on that roller coaster, and all the fears and insecurities from my past came roaring back. *You can do this. Stay strong.* "It was a martini … not tea. And don't be patronizing. I do it all the time in my consulting business."

"With reputable companies … Janice Gamblin's a whole different matter."

A Glass House

"I'm sorry. We only hire males for our technical division. Females can work in the marketing department, but you have to be married."

My interviewer wore a slim black necktie with his steel-gray, pin-striped suit with slim trousers and slim lapels. Everything about him was slim until you got to the fat, black owl-eye frames of his glasses. "Of course, if you type and take shorthand, I can find something for you."

Or if I were a man. It was during those months before graduation when everyone tries to land a job; I was interviewing with IBM, well known for their conservative stance. With that in mind, I carefully dressed in the classic Jackie Kennedy look—a navy blue sheath, pearl necklace and white gloves. "My degree is in mathematics. Surely you have job opportunities for mathematicians."

"Sorry, Lady. You're the wrong sex."

"You can't do that ... You're only a girl."

Admonishments that had started with my father followed me to the playground marble games and into the offices of school counselors. They tagged along with me still.

Graduation day came and went. Most of my friends set dates to marry and lined up their dream jobs as elementary school teachers, choir directors, music teachers, minister's wives, secretaries, or, best of all, stay-at-home moms. Those who were not marrying right away left to share apartments and find work in Dallas, the Texas mecca for single women. But I hadn't gone the recommended, traditional route for young women and found myself unemployable. With no means to support myself, I was forced to move home.

"You aren't in love with him." Mom sat small on the corner of the couch winding a tattered handkerchief around her fingers, first one way and then another. Dad was in his favorite armchair sipping a bourbon and water.

"How do you know that?" James, my boyfriend from college, had returned to his home in Texas following a weeklong visit with my parents and me to plan our upcoming wedding.

"I can tell. Mothers just know things like that. Why he didn't even offer to help when I talked about needing to fix the fence."

"Seems to me he didn't talk about anything." My father gulped the last of his drink and headed into the kitchen for another.

"Mom, you and Dad didn't even give him a chance. He is exactly what you said you wanted for me. He's smart, serious about his studies and a good Southern Baptist. He will make a fine husband and father."

"But the spark … there isn't a spark between you."

Dad returned to the living room with a fresh drink boisterously contributing to her argument. "And he is so quiet. What ever happened to telling a few jokes and having a little bit of fun?"

"You're right Dad, he is not a backslapping, drunk salesman like you." I slung the words over my shoulder and walked out of the room. I was twenty-two years old, and this was the first time I had ever spoken disrespectfully to my father. It felt good, but Mother would be upset.

The day my engraved wedding invitations arrived with *Mr. and Mrs. Noel Chester Dickson proudly invite …* Dad went into a tirade. "Don't you dare send those to any of my business associates. I won't be humiliated at work." He never used his given name of Noel Chester; it embarrassed him; he preferred the initials, N C. and proudly boasted they stood for "No Count."

Despite the tension in the house my mother performed her magic with the sewing machine. I'd found a picture of a sedately elegant wedding gown, and Mom recreated it perfectly. There was nothing frilly about the dress; it was white silk linen trimmed at the neckline and sleeves with scalloped satin piping. A six-foot long train, outlined with yards more of the scalloped piping, trailed behind the floor-length gown.

"Sharleen, you must make the walk by yourself." It was moments before the ceremony was to begin, and I could hear the opening strains of Mendelssohn's *Wedding March*. "Your father just had a heart attack. We're going to the hospital."

I recall hearing the wails of the ambulance siren as the minister intoned: "Sharleen Marie Dickson, do you take this man ..." Dad would recover and live another twenty years, but my parent's absence on my wedding day left a large hole in the memories of what was supposed to be a very special day.

James and I secured high-school-level teaching jobs at two different schools in Newport News, Virginia. I taught mathematics; he taught chemistry. During our stay, I took advantage of a National Science Foundation program called "Train the Trainers"—high school math teachers were given the opportunity to attend classes at a local university on the weekends and school holidays to secure a master's degree. My graduation from this program prompted my husband to apply and ultimately attend graduate school to pursue a PhD in physical chemistry. We moved to Blacksburg, Virginia, and he enrolled in Virginia Polytechnic Institute. I needed a job, and the local high school was the obvious place to start.

"I have two years of teaching experience behind me and a Master's of Mathematics."

"I'm sorry. Your credentials look fine, but we don't hire wives of graduate students."

"What if I was the husband of a graduate student? I'll bet you would give me a job then, wouldn't you?"

The secretary's eyes softened and she made a slight nod. "I didn't make the policy." Her words were spoken through the tight lips of a strained smile. Then she leaned over the counter and said, "Down the way, toward Radford, there's a very secret Department of Defense computer installation." Her words were whispered in a conspiring manner. "It's under a mountain, and you have to get a Top Secret clearance from the government to go there. I've heard they are looking for people."

Fate controls things in mysterious ways; this rejection turned out to be fortuitous. At this time, computer science curriculum was not yet taught in the universities, and my math background was just what the government was looking for. I was hired as a mathematician at the GS-7 level, the first rung of the Civil Service professional track. My starting salary was more than double what I could earn as a teacher. Three weeks after my security clearance was announced, I headed to Washington D.C. courtesy of the US government, for training as a computer programmer/ systems analyst.

The next five years were happy years. I felt accomplished and my performance reviews were such that I continued to take on new responsibilities in my job. I was fulfilled and I felt needed. I headed a team of six men and was routinely called into management strategy meetings. My earnings enabled my husband to pursue his degree, and the Department of Defense installation where I worked held a key role in the security of my country. The computer training I received gave me a head start in a field that for decades would shape not only my destiny, but also the world's. There were no parents or churches to tell me how I should behave. My husband was immersed in studies, so there was no time or place to play a submissive role.

I didn't talk to my family about how much I loved my job. When I was growing up Mom only worked when finances were tight. She passed the tests to become a real estate agent, she used her self-taught accounting skill to do the books for JC Penney, and she studied and became a Notary Public. When her success in a job—she was always very successful—had pulled us out of the hole, my father would rave: "No wife of mine is going to work like a commoner. It is demeaning to a husband." She would always quit her job and go back to being a doting housewife.

It was the week of Thanksgiving, and I flew to California to visit my parents. Years earlier, after the heart attack that took place during my wedding, my father retired from the Singer Company, and Mom and Dad moved back to their home state. They were hosting a big family reunion at their house in Hemet. My sister and her family, aunts and uncles, cousins—everyone would be there. Everyone except my husband; he had to stay in Blacksburg for classes.

"Mom, Dad, I have some great news I want to tell you." It was late in the afternoon before Thanksgiving; my mother was working on the pastry for her traditional holiday mincemeat pie, and Dad was doing a taste test on the brandy sauce that would be served with the pie—one shot of brandy for the sauce, two shots for himself. "I got a promotion and pay raise in my job." Mom looked up; Dad poured himself a full glass of brandy.

Mother was quiet; she always waited for Dad to speak first. "Are you still working for the military? Under the mountain?" he asked.

"The Department of Defense. And yes, I am still working for them. James is in graduate school. We need the money to live." The kitchen went quiet except for the thuds and squeaks of the rolling pin against the stiff dough. "My raise put me at a little more than eight thousand a year." I heard a sharp intake of air and looked into Mom's wide-opened eyes.

The subject of finances was never discussed in our home, but there was a good chance my new salary was significantly more than my father had ever earned. Dad loved to act as a big spender, often to the detriment of the family budget. Whenever we went out to eat, it was at a "fine" restaurant—no family diners for us. Come time to leave, Dad would put down a large bill for a tip and find the manager to slap on the back and boisterously compliment on the meal. Mom always left something at the table and would go back to retrieve the forgotten item. She'd glance quickly to ensure my father's back was turned, scoop up the large bill and replace it with a few ones. I suspected this was the way she collected the "stash" that purchased my red sequined dress.

"So what is the news you have to tell us?" My father gulped down the first glass of brandy and poured himself another.

"That was the news."

The silence was palpable.

"I guess I do have something else, but you can't tell anyone until I know for sure." I paused, not for drama or to get their attention; I was uncomfortable telling them so soon. "I think I may be pregnant."

"That's wonderful news." Mother dusted her hands on a dishtowel and tears welled.

"God damn it, Sharleen." Dad took a swig of brandy and set down the glass so he could give me a hug. "I've never been prouder."

Little did I know that getting pregnant was all it took to make my dad proud of me. My face burned, Mom thought I was blushing, and my throat constricted making it difficult to speak. I'd spent my life trying to gain his approval, but not like this. I chose not to explain my reaction to his comments. It felt disrespectful and would have been upsetting to my mother. A confrontation would have made for a very uncomfortable Thanksgiving. So, like the young girl, I buried my feelings of hurt and rejection deep inside. Somewhere else was now over two-thousand miles away, and I retreated from my parents.

Fourteen family members and friends graced our Thanksgiving table the following day. Mother and I carried in steaming bowls and platters of food. When everyone was gathered and the wine poured, my father stood slowly and ceremoniously raised his glass. "I want to propose a toast," he said. "Sharleen," he nodded my way, "will soon give her mother and me a baby boy!"

Contrary to my father's prediction, my first child was a girl. And twenty-three months later a son was born. Thankfully for me, it was still imperative that I work. Five years after moving to Blacksburg, James finished his graduate work, took a job as a research chemist with a Fortune 500 company, and our family moved to Lancaster, Pennsylvania—a provincial area deeply influenced by the surrounding Amish and Mennonite communities. It seemed the perfect place to raise a family.

Our children were ages one and three when we moved into a neighborhood that had seen three generations of growth before us. The people around us were retired grandparents, parents of high school students, and those like us, families with young children. We had no friends or family nearby and no support system. Out of necessity, I stayed at home to be a "mom."

"So what does your husband do for a living?" It was the opening question asked upon meeting anyone new. Attitudes and opinions were not subtle here. I soon tired of answering and stopped going to parties. Neighborhood coffee klatches became my only outlet, but I soon gave these up from the boredom of talking about children and recipes. My whole being screamed, "Look at me, I am a real person." But the demons shouted back: *only a girl, not good enough, unworthy, unlovable.* I fought an ongoing battle with my nemesis, depression. Help from the medical community came in the form of a prescription for Valium, which I refused. And so, to dull the pain, I looked to alcohol.

The constraints imposed by the university I attended helped me to make it through college without drinking. It was during my high school teaching years in Hampton, Virginia that my husband and I were introduced to the pleasure of a Perfect Manhattan—blended whiskey served up with a dash of bitters and equal parts of sweet and dry vermouth. One drink, and then two, became a nightly ritual.

Like a dutiful daughter, I phoned home every Sunday evening, purposely waiting until after eight o'clock, California time. The three-hour time difference ensured Dad would be drunk and in bed.

"Hi, Mom, how are things going?"

"Hi, Honey. We're both fine, but I must say, a little worried about you."

"Why? Nothing has happened."

"Well, you know. The last few weeks you've sounded sort of low. Well anyway, this morning we were listening to Jerry Falwell on the radio. They were talking about a monthly newsletter they are putting out with daily meditations and scriptures and all. So your dad and I are sending them money for you to have a subscription."

Silence.

"You ought to get the first one in a couple of weeks. I know you'll enjoy it."

The day my newsletter arrived with the lead article titled, "Women Praise God by Being Submissive to Their Husband," I called the post office and placed a hold on future deliveries of this type. I called it pornographic material.

NOW Comes to Lancaster. The National Organization for Women is forming Consciousness- Raising groups in the Lancaster area. Interested? Call 717 391-1NOW.

I cut the newspaper advertisement out and taped it to my vanity mirror. It took a week to find the courage to call. "Of course." The woman on the telephone sounded both professional and friendly. "Actually our first session is tomorrow night, at seven. We're in a brick row house, sixteen B, near the corner of Mulberry and Lemon." My anxiety rose—it was not a particularly safe part of town, especially at night. "Just come down Prince and take a right on Walnut to get to Mulberry."

"I lied to my husband about where I was going tonight." Muffled laughter came from the five faces that stared at me. "Told him I was taking some bridge lessons."

"Is it necessary for you to lie to get out of the house?" Leslie asked. She lived in the home where we met and was our facilitator.

"Not really. Guess I'm a little embarrassed by being here."

Joy was the next to speak up. "We can understand that," she said and clutched the hand of the woman sitting next to her. "We're lovers, and there aren't many places we can be together in Lancaster County."

Miriam sat directly across from me in our small circle. She dressed in traditional Old Order Amish garb—a navy blue dress with long sleeves and a full skirt, covered with a cape on the bodice. Her blouse was fastened with straight pins, her stockings were black cotton and her shoes were also black. "Yaa … I be shunned for not acting the way of my people. So can't go anywhere they be."

That only left one more. Candy, short for Candice, sat with crossed legs covered in black fishnet stockings. Candy wore a black leather mini skirt with a tight fitting red sweater that exposed a great deal of cleavage. Miniskirts hit the fashion stage in 1966, but seven years later they were still an anomaly in our conservative area. "My husband liked to beat me up. So now, when I'm not waiting tables at a lounge down on the south side, I work the streets."

I attended meetings for almost three years, for two hours every Thursday night at Leslie's home. It became my new "somewhere else." The disparateness of our social circles allowed the group comfort in revealing intimate details of our lives. In Leslie's modest, dimly-lit living room six women became confidantes, providing an ongoing support system to one another. Talk was of many things, but always came back to that empty shallow feeling of being a "non-person." Husbands weren't solely the cause—it was society that was doing the job on us.

When I talk to friends or my grown children, I refer to this time as my "nervous breakdown." They were also my angry years. This anger drove a wedge between me and my husband, my parents, my friends, and most regrettably, my children. I look back on this time with guilt—lying on the couch in my nightgown and robe as Shelley and Chris played alone in front of the television; getting dressed minutes before my husband arrived home from work; listening to my daughter tell her younger brother to be quiet so he would not bother me. But most of all, I missed those special bonding days with my children.

"Be good, Chris, don't make Mommy mad."

My daughter's words, so like those I had heard as a child: "Sharleen, don't upset your father. Don't make too much noise. No, you can't have a friend over, it would be disruptive. Turn the television to a different channel; you know your father doesn't like Ed Sullivan."

The day I heard my daughter speak those words, I decided to go back into the workforce. My son was old enough to go to pre-school, and I wasn't doing them any favors by staying home.

"Do you know COBOL?"

The name was an acronym for COmmon Business-Oriented Language, and it was the primary computing language used in the world of business and finance. My "interviewer" was not at all like the man from

IBM. He was tie-less and wore a crumpled shirt with the sleeves rolled up. His feet were propped on the desk as I entered his cigar-smoke-filled office.

"I've programmed for five years in Fortran. It will be very easy for me to learn COBOL."

"I've never heard of this Fortran."

"Actually, it's one of the oldest programming languages. Most of the newer languages like COBOL have Fortran as their basis." I was feeling good about the interview. He was at least giving me an opportunity to talk. "It's a procedural language mainly used for scientific computing and numerical analysis."

He lowered his feet to the floor and put the cigar into an ashtray. "Have any children?" he said, and leaned forward with elbows on the desk.

"Yes," I answered and smiled. "My oldest just started first grade, and the youngest is in a pre-school class."

"So, what would you do if we needed for you to come in during the middle of the night and one of your children was running a fever?" My interviewer put the smoldering cigar in his mouth and lifted his feet back onto the desktop.

I started to cite all the times my former employer had called me in the middle of the night, but I knew from the question that any thoughts of the interview going well were dashed. He might as well have said: "*You can't do the job … you're only a girl.*"

"I think I would do exactly as you would in that situation." I stood slowly, gathered my things and walked out of the office.

Rejection is a pervasive thing. Thoughts of not being worthy consumed my days. I went through weeks of being unable to have a conversation about anything without crying. Trying to stop the tears only made it worse. Childhood taunts played constantly in my head. *Crybaby, crybaby … Sharleen is a crybaby.*

A dozen people of all ages and sizes sat in a circle of gray metal folding chairs in a brightly lit Sunday school classroom. The woman sitting directly across from me looked to be in her fifties. Her hair was bleached blonde and tightly permed; she seemed obsessed with scraps of paper with jotted notes—she read them, put them in her purse, and moments later pulled them out again. I stared at a bulletin board filled with pictures drawn by children about the same age as my son to avoid making eye contact with anyone in the group.

"Good evening. Glad you could make it tonight." The minister's eyes shone with acceptance and friendliness. He looked comfortable in the manner in which he was dressed, not at all standoffish like on Sunday mornings when he wore the long black robe. "There's coffee and pastries to enjoy, and facilities are down the hall to the left. We're going to go around the circle and introduce ourselves. Tell the group what it is that you hope to gain from being here."

Pastor Ted started with the woman sitting to his right, the one with the notes. She read from them: "My mother is dying, and I need to get help in caring for her. I am unable to cope with all her demands." The next person: "It's a money thing. My husband just lost his job, and we don't know how we're going to pay our mortgage." And on around the circle; my body tensed as my time to speak approached.

"I want to be able to talk to people without crying." I blurted the words out just as the tears began to flow heavily. My throat ached from efforts to hold them back. Silence. A deafening silence.

"Sharleen," Ted spoke gently, "you must first learn to love and accept that part of yourself that needs to cry."

Eventually I did learn to love and even nurture the part of me that was able to cry, but in the inviolability of the group, I was able to make another discovery—a discovery that would serve me well. I'd known for some time that my mother had no voice against my father, and, with the help of therapy, I came to see that I, too, had no voice to be myself. It had begun with my father, but was now pervading my entire being.

"We're going to free write in this exercise." Ted, my minister-marriage-counselor friend, smiled and passed around exam "blue books" and sharpened yellow pencils. I was at a retreat center with seven other women, the survivors of the first therapy group.

"I want you to think about being a house … and I want you to write about the kind of house you would be."

My house sits high on a rock cliff—its walls are glass, it has a narrow stairway down—the lines are clean and uncluttered. Strong, heavy beams support, and yet the glass walls are quite fragile. I leave the lights on most of the time, but there is hesitancy for people to climb the stairs to come in. They think I am aloof. I am strong, set apart, yet very vulnerable. By being glass and leaving the lights on, I feel others must surely know what goes on inside.

There is a room furnished very comfortably—perhaps in Early American. Here are located all of the traits I have been told are desirable for women to have: love of home and family, sentimentality, humility and submissiveness. This door is closed most of the time. There is another room—not surrounded by glass. It is bare, with only a rug and, perhaps, a fireplace. This is where I hope to entertain my friends. I try to bring my children here often. I wish my husband would come; he says he wants to, but it is difficult for him. There are so many demands placed on us. So far there have been a very small number of people ever to come to this room. I have decided they won't climb the stairs alone—I must go down and guide them. This is the center of my house, my most important room. There is pain in this room—happiness, too.

Out of here, surrounded by glass for all to see, is the room containing "appearance" type things: my prize possessions, my equipment to display my talents, previous career experiences, my education, my mind and its interests. I feel they are important. They sit high on a pedestal. I wish I could take them down, but for the time I keep hoping someone below will see them and in some way place importance on them. This room I would like to keep, but wish it could be moved further back in the house and no longer surrounded by glass.

The group was silent—they didn't know how to respond to what I had written. Later that afternoon one of the women told me she would pray for me.

In the fall, just as my youngest started first grade, I was hired into the Business Information Systems department of the company where my husband worked. My struggles with Lancaster County began to take a different shape. No longer was I the only one exposed to feelings of isolation at being different—now it was my children. There was the mother who would not allow my daughter to join the neighborhood carpool for Brownie meetings because I could not adequately meet my part of driving, and the teacher who took it out on my son because I was not able to be there during "Mother Help Days." There were missed award ceremonies, music concerts, sporting activities and field trips. Schools in Lancaster County in the late '70's were not quite prepared to accommodate children whose mother worked.

The growth and changes in me took a toll on my marriage. Learning to love myself, especially the self who needed to cry, also meant recognizing those basic needs that weren't being satisfied. Alcohol became a stronger crutch. The comfortably furnished glass room in my house went away, and with it, all the trappings that my husband, my parents and society expected of me. The room where my successes and accomplishments were displayed went also.

In 1980, during the sixteenth year of our marriage, my husband and I were back in that Sunday school classroom seeking the help of marriage counseling. Pastor Ted offered Thursday night therapy sessions for couples that felt their marriages needed help.

"Good evening everyone." Ted made the perfunctory housekeeping announcements while I scanned the faces of the other two couples in our circle. "I want to compliment all of you on the courage it took to show up this evening." The slight smiles and head nods of others told me I was not the only one with a queasy feeling in my stomach.

"I usually begin my sessions by asking everyone to introduce themselves and to tell the group why you are here and what you hope to get from our work together." Ted turned to the couple on his right and suggested they start things off.

John and Sally set the standard for the rest of us—one spoke up, the other remained quiet. "I guess my problem is jealousy." John reached over and took his wife's hand. Sally was gorgeous—a voluptuous Cher Bono and overtly sexual in the way she dressed. "I would like to learn to trust that my wife is being faithful."

The wife spoke for the second couple. Her elderly mother was living in their home and her husband resented the attention given to the sick woman. The wife wanted help with a plan to restore their marriage.

And then it was my turn. There was no question I would be the one to speak up; James had resisted coming at all. "Our relationship is matter-of-fact," I began rather hesitantly, and then, as I realized I was not going to cry, my voice gathered strength. "Sexual encounters are perfunctory, and we have minimal communication. I want to regain intimacy in our marriage."

Ted thanked everyone for being so open and honest about his or her issues. The remainder of the two-hour session was spent getting to know one another. During this and subsequent meetings I said very little; James said less. Not so with the other two couples.

We were well into the fifth session—most of the time had been spent with an ongoing argument John and Sally were having. John complained about the stares of men brought on by Sally's provocative manner of dress; she made no apologies. "I should be able to dress however I like. They are the ones who have a problem." And then the fatal slip came. "James likes the way I look."

My husband ... Sally was talking about my husband. The room went silent except for my audible intake of breath. All eyes turned to James. "It's really nothing," he said. "When Sally asked me if I thought she dressed too sexy, I told her she looked nice." With some prodding by Ted, James described daily phone calls from work to Sally. "We just talk," he said, "about how each of us is feeling and things that are going on. It's not a big deal, just somebody to listen to me."

His words ripped through me and shredded any semblance of hope for our relationship. All I'd ever really wanted from him was the intimacy of talk. And when I put myself next to Sally, I became that skinny, pimply-faced girl that hated the way she looked. The night after that group meeting I wrote in my journal: *I'm scared—I want to cry. I want to retreat deeply into myself. If it were possible to go somewhere else now, I would.*

The next Thursday night arrived and the part of me that withdraws into myself hated the thought of sitting in the room with James and Sally. "Sharleen, you seem unusually quiet this evening." Pastor Ted said. "What is going on?"

"I don't know. It's as though I need a sign of reassurance that James does still love me and won't walk out." Once again, the words came without the tears. For the past week an old phrase from my journal—*I am not lovable ...I am not lovable*—played constantly in my head. It took me back to that time of my life when my diary was filled with self-loathing. And it took me back to the night I wore my magical red dress.

The night of the Sing at Hardin-Simmons finally arrived. Red satin stiletto heels and dangling rhinestone earrings gave the finishing touch to my red-sequined dress. I walked into the back-stage area transformed into a beautiful, self-confident woman. Bustling activity ground to slow motion and then stopped. All eyes riveted on me. Sounds hushed. People whispered. My face and neck tingled with a flush of heat. The Chicago magic vanished.

Memory of changing into costume for the performance, and the performance itself, is a blur. After the Sing I cried in the arms of my boyfriend, James, and made up stories about what the other girls said about my dress and me. He reassured me and told me the dress was beautiful, but more importantly, I was beautiful. I knew at the time I was being dishonest, but it felt okay to make things up when all you really wanted was someone's love and approval.

A year later, James and I would be married.

I refused to openly go back to the place where I lied to James or anyone else to solicit comfort and reassurance. I had worked too hard on learning to love myself; never again would I claim to be a victim looking for rescue.

The minister breathed deeply and said: "Does this insecurity come from James' admission to calling Sally?"

"Of course. He is giving to her the only thing I wanted. I hate to feel this way. I don't want to be so dependent on him. In fact, I don't want to be dependent on anyone but myself."

After several moments the minister looked to James. "What do you think about what your wife said?"

"I'm left to wonder. If I don't choose to share feelings with Sharleen, thereby hurting her, how much of her problem must I accept as my own?"

I sat in stunned silence listening to the background murmur of Ted's voice. "Why are you unwilling to share your feelings with Sharleen?" I didn't hear an answer.

We stopped going to therapy sessions, and I retreated to the bare room of my glass house. I wasn't willing to give up my need for a husband who could share with me the intimacy of both our strengths and weaknesses. I needed to bring my "whole being" to a marriage without fear that some parts of me would be rejected or unacceptable and, in return, I needed a mate who could do the same.

Six months later I gave up Perfect Manhattans and filed for divorce.

Double Doll

I pulled into the driveway of my parent's small California-style condominium in Hemet; it had been sixteen years since that regrettable Thanksgiving dinner.

All the lights shone brightly, and there were several vehicles parked out front. I took a deep breath and let myself in the front door. The living room was empty with the only noise coming from a television that played quietly in the corner. A shaft of light led me down a narrow hallway to the open door of my parent's bedroom.

"Thanks for coming." Mom gave me a hug.

"You knew I'd come. How are you holding up?"

"The minister is here, and hospice. Hospice is what keeps me going."

My eyes were drawn to the massive bed that dominated the room. A sheet covering a slim body rose and fell only slightly with the form's labored breathing. I had to study the face to make certain it was Dad— the large rotund body that towered over me, as a child, that made me feel small and insignificant, was skeletal. Mom and I stood quietly, holding hands and listening to the minister read Bible passages intended to comfort when death approached.

"I am glad you made it," the woman from hospice said. "Your father's time is very near." She motioned for me to follow her into the living room.

"Your sister and mother have said their goodbyes; I would suggest that you do the same."

"He's asleep now, and my work is done," the minister said when he came out of the bedroom.

I changed clothes in preparation for a long night and entered the dimly lit room. Staccato hisses made by the oxygen machine provided a background rhythm to Dad's calmer, shallow breathing. I walked to the chair at his bedside, cupped his fragile hand and laid my head on the edge of the bed. It was sometime before dawn when I awakened to the raspy sound of his cough.

"Dad … it's me. I'm here."

"So you did …" His words were cut off by another fit of coughing. I held the straw in a glass of water to his lips and stroked his full head of black hair. Dad's body had withered, but his hair never turned gray or thinned.

"You know, despite the differences we've had, I do love you." My words belied the years of anger and resentment stuffed deep inside; but he looked so frail and vulnerable. "Is there anything you would like to tell me?"

"Give me my Bible." The leather cover was cracked with age and the pages dog-eared. It took him only moments to open to the place. He stabbed at the spot on the page with a bony finger. "Now read, Girl."

He pointed to Ephesians 5:22. Memories surrounded this passage; I could say the words without looking at the page. "Wives submit yourselves unto your husbands …"

"Go on," Dad insisted when my voice faltered.

"For the husband is the head of the wife." I closed the Bible and stood up.

"Don't you leave," he shouted. "We must pray." He groped for the book I'd left on the side of his bed and began to wave it in the air.

"Dad, I'm not your little girl anymore. I know you think I am at fault for my marriage failing, but I'm forty-two-years old and must do what I believe is right for my children and me. You don't have much time left; I really would like you to accept me for who I am."

"You shame your mother and me with your actions." His fervor brought on another coughing spell.

When I left his room, I couldn't sleep. I made a pot of coffee and sat at the dining room table trying to make sense of what had just happened. Unconsciously my eyes scanned the room and all the familiar objects that held a lifetime of memories: the oil painting of an adobe house nestled near Taos in the foothills of the Sangre de Christo mountains with chile ristras hanging on the walls, and the watercolor of a small stream close to Chama running through stands of brilliant yellow aspens with the Brazos Cliffs in the background—both given to my father as payment for his sewing machine repairs when he worked the northern regions of New Mexico; the crudely woven rug given to Dad when he picked up an elderly Navajo man walking from the reservation to Gallup to sell items his wife had woven; various macramé wall hangings I'd created and sent to Mom and Dad during my "nervous breakdown" period; and the antique Grandmother clock with the glass door over the face that my sister broke when she swung the croquet mallet at my head, and I ducked.

Memories flowed; I started a list of all the things I wanted to say to my father: *Why couldn't you just love me for who I was? The only time you talked to me was to show your disapproval over something I did. When we did talk, everything you said to me was either teasing or sarcastic. Do you know how badly sarcasm hurts? You preached about church and the Bible, but then you drank and cursed. I couldn't bring the two together. Sometimes I wanted you to listen to my pain, but really all I wanted was for you to look at me. Every time we got close to one another, you would tease me. Is that the only way you could relate to me? Most of all, I hated the way you made Mom give up who she was. I hated your story of how she stepped out of line for college.*

"Sharleen, it's now." My mother laid her hand gently on my shoulder. Sometime in the middle of the night I had moved onto the couch in the living room. "Hospice is here."

My sister, Sherry, Mother and I stood with the hospice volunteer as Dad's breath got increasingly shallow. He never regained consciousness and died peacefully in his sleep. The man who dominated in varying degrees the lives of all three of us was gone. We grieved differently. Mom needed to sleep, but she was unable to be in the bed where Dad had died. She took to my bed in the guest room until hospice was able to remove the hospital-issued bed made available to us. My sister cried openly. I retreated into stony silence.

I stayed on with Mom for more than a week—there were funeral arrangements, calls to friends and family, insurance claims to file, and papers to sort. I spent days going through boxes of pictures and memorabilia while Mom slept. In the bottom of one of the boxes was an unopened letter addressed to me at Rockford Lane, Lancaster, Pennsylvania. Yellowed, unlined paper held multiple pages, front and back, of Dad's familiar scrawl. The letter was dated 1977.

Dear Daughter,

Thank you for the very nice father's day card ... but most of all for a most beautiful letter which not only conveyed many, many thoughts but relayed a message of true concerned love for both your mother and I. With the Lord's help and guidance, I will describe two men as I have observed them—both known to you as your father—namely Noel & "Pete" Dickson ...

The letter explained that during high school he was the smallest member of the football team and was nicknamed "Pee Wee" which later developed into the name of "Pete."

The first person, Noel Dickson, was born of hard-shelled Baptist Christian parents …Noel received Christ at the early age of 11 years and was baptized at the Tower Grove Baptist Church in St. Louis, Missouri. He recognized himself as an introvert—so consistently, to overcome this withdrawal, he felt the need of being a ringleader of his friends and associates, thereby always going further and doing the unexpected to gain the attention and esteem of those that were his associates. Needless to say, Noel gradually developed the introverted personality into Pete, an extrovert.…

In retrospect I would list "Pete's" priorities as follows:

1. *Job (Pete felt without a job, all else would be impossible.)*
2. *Marjorie*
3. *Self*
4. *The Lord*
5. *Others*

"Pete" was never unemployed, but always had the offer of a better position with more lucrative possibilities. During the early childhood of "Pete" and Marjorie's two daughters, "Pete's" overwhelming desire for <u>self-esteem</u> brought him to take a job with the Singer Co. (a large company that could offer the fulfillment of "Pete's" burning ambition).

At this particular time of "Pete's" all-out effort of achievement, to list and compare his priorities seems very necessary:

1. *Top rung of the corporate ladder*
2. *Self-esteem & gratification*
3. *Wife & daughters*
4. *God (when it didn't interfere with # 1 or 2)*

The litany continued for another ten pages stepping through each phase of his life and work and health—successes and failures. After citing several heart attacks and subsequent job limitations, job successes prompted him to write:

This new assignment renewed his badly shattered ego to the point that his self-importance stirred up again the urge to pursue the climb up the corporate ladder to the tenth rung. A coincidental parallel between "Pete's" ten rung ladder, created in his own high-minded, self-centered being, and the <u>Ten Commandments on the stone tablets given to Moses by our Heavenly Father</u>....

The more successful I became as a businessman, the more addicted "Pete" became to alcohol. At this point I believe that you and your sister are quite aware of your father's apparent arrival to the point of no return. However, through a short, but timely suggestion of your mother, "Pete" surrendered his complete worthless self to our Lord Jesus Christ and by His grace a total new life is being experienced by "Pete." His new priorities are as follows:

1. *<u>Jesus Christ</u>*
2. *Marjorie*
3. *Daughters & family*
4. *Others*
5. *Self*

Sharleen, this is me, your father speaking now—I hope there has been a pattern of continuity followed that allowed you to understand the true me. ... Yes, your mother and I are having problems, however, as a rather new Born Again child of God there remains a good deal of cleaning up yet to be done through my continued maturity in His word.

Mom came into the bedroom as I was finishing the last few lines of the only letter I can remember my father writing to me. "I found this in the bottom of the box," I said and handed the letter to her. "It was never mailed."

"Oh my. I'd forgotten all about it." She pursed her lips and twisted them to the side so she could chew on the skin inside her mouth. It was a nervous habit—I can't remember a time she did not do this—a habit that I recognized in myself. "Your Dad and I were having so many problems then. We decided it was best not to send the letter to you."

"I knew about his health … the heart attacks and the emphysema. And, of course, I knew about the drinking. What other problems were there?" It was the first time my father admitted his failures. Perhaps we could have had a real relationship these last eight years. Perhaps we could have gotten to know one another and found love for each other on his deathbed.

"It wouldn't have done for me to tell you girls. But I guess it doesn't matter anymore." She lowered her eyes and kept her head bent as she continued. "You know we were trying to run the dealership here in Hemet. And you know your dad always wanted to be on top. I lived in constant worry that he was working too hard. The doctors repeatedly warned that stress and strain would inevitably bring about a final crisis." She gave a long sigh, and we sat in silence for several minutes. "The doctors also told me I should not worry your father with these facts. And I was told to avoid disagreements and arguments." Tears slid slowly down her cheek and, when she looked up, there was pleading in her eyes. "They also told me to avoid any bedroom activities. Knowing your father, you can understand the precarious position that put me in."

"You lived like that for seven years and didn't tell anyone?" I pulled Mom to me and wrapped my arms around her; we sat in silence until her tense body softened.

"I must sleep now," she said and headed back to her bedroom.

And then I wept. At first it was for my mother and all the years she'd lost, but as the tears came harder, I realized they were also for me, for what I had lost, and for my father and what he had lost. For fifty years, her entire married life, Mom gave up her own needs and dreams to follow my father; he spent most of his seventy-one years making up for his perceived inadequacies by working harder to prove himself. My entire life I had been in retreat—building that protective shell around me so I would not have to face the pain of rejection and failure—a retreat where there was never the need to use my voice to defend the person I wanted to be. My roots were planted in California—where I was born, the place of my extended family—and they had not yet found a safe place for replanting.

I retrieved my scrawled list of words I would never have the opportunity to say to my father and wrote over each statement with a red marker, *I FORGIVE YOU*. I saw this as the beginning of my healing.

Several days later, on the top shelf of the storage unit, I found a box— stashed away and untouched for over thirty years. I pulled out the map Dad used to navigate the Navajo Reservation; he'd highlighted roads, scribbled notes and drawn arrows pointing the way to the homes of his customers. And then I found my double doll. She lay crushed in the bottom of the box, under framed photographs and albums of newspaper clippings; the thunderbird pendant with its embedded chips of colorful stones was still attached to the chest of the Navajo girl.

"Mom, look at this." I lifted the doll out of the box and held it for my mother to see. "Do you remember the day I got this? I think I was eight or maybe nine-years-old." Mom nodded. "I thought Dad threw it away."

"He was drunk. I hid the doll. I always meant to give it to you. Guess I forgot."

"Did you know about the Navajo girl I met and the corncob doll she gave me?"

"I remember your dad being very angry and ranting about heathen idols. That's when I hid the doll."

"It was the corncob doll he thought was the idol … he threw that one away."

"Your dad had his ways, Sharleen. And I have mine."

"What's that supposed to mean?"

"Your Dad was too angry. Something about you being in a cave … it wouldn't have done for me to get in the middle."

"But you did … you hid the doll. You just never told me." I turned the double doll back and forth from the white face to the brown. "And I never told you that for a long time I prayed for God to turn me upside-down and make me into an Indian. The girl, the one in the cave, her name was Nanabah. We couldn't speak each other's language, so we exchanged gifts. It was a promise to be friends. She gave me a corncob doll, and I gave her my gold locket."

"The gift from your Aunt Dorothy?"

I nodded.

"I never understood why you stopped wearing it. So where did you get the double doll? And what happened to the corncob doll?"

"Dad bought this one at a roadside stand. He threw the corncob out the car window."

I told my mother that work-related issues prohibited me from attending my father's funeral. Mom seemed fine with my decision. "You were here before he died," she said. "That's the important thing."

I couldn't explain my relief in being unable to attend. Slowly, in my own time, I knew I would make peace with the memory of my father; it was the other family members I couldn't bear to face. My sister, her children, aunts, uncles, business associates, even Mother—they would all expect a certain level of openly expressed grief from me. I couldn't do it. I could not pretend to be sorry he was gone. I could not bear the thought of listening to all the glowing eulogies or hear what a God-fearing man he'd been or see the hankies dab wet eyes or receive the hugs and condolences from people who did not know me. I did not want to watch the face of my mother as she pressed raw skin of her cheek between her teeth. And I could not feign tears.

Hospice left brochures telling us that the purpose of funerals was to pay respect to those left behind. Mom was the one left behind. It was not me. So I retreated from my father's funeral and went to that safe and comfortable "somewhere else." The doll and Dad's reservation map, my reminders of a childhood time and a place when I was a real person that did have a voice, were repacked carefully and put back on the storage room shelf.

TO LOVE, HONOR and COMMUTE — *Lancaster, PA New Era* — *Tuesday, August 27, 1985*

Sharleen Daugherty, an independent computer software consultant who resides with her husband, Len, a manager at Armstrong World Industries, knows the meaning of "Trying to keep it all—family and job—in perspective." The mother of two teen-age children (as well as three step-children) says she wishes that she did not have to spend so much time on the road. Yet her job requires her to travel—often by train, more often by plane—around the country. That, the 43-year-old woman explains matter-of-factly, is something she and her husband accept.

Giving up her career was not an option when they married. "One of the things that drew us together was our mutual respect for our abilities in the working environment," she says. So they both have learned to take her traveling in stride.

My current income, coupled with travel awards, enabled me to splurge on my mother. It was her seventy-fifth birthday, five years after the death of my father. Mom and I sipped champagne as we stood on the balcony of our room at the Ritz-Carlton, Laguna Niguel—a AAA Five Diamond Southern California beach resort billed to cater to the world's most discriminating guests.

"Your father had other women."

I felt the air leave my body, like being kicked in the stomach. "How? ..."

"It started when we were in Albuquerque." Mom twirled the flute of champagne and gazed into the blue waters of Dana Point. "Your dad called and told me he had to stay over another night in Gallup for business. I had a dream ... I saw the name of that Thunderbird motel out on Central Avenue and a door with the number two-thirteen. They were big brass numbers in my dream ... just like on the door."

Her voice was monotone and matter-of-fact, but she sipped more of the bubbly, squared her shoulders, and the words tumbled out. "You know, Sharleen, I drove right to it. I knocked on the door of number two-thirteen, and your dad answered."

Silence.

"He sure had a surprised look on his face when he opened that door and saw me." She started to giggle.

I managed to say, "I'll bet," between gulps of air as we both laughed uncontrollably.

"I have to go inside," Mother said. "I think I'm going to wet my pants."

When she returned from the bathroom, I held her in my arms and guided her to sit on the bed. "Mom, thanks for telling me this. I've never felt so close to you." We sat in silence, listening to the pounding surf outside our balcony. "Dad aside, your story is incredible ... like you are prescient, or something? Have you always had dreams like that?"

It took her a long time to answer, and I saw that nervous habit again—the hand pushing raw flesh from the inside of her cheek against her teeth—a habit that I emulated resulting in knotty sores on the inside of my mouth. But when the words came, they tumbled fiercely as though a dam had burst. "Lots when I was a child. Your grandparents were Pentecostal; you might call them Holy Rollers. Well, they took me to tent revivals, and I experienced miracles, prophecies, speaking in tongues, the whole gamut. That can be pretty scary when you're only seven or eight years old. So I forced myself to ignore the dreams. I was afraid they meant

70

I was becoming like some of the crazy people I saw in church. It was hard to give them up because I flew a lot in my dreams. I loved flying ... it was so beautiful and calm up above. And finally, one day I noticed that I wasn't remembering my dreams or flying anymore."

"Amazing! I used to fly in my dreams, too. I know what you mean about it taking you somewhere else. What happened to me is that it got increasingly difficult to get myself in the air. I remember feeling like if I just flapped my arms harder I would be able to get up. Sometimes I even crashed into trees or electric lines because I wasn't working hard enough. I would be exhausted when I woke up."

"Oh, Honey, we've missed so much." Mom cradled my hand in hers. "I know there was a time when you were angry with me. I couldn't get to you through all that anger."

"I think the anger was about that horrible story Dad used to tell of how you stepped out of line at the registrar's office. I hated that story. And the way you would get a good job ... you loved working ... and then Dad would get a pay raise and make you stop. I was angry with you for letting him do those things to you. I vowed it would never happen to me."

"Is that why you pulled away from the family?"

"I think so. That and the fact Dad never approved of the way I lived my life. Do you remember the time you both came to visit me in Pennsylvania? Chris was about twelve at the time. Dad started with his sarcastic teasing, doing to Chris what he had done to me at that age."

"I remember. You and your father got into a row. You told him you weren't raising your children to accept or listen to teasing or sarcasm."

"Dad couldn't understand. I remember it upsetting you because Shelley and Chris didn't want to be around while you were there. It wasn't you, it was their grandfather."

"Oh my. We all missed out on so much. If I had just stood up to your father."

Later that evening, while we enjoyed a meal that featured Pan-Latin cuisine overlooking the ocean, I posed the question that haunted me. "I don't … I don't understand why you stayed with him?"

"What would you have had me do? You know he didn't want me to have friends or go places without him. He was my life."

"And you never told anyone about the other woman?"

"It wouldn't have done for you girls to know. But I preached to you to never become dependent on a man. I always felt so very proud when you were having success in your jobs. I just couldn't say so in front of your father."

A memory from days past came flooding back. I was in the kitchen drying the dishes, as my mother washed them. *"Sharleen, money is control … you don't want to end up like me."* Her arms were in soapy water up to her elbows, and her eyes pleaded when she looked at me over her shoulder. *"Don't ever become dependent on a man for money."*

Six months later my sister summoned me back to the California condo. Mom was dying from pancreatic cancer. We hired a nurse to be with her during the night, and my sister and I took turns sitting at her bedside during the day.

I purchased a picture puzzle—a beautiful rendering by Thomas Moran of the Grand Canyon of the Yellowstone—and sat for the deathwatch at the same dining room table I'd sat at six years earlier. The puzzle, with its magnificent rock outcroppings, canyons, waterfalls, and untamed wilderness gave me mindless relief during the time my sister was with my mother. Often, when Mom slept, Sherry would come and sit with the puzzle and me.

"So, are you going to stay for the funeral this time?"

"Yes, Sherry. I'll be able to stay the course with you."

"You know it was hard on Mom when you left before Dad's burial."

"She didn't tell me. She seemed fine that I was going."

"You should know better. Mom would never put her own needs above yours." My sister was right. Mother's voice was muffled by the presence of my father, just as mine had been. "In fact, it seems to me you've never been present, even when you came out for visits. It's like you were here in body but not in spirit."

"I've never felt comfortable coming home."

"What do you mean? We all loved to have you visit."

Visits where my sister and her family were present always included Sherry's stories to her children about how much of a brat I was when we were growing up. "She was such a little snot. I would have boyfriends over, and Sharleen would charge admission to let her nerdy little friends peep in the windows at us. And tattletale ... the goody-two-shoes always told Mom and Dad. I'd get in trouble, but I gave it back to her in spades." It would end with raucous laughter and me leaving the room.

"Right. It was great sport for you. All you wanted to do was relive the past ... about how wonderful you were and what a bratty sister you had. When you weren't around, I got the same treatment from Dad. He harped on me about my job, and how I wasn't staying at home to take care of my family."

"You know you were always the favored one. You got the fancy education and the nice big house. You've had a very easy life."

"Sherry. You had the same opportunities I had. We made different choices, that's all. But now I understand why you teased. You are jealous."

"I may have been jealous once, but not anymore. Now I'm disgusted and angry."

Her words took me by total surprise. "I don't understand."

"James. You walked out on James, just like Johnny walked out on me."

I was caught off guard. Never would it have occurred to me that the anger she placed on her cheating husband was now transferred. I answered in a loud voice. "I wasn't the one having an affair."

The baby monitor signaled that Mother was awake and calling for my sister. The voice that came through the device when Sherry entered Mom's room was weak and shaky. "Honey, I am dying. Please don't let me die with you and your sister arguing with one another." Waves of guilt swept over me. Mom was the peacekeeper in our home, and nothing had changed ... even on her deathbed.

Dying was not easy for Mother; she may have starved to death. No matter how alert we were, Mom managed to pull out the feeding tubes. She wanted to die and to be done with the misery. The long quiet hours gave time for my sister and me to heal our grievances toward one another. The day Sherry said to me, "You know, Sis, it's a good thing we are blood relatives and must love one another ... as different as we are, if we were just acquaintances we wouldn't even be friends," I knew we had arrived. Our relationship was as good as it was going to get.

Over several weeks, Mom flitted in and out of lucidity. "I love that you and your sister are both here with me. We'll have such great fun together. Maybe we can all go back to that wonderful restaurant in Laguna Beach. I see your grandfather, he is calling me. I should have listened to your father. He said I would go to Hell if I weren't born again. I've gone there already. I am there. I'm in Hell."

Towards the end Mother suffered from convulsions; it was important for both my sister and me to be at her side. One of us had to hold down her tongue and one had to administer the medications. "Mom, Sharleen and I have made our peace with one another." Mother was just coming out of a particularly intense seizure and mumbling about being in Hell. "You don't have to stay for our sake. It's okay to just let go and be with Dad."

"Maybe she doesn't want to be with Dad," I said and looked into her tormented eyes. "Maybe that's why she thinks she is in Hell."

Despite the presence of her children, Mom died alone. I grieved for the forty-some years "it wouldn't have done" for us to be friends and confidantes. Mom was a kind and generous person; she was always there if someone needed her. Dozens of family members and people whose faces I did not recognize were at her funeral to give testimony to the impact she'd had on their life. Dad was cantankerous and selfish. His death was calm; hers was not. I wondered about a God that would allow this to happen.

When I first arrived at the condo, I'd unpacked the box with the double doll. In the nights, sleeping in the guest room of my sister's condo, I often pulled the covers over my head and curled into a tight ball, hugging my doll. It was during those long nights that I sorted through my memories to try to make peace with the woman I'd become. I replayed the childhood teasing that drove me to my secret places of somewhere else; the teenage rejections and ridicule when church became my sanctuary; the lack of approval by parents, church and society as a young woman that sent me hundreds of miles from home and family; the longing for intimacy in a relationship that forced the dissolution of my first marriage. My mother's legacy was that of "peace keeper," a trait I only partially inherited. I did not confront or stand up for what I believed in or needed, but, unlike my mother who quietly stayed to bear the consequences, I chose to walk away. That was my way of surviving and keeping an identity. That was my defense.

PART TWO

Crow Canyon

"**K**eep your shoes next to the bed and shake them out before putting them on."

I was one of ten women attending the opening night reception for a weaving workshop at Crow Canyon Archaeological Center. I'd seen the advertisement for the weeklong program in *New Mexico Magazine*, a publication that was one of my favorites since leaving the Land of Enchantment in 1959.

"That way you'll avoid a scorpion bite." The speaker followed his words with an elongated pause intended to emphasize. "We have mountain lions, bears, coyotes and snakes." His slight build and lily-white skin suggested the young man hadn't actually seen any of the aforementioned creatures. "Use your flashlight when you go to the bathrooms and, whatever you do, don't hike the trails alone."

A woman in designer jeans and a leather cowboy hat cupped her hand over her mouth and leaned toward me. "Who is this guy?"

"He's an anthropology student from Michigan State … at least that's what the information packet says. He's doing an internship."

Two women sat on the stage behind the speaker. Their clothing was similar and a style I could identify as traditional Navajo. They wore brightly colored velveteen blouses, adorned with an abundance of jewelry, over three-tiered ruffled skirts. In my high school days, we called them broomstick or squaw skirts. The woman directly behind the speaker looked like an ornate Christmas tree. She wore a blood-red blouse and green skirt, twined ropes of silver, coral and turquoise hung from her neck, and a woven sash-belt stretched around a substantial middle. The V-shaped neckline of her blouse was held together at the collar by a large silver disk embedded with turquoise chips—identical to the wheels of color atop cuff-bracelets on both wrists.

A slender woman wearing a royal purple blouse and a cerulean skirt sat next to her. She wore a magnificent squash blossom necklace. Hand-forged silver pieces, made to look like the trumpet-shaped flower of a yellow squash plant, hung, ten to a side, on a double strand of silver beads that held a massive chunk of sky-blue turquoise surrounded by a horseshoe-shaped piece of silver.

Suddenly, I felt self-conscious about my crudely made thunderbird pendant and discreetly took it off my blouse. The bravado that propelled me out of the Stock Exchange boardroom and through the lunch with Janice was dissolving. What did I know about the Navajo culture? I'd spent one summer riding through the reservation with my father and a small portion of an hour with a girl named Nanabah. I was out of my element.

"I'd like to introduce our special guests." The speaker stepped aside and motioned toward the women. "This is Jessie Begay." Christmas Tree hunched her shoulders when she stood. "Jessie is from Teec Nos Pos, not far from the Four Corners area. Her brother built the loom stands you'll receive in class tomorrow." Jessie had small eyes that flitted from one thing to the next, never coming to rest. "And Lola Tsosie." Lola rose slowly, exhibiting an elegant and regal stance. Her hair was tied back in a bun, the traditional style for a Navajo woman. "Lola also lives in Teec Nos Pos. She and Jessie are sisters. They'll be your instructors for the workshop. Lola doesn't speak English, so you'll have to direct your questions to Jessie."

The intern droned on with information about schedules and the timing of events. I made a beeline for a telephone to call Len when the meeting was over. "You wouldn't believe it out here," I said and looked around to make certain no one was within hearing distance. "It's the poverty. I don't remember it being so bad. And the land is so drab and desolate."

"You were a kid," Len said. "Things look different when you're young."

"I just came from the welcoming reception. Not a drop of wine."

"Will you get what you're looking for?"

"Hard to say." I didn't want to tell him how inadequate I felt. Len and I weren't in agreement over my trip to Crow Canyon or my new business. Despite my efforts to explain the dream and the strong message it sent me, he passed it off as *woo-woo* stuff. "They introduced the two women who'll teach the class. They're Navajo, at least."

"What's the place look like?"

"The lodge is beautiful, and the weather has been good ... warm during the day, cool at night." It was mid-October, and the temperatures on the high desert still showed signs of summer. "Did I mention the air conditioner on the rental car didn't work?"

"What else?" he said and chuckled. "Are you taking your blood pressure pills?"

I knew his question was rhetorical. In the six months since the day I cradled the pigeon on the sidewalk in New York, my blood pressure had reached new heights. My doctor was routinely changing my medication in efforts to keep it under control. I'd spent those months visiting my customers and developing project plans to turn over accounts; woven into my travels were trips to local libraries searching for any shred of information about the Navajo Indians. I was trying to give myself a crash course in the rewards and pitfalls of working within another culture. By adamantly insisting I could do this on my own, coupled with grandiose ideas, the bar for my success was high.

"One of the fun things is, we're sleeping in hogans. You pronounce that hoe gone." There was a long pause from the other end of the line. "I'll read you the Crow Canyon spiel. 'It's a traditional home for the Navajo: an eight-sided dwelling made of logs chinked with mud and a door that faces east. Most have a dirt floor with a wood burning stove in the center and a hole in the roof for smoke to escape. Typically there is no electricity or water. Today, many Navajos have modern houses or trailers and only use their hogan for special occasions or ceremonies.'"

"Sounds charming. Glad I'm not there."

"Actually, these are pretty nice. They have a concrete floor with baseboard heat and regular style furniture ... you know, a chest of drawers, a couple of twin beds with a nightstand, and a small table and chair. There's plenty of space. And we do have electricity. But on the downside, the bathhouse is about twenty yards from my hogan."

"Good thing you took a flashlight."

Len told me the news from home, and we concluded our conversation when I heard the dinner bell ring. Much to my surprise, the cafeteria food was extraordinary: platters of steaming tortillas, tamales, enchiladas and chili rellenos, accompanied by bowls of spicy red and green sauces— cuisine that combined the best of the Native American and Mexican foods. I grew up on food like this, but hadn't had any since leaving New Mexico. The aroma coming from the kitchen took me back to Saturday mornings in Albuquerque when a young boy pulled his wagon through our neighborhood selling hot, freshly made tamales. Most of the time I paid a quarter for cornmeal stuffed with spicy pork and green chilies wrapped and steamed in a cornhusk. Some days, when money was tight, I paid a dime for the same cornmeal stuffed with cinnamon, raisins and brown sugar.

We were on our own after dinner. I was still acting like an insecure and withdrawn child and was not in the mood to be sociable, so I headed for my room. The Navajo women were on the path, a few paces in front of me, and they entered the hogan next to mine. A black pickup truck was parked in front. The sides were splattered with a thick coat of reddish-brown mud, and the fenders I could see were dented; the windshield was a maze of cracks, and a bungee cord held the hood down. I felt uncomfortable about approaching the women. I hadn't developed a sense of how to behave in this foreign culture or what expectations were placed on me—so I fell back to the security of my professional persona and reviewed of my business plan.

Several bullet points followed the strategy entitled *Visit Crow Canyon*: the first was, *Document the tools required for weaving a rug*; the second, *Understand the process and the technique*; the third, *Learn how to discern the quality*; and the fourth bullet, *Recognize the names of the different designs*. I quickly scanned the notes, which were ideas on how to acquire this knowledge penned under each bulleted entry. Then I reread the statement at the bottom of the page, the one in bold print and highlighted. ***In order to reduce costs and eliminate the middlemen, BUY DIRECTLY FROM THE WEAVERS***. I saw the middlemen as traders and gallery owners. In this enterprise the middleman would be me.

I watched my travel clock, giving the women an appropriate amount of time to settle themselves, put my papers back in my briefcase and, emboldened by my plan, headed out. The first knock on their door was too timid. I was back in my business-like mindset and impatient, plus I needed to establish who was in control of this meeting. I knocked again, louder this time.

The door opened only a crack, and I looked into the eyes of Jessie Begay. She said nothing. *Okay, what do I do now?* I stood awkwardly and finally muttered something about a business proposal. She pulled the door wide and stepped aside. Once inside I could see Lola sitting in the room's only chair. She worked a long slender dowel with a round disk close to the bottom, pulling clumps of raw wool from a bag, twisting it through her fingers and around the tip of the dowel. The stick came alive with the quick back-and-forth motions of her hand twirling the dowel against the top of her thigh, and the wool around the slender stick gathered as spun yarn on the disk. Without a word spoken, Jessie moved to sit on the edge of one of the beds. I stood just inside the door; several minutes passed in total silence.

This was my first personal encounter with Navajo women. It would take dozens more before I became comfortable with silence. Eventually I would learn that, in the Navajo way, silence is acceptance, an expression of harmony between the human and natural world. But I still operated on a timetable that forced efficient use of every minute. Unable to tolerate the quiet any longer, I walked to the other bed and sat down, opened my briefcase and pulled out the pages of my business plan entitled *Visit Crow Canyon*.

"Ya gots money in there?" Jessie broke the silence.

"A little." I felt heat creep up my face. Back east new acquaintances didn't ask personal questions. "You know, for emergencies."

The women exchanged comments in Navajo. Jessie reached for the purse that was next to her on the bed. I'd observed earlier in the day that both women had similar pocketbooks, an old-fashioned style—a pouch in black vinyl with a clasp to open or close, and strap handles for carrying. I also noticed that the bags never left their sides. Jessie opened her purse and held it out for me to see; the bag was filled with ropes of turquoise and silver beads, bracelets and pendants—enough jewelry to start a retail business.

"For emergency," Jessie closed the bag. "How many dollars you pay for your purse?"

Another question that caught me off-guard.

"You knows. What did you give the trader for it?"

"I really don't remember. It's old."

Similar to the lack of conversation, questions regarding the cost of things would be another cultural hurdle I had to cross. In retrospect, I think it comes from generations of dealing with the traders—bartering for necessities without knowing the dollar value of goods. But that evening Jessie's questions served to highlight just how far out of my element I was. I wanted to run and hide, retreat into my somewhere else. Instead, I changed the subject. "Tell me about Lola. She's your sister but you don't look at all alike."

"Same father, different mothers."

Silence.

"And she doesn't speak English?"

"That's 'cause parents hide her from bus drivers."

"What?"

"Boardin' school. When government says all Indians have to go to school, parents save out best to teach old ways. My momma tried, but trader told on me."

"Why wouldn't they want their children to go to school?"

"Grandmother's afraid. They think if we goes to white man school, we'll forget what it means to be *Diné*. You know, think with head instead of heart. So best children kept at home. That ways they learn how to care for sheeps an things like that."

In the simple words of her grandmother, Jessie had just articulated what I was seeking—that ability to think with my heart. I'd read many books about the Navajo. I'd learned they call themselves *Diné*, a word that means "the People." The name "Navajo" actually translates to everything from "the enemy" to "great planted fields," depending on the language. I'd read about the forced boarding schools and the fact that the Navajo

Reservation was the largest Indian reservation in the country, but none of the written words had described the essence of the people as succinctly as Jessie's grandmother.

"So you went to boarding school?"

"In Utah, up by Salt Lake City. I hates it." Jessie's voice lost any tones of enthusiasm; she spoke in flat monotone. "They beats us if we talk Navajo or tell stories. Every year they takes me after we bring sheeps down from mountains."

I'd read that in the heat of the summer, the Navajos took their sheep up into the mountains for water and better grazing. Then they brought them down, into the arid desert land, for the winter months and for lambing. As Jessie talked, I concluded that the boarding schools hadn't done a very good job of teaching her the English language. But I would come to realize there were speech issues common to most of the Navajos I met. "G" was rarely pronounced in a word ending with "ing," and the sibilant sounds were difficult for them. More than one sheep was sheeps; multiple trading posts became tradin' postes; two boys were called boyses; and artisans were artises. I determined, in most cases, it was not a matter of education, or lack thereof, but a situation where English, as a second language, presented speech patterns and sounds that were in competition with their native tongue. I also learned that the Navajo were much more successful at speaking my language than I was in speaking theirs. The glottal stops, glottalized consonants, gliding vowel sounds, diphthongs, and speech intonations that rendered the same basic word with multiple meanings were beyond my ability to produce or learn.

When I asked if the children were still being forced into boarding schools, Jessie told me the people had gotten angry and demanded an end to the program. "We starts own schools," she said, "here on reservation. Lola teaches at Head Start."

"The Navajo language?"

"That, an' how to weave, tend sheeps. Them kind of things. We got whole bunch of parents my age that don't know 'bout the old ways."

I glanced at Lola; she lifted her head and gave me a shy smile. "Lola can understand English?" I asked.

"Little bit, but nots like me. Boardin' school teaches me lots 'bout White Man's world. So's I do all the talkin' for both of us."

And then we sat in silence.

"I'm starting a new business and need to buy weavings."

Jessie's face broke into a smile; she pulled out a cardboard box stashed under her bed—it was full of small rugs. "I'm good at business." She said and laid the rugs out on the floor. "Gives you a good price on Storm."

Jessie held up a weaving with a gray background that was framed in a border of black yarn. The top and the bottom of the long sides were electrified by zigzags of red and white; in the middle there was a red square outlined in white with similar but smaller squares in each of the four corners. Strong black jagged lines joined the corners with the center, as if charging the entire rug with slashing thunderbolts.

"I recognize that design." I was pleased my time doing research and studying was paying off. "The zigzags are lightning bolts, the square in the center represents the hogan, and the smaller squares are the Houses of the Wind or Four Sacred Mountains."

"*Aoó,*" Jessie nodded.

I sat on the floor to examine the rugs more closely. The third bullet of my business plan was to learn how to discern the quality. Like a man kicking tires in a used car lot, I fingered the wool and looked closely at the tightness of the weave.

"Gots to do this," Jessie said and dropped to her knees in a dramatic gesture. She folded the rug and held the edge of one end against the other. The widths of the ends were off by at least an inch. "They don't match. That's how comes I give you a good price."

"How much?" I held the skewed rug in the air.

Jessie looked at Lola and motioned for me to follow her outside. "Two-fifty. An don't tell them what I say. I'm givin' you a deal."

I'd done a quick estimate on the size. "If that Storm costs fifty dollars a square foot, what would a quality weaving cost?"

Jessie looked puzzled. "Its two-hundred-and-fifty dollars," she repeated.

We went back inside.

"Okay. Here's what I want." My voice was back, and Len's words to me as I boarded the airplane, "Don't let them take advantage of you," played loudly through my head. "I'm starting this new business and I'll need a lot of weavings. Only good ones." I stared directly at Jessie. I felt back in my element, and the words flowed easily. "I want weavers I can depend on to do custom orders." Jessie folded her rugs and put them back in the box. Lola's head was down; she hadn't uttered a word.

"Like consign weavin'?"

"Right." I handed Jessie my business card. "I have an eight-hundred number. You can call me for free."

"How much you pay?"

"That depends." I turned and headed for the door. "And one more thing. I want a Master Weaver. Someone who can weave sandpainting rugs."

"How did everyone sleep?" It was the intern from last night. The woman sitting next to me had dubbed him Scrawny. "As you can see, each of you has your own loom."

The loom stands measured about a foot-and-a-half wide by two-feet high. Stripped tree limbs formed a frame that stood vertically and attached to a flat wooden base; a continuous warp thread was strung in a figure eight between two dowel rods, and the dowels were wired to the top and the bottom of the frame to form the loom.

"Let's all give Jessie Begay a round of applause for providing the stands." Jessie smiled broadly, and Lola stared at the floor. "The Navajo believe that Spider Woman, a mythical character, taught the women to weave. And Spider Man instructed the men in making the looms. There are no printed patterns; the designs all come from the women's heads."

"We just knows how to do it." Jessie tapped her temple with an index finger.

"And with that, let's learn to weave." The intern made a broad wave with his hand and nodded to Jessie. She puffed herself up and stood to address the group.

"The weavin' at the bottom of everybody's loom ... that's a hard part. So's we just did it for you." She glanced down at a crumpled piece of paper in her hand. "Later this week you're gonna learn about stringin' the loom, spinnin' and dyin' wool, too. But now, just weavin'." She nodded to Lola. Both women went in different directions, positioning themselves next to a participant. Lola came directly to me.

As the week progressed, Jessie spent the days showing her box of rugs—all done by her, of course—to anyone interested in buying. It was Lola I was drawn to; she quietly moved from one person to the next guiding their hands through the intricacies of weaving. She spent more and more time by my side, as though I were having private lessons. The motions of Lola's hands at the loom were strikingly different than what I was used to with my computer or the act of writing with a pen; they were fluid and graceful in a musical way. And the gentle thudding sound made by the wooden comb, as it beat down the weft cords, was calming and soothing. I became convinced that learning to weave was the answer to lowering my blood pressure.

It was the last day. I rose early to finish a difficult part of the design before my instructor was gone. My driven self was back. I felt an urgency to understand the process, as though the knowledge was the only thing that would enable me to make the right business decisions. Lola was already at her loom which was a much larger version of the tabletop looms we were given.

"*Yá'át'ééh*," I said in greeting. I worked hard to get the proper inflection in the Navajo word for hello. Lola nodded and came to sit next to me at my loom. She watched my hands move clumsily and nudged herself close to guide me. On one of my returns from the coffee pot, I caught her undoing several rows of weft and threading the yarns back through the warp. A smile crossed her face when she realized I'd seen her redoing my work.

"You learn good," she whispered. "Just little mistakes."

"Thank you." I followed my words with an embarrassed laugh. My weaving looked like a figure eight; the sides pulled in at the middle from threading my weft too tight. If nothing else, the week had taught me I would never be a weaver. It would take several reincarnations to make me able to recreate even a not-so-good weaving like Jessie's Storm.

"I thought you only spoke Navajo."

"English not good."

In broken sentences, punctuated with shy smiles, Lola told me she understood the spoken word fairly well. She was merely hesitant to talk in front of people. She also cautioned me against buying a weaving from Jessie; they were borrowed rugs from a nearby trading post, and Jessie sold them at a marked-up price. I learned that Jessie didn't really know how to weave—one of the results of going to boarding school instead of staying home with the grandmothers—but that she was masterful at making money off other women. She was their broker and always got a piece of the action. This was information I logged in my mind for future reference.

I asked Lola about buying directly from her, but she shook her head and said the school program kept her too busy. She motioned for me to follow to her loom. Her work was used to demonstrate techniques throughout the week. It was a sampler of designs. "I wants to tell you about weavin'," she said and slowly positioned herself. Lola sat on the floor, drew her shoulders back, and took a slow deep breath like a concert pianist ready to perform. And then her hands came alive. They moved deftly, pulling sticks to separate the warp cords as she wove her batten through them. When the warp was separated, a fast-moving hand grabbed a weft strand and threaded it through the warp. All this happened so quickly that the thudding sound of the comb beating down the weft never paused—it became a heartbeat of the silence.

I shut my eyes and tried to embrace the beauty and calm of the moment, so different than the ticking clocks and the scratching pencils in the boardrooms of countless companies. The thud, thud of the comb became my own heartbeat, as it pounded with anxiety. I was unable to let go of my fear of failure. The same fear that doggedly trailed me into those business meetings, sat beside me still.

"All 'bout *hózhó*," Lola said and set her tools aside. She ran her fingers across the warp cords as though they were the strings of a harp. "Gots to be just right ... not too loose, not too tight." She placed her hand over her heart. "Gots to be right in here, too." Lola went back to her weaving. Designs magically appeared, rising out of the earth tone yarns like the snowcapped mountains on the horizon of the high desert. Last week's memory of a drab and desolate landscape faded into the beauty of her tapestry. This was my first lesson in learning to think with my heart and creating a kinder, gentler business. I was back on the reservation, dancing my double doll amongst the storybook-shaped rock formations.

"The time has come to say good-bye." It was Scrawny. "I hope this has been a meaningful experience for all of you, and that you will come back."

My mind only half listened; I scanned the room for Lola. I'd looked up the Navajo word "*hózhó*" and wanted to talk with her about it. It meant: Everything in balance and harmony. How did she do that? All the years I'd struggled at being a wife, a mother, and a woman that was driven to make it in a man's world left little time to think about bringing my life into something as obscure as balance and harmony.

After the meeting everyone dispersed to pack belongings and head for home. I was going to do some touristy things—visit Cañon de Chelly and take a tour that included Spider Rock, the mythical home of Spider Man and Spider Woman. One story I'd read told how Spider Man took the Eastern Horizon to make one side of a loom frame; he took the Southern Horizon for another side, the Western Horizon and the Northern Horizon. The four horizons to make the loom frame. Then he took Father Sky and Mother Earth, and threaded the Female Rain Showers between the two to form the warp. And he brought all the twelve Sacred Mountains together to harness Father Sky, Mother Earth, and Female Rain Showers to the loom frame. He used the Sun Rays to form the heddle, and the Lightning to bring the tension.

I carried the first load of bags out to my rental car and, on my way back, I noticed the black pickup hadn't left. Jessie was loading cardboard boxes into the back.

"*Yá'át'ééh*," she hollered and walked toward me. "Need help?"

"Thanks." I motioned for her to follow me into my hogan. I gathered up things for my briefcase and nodded to a large black duffel bag. "You can carry that," I said. "It's light."

She pulled the bag up and down in the air and laughed. "What's in it?"

"Quilts. Take a look."

Jessie unzipped the bag and smiled as she pulled the colorful Amish samples from the bag. "Whatcha gonna do with these?"

"I'm taking them to gift shops. I want to find one that will display them as wall hangings. They're samples of designs people can order in full-size bed quilts."

"Custom orders like you wants for rugs?" She arranged the quilt samples on the floor and stood back to view them from a distance.

"Same thing."

"You wants to do some tradin'?"

"What do you mean?"

"Quilts for rugs. I knows lots of women who'd do it."

"Sure." That thought hadn't occurred to me, but why not?

"My house is pink. Across the highway from tradin' post in Teec Nos Pos. Meet me next Saturday. I'll take ya to them."

I worked hard not to show my excitement. This was my first indication that Jessie might be an inside source for finding Navajo weavers. "I'll be in Chinle at the Thunderbird Lodge if you need to get a hold of me. But you can always call the toll-free number on my card. I pick up my messages every day."

Crow Canyon gave me a new reality. My attraction wasn't for the weavings—for me it was about the women. The weavings provided a vehicle. The symmetrical stair step arrangements of natural colors were Lola's reflection of being "just right." She didn't look to money, or the approval of others to find her place; it all came from within. Lola possessed something I longed for in my own life, something I could be essentially good at, deft and graceful as Lola, something from deep in my own soul, my essence, something that would bring love and acceptance from within. My double doll dream started me on this journey; the women would be the ones who sustained me.

How would I incorporate that in my business plan?

Doing Business the Navajo Way

The Indian Country map indicated a one-and-a-half hour drive from Chinle to Teec Nos Pos; the route made a wide circle that stayed on paved roads, but took me more than sixty miles out of the way.

"This road over the Lukachukai Mountains." I turned my map toward a young woman at the motel desk, "Is it passable? I'm driving a Ford Explorer." Navajo 13 showed as "improved gravel" and made a direct line, squiggly in places, to Teec Nos Pos. Even if I traveled at a speed of twenty-five miles per hour, it looked like this route would save thirty minutes.

"Road's good. I take it every day."

I headed northeast from Chinle, a town that got its name from its location. The Navajo word, *ch'inli'*, refers to the mouth of the canyon where the water flows out. I'd ridden in an open jeep driven by a Navajo guide the day before, across streams of water that snaked through the sandy floor of Cañon de Chelly. I learned that Chelly is pronounced like *shay*. Outsiders require guides because of the prevalent quicksand, the immensity of the place, and the lack of formal roads. A more important reason for a guide is the sacredness of the canyon to the Navajo. Throughout time it has served as a refuge and fortress to the People.

Today my route passed along the rim of Cañon del Muerto, the northern branch of the larger Cañon de Chelly. It took me past Mummy

and Massacre Cave Overlooks to Diné College in the town of Tsaile. The
rim road sat at an elevation of seven thousand feet and traversed high-
desert country; the landscape was both stark and magnificent, making
me glad I chose the more direct route. I thought of my comments to Len
about the countryside being drab and desolate. I just hadn't been looking.
The mesa was alive with color and irregular shapes: the yellow/gold stands
of sunflowers and blooming rabbitbrush interspersed with the scarlet red
of a lingering Indian paintbrush. At Tsaile I turned to the northwest, on
a highway that skirted the Lukachukai Mountains, and then east again,
to the community that sat at the base of the mountains for which it was
named. Navajo 13 turned to gravel after I passed through Lukachukai
and then to a boulder-riddled trail that climbed steeply through cuts
of red rock stained with fields of orange and gray lichens and stands of
ponderosa pine.

At the top of Tunecha Pass an overlook provided me with a place to
take a few deep breaths; I wondered at the kind of job that would be worth
making this drive on a daily basis. My answer came when I stepped out
of my vehicle and looked across Red Valley—a spectacular panorama of
a multi-colored desert and, looming in the distance, the imposing lava
and rock formation of Shiprock shrouded in an atmosphere of soft pink,
lilac and rose colors.

Despite the uphill drive that shook my nerves as much as it rattled
every nut and bolt in my rental car, I made good time and still had an hour
before my appointed meeting. The trip down the mountain went much
faster. I thought I was over the worst of the drive when I passed by the Red
Rock Trading Post and found myself on a stretch of recently blacktopped
pavement. My foot got heavy on the gas pedal. And then, instantaneously,
in sickening lurches, I went from a smooth highway to a dead stop in a
wide expanse of deep, fine sand. There was nothing but large boulders,
pieces of timber that were carried down from the mountains when the

rain made the washes run like raging rivers, and a few animal trails. I was in a dry riverbed; some would call it a goat path, with sides that cut deep into the sandstone.

I grabbed my map and got out of the vehicle. All four wheels were buried in at least six inches of sand. A scan of the horizon revealed nothing but stands of spiny cholla cactus that stood watch over my predicament. The road that went over Tunecha Pass, according to the map, continued north, through Red Valley, for about fourteen miles. It followed a wash through the Carrizo Mountains. I'd found the wash.

I climbed back into the driver's seat, started the engine, shifted into 4-wheel low and listened, as the powerful machine drove the tires deeper into soft sand. There hadn't been any Pavement End signs, and I had been going too fast. I killed the engine and went to the back of the vehicle; the only equipment available was a long handled ice-scraper, a plastic throwaway bag I was using for trash, and my quilt samples. After much deliberation, I dug the sand away from the wheels with the ice scraper and pushed a quilt behind each tire for traction.

I drove in reverse back to the paved route that took me due east, north to the town of Shiprock, and then west into Teec Nos Pos. I arrived more than two hours late. Jessie's house was easy to find. I pulled into the yard of a bright pink cinderblock dwelling with a mud-covered hogan fifty paces off to the side.

"Sorry I'm late," I said when she opened the front door.

"Don't matter. Wasn't even for sure this was the right day."

"Well, it matters to me. When I tell someone I'll be a certain place at a certain time, I'm there." I stopped myself and let a wave of frustration pass. Thirty-five years in corporate America was showing. The belief that "time is money" served me well in my consulting business, but didn't have much to offer here. After my walkout at the stock exchange, when I decided to trade the fast pace and competitiveness of the business world for a gentler way of making my fame and fortune, I hadn't realized I would be replacing one stress-producer for another. I needed more practice in living on Navajo time.

Jessie gathered her belongings, and we started out for Lola's house. Her directions were spare. She gave no indication of approximate distances; landmarks were comprised of big rocks or lone trees, and turns were down dirt roads marked by piles of old tires. I realized that Jessie didn't know left from right; she used the thrust of her chin in the appropriate direction when she wanted me to turn, and several times we had to backtrack when the tire-rutted trail ended in someone's front yard.

We drove in silence until Jessie spoke. "What you gonna do with all them weavins you wants to buy?"

"They're for a show back east." I was grateful for some conversation. "I'm planning a culture and art exchange, my company's kick-off event. I'll have Navajo weavings on display alongside Amish quilts."

Silence.

"The event will give people a glimpse into two different cultures. That's why it's important I have a lot of weavings … especially a sandpainting weaving."

Jessie was nonchalant and stared out her passenger-side window.

"The real beauty of an Amish quilt isn't the design; it's the meticulous hand stitching."

After a long pause, Jessie turned toward me and asked, "What's that word, 'meticus'?"

"Me-ti-cu-lous. It means being extra careful with detail. The stitching is where an Amish woman shows her heart and how much she loves her family."

We continued to drive in silence.

"So you gonna sell at the big show?"

"This show won't be the right place for selling. I want orders, not sales."

The area surrounding Lola's house spoke to the complications of her life. A padlock on the door made her hogan look old and unlived in. When I asked Jessie, she told me it was used for ceremonial purposes, but now is a storage shed—not like the hogan Jesse lived in during the winter months because her modern house was too cold. Close to the hogan was another small, rectangular house built of handmade-adobe bricks. The high window frames, from hand-hewn lumber with panes of stretched oilskin cloth, made this dwelling look even older than the hogan. Smoke rose from the chimney of the adobe house, and I saw the door open far enough for someone to peek out. My attention was drawn to a bright orange extension cord; it threaded from one of the windows, across a makeshift driveway, and into the window of a newly placed prefabricated home.

The house was a garish blue with glass windows framed in low-maintenance white metal. In front there was a postage-stamp sized patch of green grass that looked recently purchased—sod rolled out over barren hard-packed dirt. A satellite dish rested in the middle of the lawn, prominently announcing that this family owned a television. Near the edge of the grass sat a rusted-out barbeque grill and a doghouse. A storage shed fabricated from a conglomeration of different materials stood off to the side. Sheets of corrugated metal, pieces of plywood, old discarded doors, stacked-up cinder blocks and a card table retrieved from someone's trash made up the shed, and a large piece of canvas served as covering for the entrance. Several sheepskins were draped over a wire strung along the side of the shed, an electric washing machine gathered rust, and scattered helter-skelter around all of this was an array of bright red, green, and yellow Fisher-Price toys.

I pulled to the edge of the grass and stopped. Jessie and I got out amidst a group of curious dogs, sheep, and goats. I couldn't help but wonder how they kept the sheep from eating the new sod. Maybe the satellite dish worked like a scarecrow. I struggled with the cumbersome duffel bag and followed Jessie inside the doublewide. Lola sat quietly in a chair spinning wool, just as she had at Crow Canyon. The room was bright; white walls smelled of fresh paint, and pieces of yarn tied back bed sheets that were tacked over the windows. Piles of framed photographs were stacked against the wall, as if Lola hadn't the time, or maybe the hammer and nails, to hang them.

And then I saw the extension cord. It came through a partially opened living room window, crossed under a loose rug near the entrance to the kitchen and became a connection for two indoor cords. One fed electricity to a large console television and floor lamp; the other stretched through the kitchen to a modern refrigerator. We'd been there only minutes when the pickup trucks started arriving. Women crowded into the small living room.

"How did they know we were here?" I whispered to Jessie.

"They seen us comin'," she replied. "And no needs to whisper. They only talks Navajo." I inwardly chuckled at Jessie's clever motivation for sending me down the wrong roads.

As the women entered, they clasped hands and greeted one another with *Yá'át'ééh. Aoó* was the typical response. Then, very abruptly, half a dozen expectant faces stared in my direction.

"Show 'em the quilts," Jessie insisted.

I felt like Santa Claus as the women watched me pull the Amish quilt samples out of the bag and lay them, one by one, across the floor. The women clustered closely together turning the room into a kaleidoscope of color. They were dressed traditionally in patterned squaw skirts, brightly colored velveteen blouses, and jewelry made of turquoise and coral. A black carpetbag-shaped purse hung over each arm.

In the middle of a speech Jessie gave in Navajo, I heard her stammer over the word meticulous. The women picked up the quilt pieces and passed them amongst themselves. They held the samples close to their eyes and then back to view from a distance, all the while buzzing with conversation.

"They wants to trade," Jessie said, "rugs for quilts." Weavings appeared—out of brown paper bags, scraps of old window curtains or laundered Bluebird Flour sacks. "Only they wants big ones. The bed kind."

"I don't have any of those. The samples are for people to choose their design."

"For making orders?"

"That's right."

Jessie launched back into Navajo. There was a lot of head nodding and *Aoós*.

"*Hágoshíí*," Jessie said, indicating that everything was settled, and turned to face me. "I got lots of orders for you." I stared at her blankly. Jessie looked puzzled and then added, "That's what you said you wanted?"

Trading for the rugs they brought wouldn't work, since I had no bed-size quilts. So we took orders. Starting with the most eager woman, Jessie determined the color, pattern, and size of quilt she desired. I recorded.

"Ask Minnie if I can see her weaving." I held out my hand to receive a rug. Minnie, a shy woman who didn't enter into conversation with the others, reluctantly handed her weaving to me. She watched the faces of the other women as I spread it out and went through my routine to determine the size and quality.

"Tell her the quilt she wants will cost a hundred dollars more than her weaving." It was Jessie's turn to have a blank face.

"I think her rug is worth about two-hundred-and-fifty dollars." I spoke in slow, measured words. "The quilt will cost three-fifty. She'll owe me a hundred dollars."

"Tradin' don't work that way. Gots to come out fair and square or you pays them. Besides, you don't have no quilts."

Nothing in my business experience prepared me for this. "But how? I have no idea … "

"That's why you gots me," Jessie said.

"So, how <u>do</u> they want to pay?" Minnie was busy folding her weaving and stuffing it back in a flour sack.

"Weavin'. I tells them what you want, they weaves it." And then the double-whammy came. "They needs to go home with cash. You gots to pay for what they brought."

"Jessie … let's talk." I stood and motioned for her to follow me out the door.

"I can't buy all those rugs. Some aren't any good."

"You got to. Else they'll think you just like the trader, goin' back on your word."

"I didn't commit to this."

"I told them you needs rugs real bad."

"Sounds like it's your word, not mine."

"'Sides, we got lots of orders."

"Right. And for those orders, I'll get paid with the same poor quality weaving that I'm looking at today."

"But they'll trust you."

I didn't trust Jessie, but somehow I knew she was right. During our conversation the childhood taunt of "Indian giver" played incessantly in my mind. There wasn't a good precedent for honest dealings between the Navajo and Anglo cultures. But at this point, Jessie was my only entrée to their world. I had to make it work.

After a lot of bartering, all done by Jessie, I handed over cash for each woman's rug—along with a scrap of paper describing the type of weaving she was to make in trade for her quilt. Once again, it was Jessie's idea. I drew crude versions of the design, colored them with crayons, and used a series of hands—a measuring trick for determining the height of a horse—to convey general dimensions.

There was one exception to the lesser quality rugs I accumulated. A young woman, unlike the others because she spoke English, brought a beautiful Burnham-style weaving. Gail, who lived in Chinle, said her boyfriend's mother, Sonya Bitsinnie, did the piece. Her efforts to explain where Sonya lived were interrupted by Jessie, who insisted that she be the one to introduce me to the weavers. To the piece of paper with Gail's rug instructions, I included my motel room number at the Thunderbird Lodge in Chinle and a request that she call me.

It was late afternoon by the time Jessie and I climbed into the Explorer and headed back to her house. "I found your sandpaintin' weaver ... name's Bertha Benally."

"Great. When can I meet her?"

"Tomorrow's good. Come back to my house."

"At nine. I'll be there at nine."

"*Hágoshíí*," Jessie said and continued to stare out the window.

I pulled into the yard in front of her house. "I did good today, hunh?" she said and opened the car door. "Boardin' school teaches me lots about White Man's world. That's hows I got so good at business." Jessie's parting words were, "Maybe you just gives me a quilt for all them orders. You know, what *Bilagáana* calls commission."

My Advice, Lil' Lady

P eaceful sleep didn't come. I tossed and turned and fidgeted, like a schoolgirl the night before an exam, with the excitement and worry of meeting a sandpainting weaver. When the alarm clock reflected five-thirty, I could wait no longer. I dressed and rummaged through my suitcase for the thunderbird pin—tacky or not, it reminded me of my new persona and was my good-luck charm.

There were two ways I could get from Chinle to Teec Nos Pos—three if you counted the dirt trail over Tunecha Pass, the way I'd gone the day before. The western route went along US 191, through Many Farms and Round Rock; an eastern route crossed the Chuska Mountains to Sheep Springs and turned north to Shiprock. I opted for the western loop.

There was no worry about deep ruts or boulders that would take out the bottom of my vehicle, so I focused on the landscape and watched for signs of life. Small clusters of sheep blended in with the desert shrubs and grazed aimlessly across barren lands; it seemed impossible for them to find anything to eat. My gaze followed wisps of smoke downward to the dome-shaped roofs of hogans. Some of the log dwellings were chinked so heavily with mud that from a distance they looked like anthills on the desert floor. I determined logs weren't a requirement when I saw hogans made with cinderblocks, stones, or plywood paneling. They all were hexagonal, octagonal or round, had a door that faced east to greet the morning sun, and a stovepipe protruding from the center of the roof.

Today, Jessie was ready and waiting when I arrived. She wanted me to follow her—something about staying on at Bertha's when my business was concluded. We drove on pavement until we turned at a sign that pointed the way to Teec Nos Pos, translated to mean Circle of Cottonwood Trees, and then into a Navajo government housing project. All the homes looked alike and faced one another. They lined up on tiny parcels of land that were laid out on a grid of streets. Any doors that faced east were accidental.

Jessie was out of her truck and knocking on the front door before I pulled to a complete stop. A small child in diapers opened the door to peek out. Jessie motioned for me to follow. We stepped into a dark room with the drapes closed. A loud noise came from a new-looking television that sat atop an empty shell of a console cabinet. A fire burned in a potbellied stove, and there was a foul odor coming from a nearby room that looked to be the kitchen.

"What's that smell?" I whispered to Jessie.

"Maybe soup … don't know."

The living room was full with furniture and people. Two couches and an armchair were arranged in a U-shape facing the television. A woman sat in the chair, children sprawled on the floor, and an elderly couple sat on one of the couches. A young man, who looked to be in his early thirties, sat on the other sofa, enthralled by the cartoon characters that appeared on the television screen.

"This here's Charlie," Jessie said and tilted her chin in the young man's direction. "He's Bertha's boy … cain't hear or talk."

The woman who sat in the armchair was introduced as Bertha. She gestured for us to take a place on the couch next to Charlie. No one spoke; they just stared blankly at the television. I felt uncomfortable and awkward—not in the same way I'd felt when I stood in the silence inside Jessie and Lola's hogan at Crow Canyon—this was a sense that I was unwelcome. I stepped over the legs of the children and made my way to the elderly couple.

"*Hágoónee*," I said and extended my hand to the grandmother. A broad smile crossed her face, and then she giggled.

"That's goodbye," Jessie chided. "You means '*Yá'át'ééh*'."

"*Aoó*," the grandmother said. The old man sitting next to her chuckled.

"They's Bertha's parents, Anna Mae and Roy Hoskie."

I was grateful for the darkness in the room; it covered the blush from the heat that crept up my neck and into my face. I continued my round of greetings, noticing that Bertha didn't smile when I clasped her hand. Deep-cut wrinkles puckered the skin around her tightly pinched mouth, and her eyes were like Jessie's, small and beady.

We sat, for what felt like hours, with only the images of a muted television and the sounds of something boiling on the stove in the kitchen. It wasn't cold outside, and yet the potbellied stove continued to belch heat into an overly warm space. I tried to conceal my discomfort with the heat and lack of conversation by examining the room. Among the other pieces of oversized furniture was an elaborate china hutch filled with dishes and crystal. On the shelves that extended beyond the area closed off with glass doors were framed photographs of children—all sizes and ages, dressed in feathers and beads and graduation caps and gowns. There was a picture of Bertha in her younger years standing next to a man in a military uniform. The rest of the walls, except the one with the wood-burning stove, were taken over by windows or kitchen cabinets. Centered in a bare spot on the wall to the left of the stovepipe was a ceramic replica of Jesus Christ hanging on the cross.

When I'd exhausted items to look at in the living room, I stared at the inane figures that danced across the television screen. The last time I'd sat waiting uncomfortably like this was in the boardroom of the Stock Exchange; the Grandfather clock provided the tick-tock, and the swirling tapestry had transported me to a different place. I remembered the scowling, discourteous attitude of the vice president. And I remembered my inner struggle before I picked up my briefcase and walked out the door. I remembered thinking that I wasn't going to be cowed anymore. I had a voice. I was going to use it. And I would be heard.

Jessie broke my reverie when she spoke in Navajo, words directed to Bertha. Their conversation was lengthy, interspersed with *Aoós* and long pauses. "She's makin' blood sausage," Jessie said when she turned to me.

"What?"

"The smell. They butchered a sheep an are makin' blood sausage."

Then, as though on cue, Bertha and Jessie both stood and headed down a dark hallway. I hesitated, not certain whether I was to follow. By this time my palms were clammy, and the smell from the kitchen rolled through my stomach in waves. I didn't want to know the details of making blood sausage.

When I couldn't stand the wait any longer, I followed the two women down the hall to an open door at the end. A large metal structure made of pipes welded together to form a frame of about seven feet on each side and constructed like the smaller loom stands at Crow Canyon was against the left sidewall. The frame was supported upright by a metal base; dowel rods marked the top and bottom edges of a weaving, and one continuous filament of yarn formed the warp of the loom. Heavy rope laced the dowels to the metal pipes at the top and bottom, and wooden sticks, threaded through the holding ropes, served as tourniquets to control tension on the warp. The loom stand held a sandpainting rug that was three-quarters complete. I caught my breath when I saw it. It looked identical to the weaving in the *New York Times* newspaper article. I'd read that it was the sacred nature of the designs that made the weavings valuable to a collector.

The colors in Bertha's sandpainting were soft and muted. Four ornate figures radiated from the center, like spokes on a wheel, with leafy branches of yellow, blue, white and black separating the figures. "These are *Ye'ii*." Jessie tilted her chin toward the loom. "Navajo Gods." The figures formed a cross with their feet toward the center and heads pointed out. Each *Ye'ii* was different in its detail—breastplates and skirts included triangles, rectangles, stripes, and intricate sawtooth patterns. The arms formed a "W" across their bodies, and their hands were crafted to show five distinct fingers.

"It's beautiful," I whispered.

"Lotsa feathers an ceremonial stuff in these," Jessie said. "Can't hardly find a weavin' like this anymore."

Gourds hung in drapes from the arms of the deities, and on one side of each *Ye'ii* was an elaborate hunting bow, on the other, a decorated prayer stick. "What do these represent?" I pointed to the colored branches that spread from the center.

Jessie scowled and then spoke with Bertha. "Blue one's tobacco, kind found up in the mountains. She ain't sure about the others ... white is maybe female corn." I stared in awe of the piece, as the two women continued to talk. "Bertha says to tell you everythin' has a meanin'. All colors and ways *Ye'ii* point—that's 'bout Four Sacred Mountains."

"Is it for sale?" I estimated this weaving at about five feet on each side. A reputable gallery owner in Durango told me the price he paid a weaver for a sandpainting tapestry, if you could find them, was two hundred dollars a square foot.

"Gots to give her six thousand," Jessie said. "Half now."

"I don't want to pay that much. Ask her if she'll take five?"

"I knows she won't. Boy's bad off. He's deaf, you know."

I hesitated. I'd spent most of the cash I brought for the trip the previous day at the quilt exchange. My business sense told me to walk away. I knew that a sizeable portion of money was Jessie's self-proclaimed commission, but I wanted that rug. I took out my checkbook and asked how to spell Benally.

"It gots to be cash," was Jessie's reply. She explained that the trader wouldn't take anything but a money order, and that Bertha didn't have a checking account. "None of us have 'em," she said. "Do all's our business at the tradin' postes. They gives us credit."

"I don't have the cash," I told her. "I'll have to come back tomorrow."

I decided to take the eastern route for my return to Chinle—US 666, the Devil's Highway to the locals. The sky was dark with black clouds that roiled across the desert and turned a landscape usually alive with color into gray, lifeless forms. It matched the color and turbulence of my mood. I'd given up my career to come to the reservation and find calm and a gentler way to do business. It wasn't supposed to be like this.

Instincts told me not to trust Jessie or Bertha, but I wanted that rug. It was more than just "want"—it was as though the entire success or failure of my new business venture depended on this single weaving. My thoughts alternated between how I would advertise the collectible piece and what I needed to do to get three-thousand dollars to Bertha Benally by tomorrow.

Off in the distance loomed Shiprock, foreboding as it floated on the horizon. This afternoon's gray skies made it look more like Cliff Monster, the name given by the Navajo. Their mythology recounts that Monster Slayer slew Cliff Monster, and the long lava dike that trails off to the southwest is said to be his blood.

I rounded a curve in the road and was greeted by a huge hawk on the post of a makeshift fence. As I passed, the hawk lifted heavily from its resting place and traced graceful circles above my vehicle. The raptor soared and spiraled ever closer to the ground. And then he plummeted, pulling up a split second before crashing into the desert floor. A small rabbit hung limp as a rag doll from the bird's talons.

The manager at the Thunderbird Lodge advised me on the bank situation, and I went to my room to call Len. The phone rang several times before he picked it up. "Daugherty, here." He spoke in his business–only voice.

Our conversation began with small talk, circle-the-issue talk, until the time and the mood seemed right. "I'm still in Chinle ... I need a favor." I could hear water running in the background. "Could you wire transfer three-thousand dollars to a Wells Fargo branch near Window Rock?"

"I thought you were in Chinle."

"I am, but there are no banks on the reservation. Closest is near Window Rock."

"So why do you need the money?"

I bristled at his question. The money would have to come from Len's account; he couldn't write checks on mine. When we married I made it clear how important it was to me that we keep our money separate. It wasn't just Mom's admonishments to never become dependent on a man for money, but involved lessons learned from my first marriage. When we divorced, my first husband and I split debts rather than assets. I took the home mortgage, he took the loan and maintenance fees for the sailboat. We divided four credit cards that were at their limit.

"Do you mind just getting the money for me?" Len didn't agree with the way I was approaching my new business; he would certainly not have agreed with the decision to pay three thousand dollars to a person I did not trust. I rationalized it was all about thinking with my heart, but even I was having trouble with that one. "I'll pay you back when I get home."

I skipped dinner that night. My stomach still hadn't recovered from the stench from Bertha's kitchen. And I couldn't seem to get the image of the dangling rabbit out of my mind. So I did what I was very good at. I made a list. Two lists actually—one with all the reasons Bertha's rug was important to me, the other listing why I felt I was being taken advantage of by Jessie and Bertha. The pros were tangible: weaving was the big-ticket item collectors wanted; Bertha was a master weaver; kickoff event for new business needed something extraordinary; possession of the sandpainting proved my ability to operate on the reservation.

The cons were based on instinct. First there had been the revelation that the rugs Jessie touted as her own came from the trading post, then her adamancy about being the one to take me to all the weavers, and the blatant way she asked for a commission at Lola's house. I felt uncomfortable and unwelcome in Bertha's home, and I was being overcharged for the sandpainting. But I couldn't point to anything definitive about their untrustworthiness—everything was a gut feeling that circled around my own sense of inadequacy and fear of failure. The "out-of-my-element" issues I understood. It was the fear I wasn't sure about.

I wrote in bold letters on top of the pro statements, *SUCCESS OF BUSINESS*, and passed off the cons as hazards of working in a culture different than my own. Already I'd learned that time didn't matter. Appointments weren't honored, the women didn't wear wristwatches, and I'd yet to see a calendar hanging on the wall. Clearly my biggest challenge was to learn the rest of the Navajo "rules" and how to run a successful business within those constraints.

Three-thousand dollars was in the bank the following day.

Since the cons from the night before were mostly about Jessie, I decided to deliver Bertha's money on my own. I could find the turn to the group of houses where she lived, but I'd forgotten which of the look-alikes was hers. I stopped at a nearby trading post to ask directions.

"How ya' doin' today?" the trader said. "What kin I do ya' for?"

"I'm here for some directions. I'm looking for Bertha Benally." The trader walked behind a counter and idly rearranged the items on a shelf. "I've been there before, but didn't pay enough attention. Do you know Bertha?"

"Shur do," he replied, in a much-too-busy-to-be-talking-to-me tone. "Been buyin' rugs from her for forty-some years now." There was a loud twang as he turned away and spat into a metal bucket. "Fact is, I got some nice ones over in the vault, if'n ya' want to see 'em."

"No, I just wanted to stop by to check on her." I felt comfortable in most of the trading posts I visited and had gotten some valuable information on the pricing of rugs from helpful traders; not so with this one. I can't explain exactly why, it was that prickly feeling you get when you're walking alone down a dark, deserted street and have the sense someone is following you. Maybe it had to do with his keen interest in my business with Bertha or maybe it was merely his seedy appearance. I shuffled my feet, anxious to leave.

"What kinda checkin' you plan to do?" When he grinned there was a large gap in the middle of nicotine-stained teeth. His shoulder-length thinning gray hair hung in clumps, and his fingernails were long, the undersides caked with black dirt. "She weavin' a rug for ya'?" Another loud twang. "Ya' gotta watch out. I spent my whole life out here, and ya' know, these Injun's, they'll cheat ya' every chance they get."

And then he looked up from his work, directly into my face. "My advice, Lil' Lady ... "

It happened so quickly. He was adding credence to my insecurity, and then came the slur. My fist slammed against his glass counter top, knocking over a rack of silver trinkets and cutting off his words. "Don't you ever call me Little Lady."

"Well ain't you the uppity one," he muttered as I turned and headed out.

Memories of doing business in a world of condescending men bolstered my determination. If the decision were to trust the trader or trust Jessie, I would choose Jessie. I went back to her house with a money order in hand so she could accompany me to Bertha's.

Anxiety rode with me as I made the drive back to Chinle. I had just turned over three-thousand dollars to someone I did not trust and whose language I could not understand. There was nothing to show for it—no rug, no receipt. Nothing. My thoughts bounced between old dreams of a "gentler way to do business" and images of the rabbit dangling from the talons of the hawk. *You fool. I can do this my way. Where is your common sense? Bertha needed the money. The trader was right. The trader was a pig.* I needed to get my act and story together before I talked to Len. If I couldn't explain my actions to myself, how would I explain them to him?

My spirits lifted when I arrived at the motel room and found a message from Gail, the young woman I'd met at the quilt exchange. She was picking me up the next morning to meet her boyfriend's mother, Sonya Bitsinnie.

The Bitsinnie home was about seven miles north of the Chinle shopping mall. We drove on a paved road for most of those miles. "Have to look for the horse corral over the way there," Gail said when she turned onto a dirt road. "That's only way I know where it is." She was excited about the meeting and her role in introducing me. "Sonya is the best weaver around here. You're gonna love her work."

After circling around the corral we crossed a small stream and pulled into a yard with several structures. The main house looked to be built from plastered cinderblock painted beige with a front door that faced east. Twenty or so paces to the north stood a log hogan with a padlock on the wooden door. Set behind the house and the hogan was a lean-to shed that formed one end of a sheep pen. A brightly painted metal sign touting BITSINNIE FOR CHAPTER PRESIDENT hung on the shed's wall. "Sonya's husband," Gail said and tilted her chin toward the sign. "His term was over last year. Best one we've ever had in Chinle." Young trees, encircled with partially buried rubber tires to hold water, gave evidence of the care given to the property—there were no trash or unsightly items lying around.

The inside of the home displayed the same attention. There were no foul smells; instead there was the vague hint of sage. A television sat quiet; the muted sounds of a radio tuned to a Navajo station came from a distant room. Walls were painted a subtle tan and windows draped with a bright red, yellow and blue floral fabric. The living room and kitchen formed an L-shape with an eat-on counter separating the two. The clutter-free countertops were wiped clean. And, hung on the wall, next to the telephone was a calendar.

Sonya's English was good. She looked to be in her early forties and wore her long black hair pulled away from her face, secured by a leather hair bun holder with a colorfully beaded stickpin through the center. Unlike Bertha, her smile came quickly and often; her blemish-free skin pulled tight over pronounced cheekbones. Sonya dressed like an Anglo, except for the silver and turquoise jewelry, in loose-fitting black pants, a red sweater, and Reebok tennis shoes.

Despite the age difference, she brought the same feelings of acceptance I'd experienced with Lola. There was an instant chemistry between us. I was delighted with the way she expressed pleasure—a young girl's giggle followed by an elongated pronunciation of the word "coool." I even had thoughts of Nanabah. It took only minutes into our meeting for me to realize Sonya could replace Jessie as my entrée to the Navajo world.

The first thing she wanted to do was show off a portfolio of her weavings. I thumbed through pages of photographs. Sonya not only had command of all the regional, sought-after designs: Two Grey Hills, Storm, Burnham, Ganado, Klagetoh, Teec Nos Pos, Crystal, Two-Faced, Twill, and the Eye Dazzler, but she pushed the art by creating new patterns and techniques.

"I call this my Rubik's Cube," she said and pointed to a Polaroid shot of a weaving that featured an elongated diamond with a burst of vibrant hues of red, orange and yellow radiating from the center. "I'm good with colors." In the picture, Sonya stood next to the rug. A blue ribbon was pinned on the corner. Many ribbons hung on her living room walls alongside two plaques stating she'd won "Best of Show" at the Gallup Indian Market for the last two years. Worry over my distrust of Bertha and Jessie softened; I'd found my Master Weaver.

The three of us talked nonstop through the morning. The Bitsinnie's had three grown sons; Gail was dating the middle boy. He was a self-taught artist in the medium of oil paints and photography and Gail was eager to show off his paintings and awards. I learned that Sonya was married to Tyler Bitsinnie; he'd attended San Francisco College and become a civil engineer. "Tyler works for the Navajo Roads department under BIA," she announced proudly. "And he studies as a medicine man."

Sonya's home in Chinle had all the modern conveniences—electricity, indoor plumbing, and even a telephone. The latest statistics I'd found had unemployment on the reservation at fifty-five percent; the Bureau of Indian Affairs was one of the few places for people to find work. I surmised that Sonya's home—very modest by middle-class standards—was one of the nicer reservation dwellings as a result of Tyler's education.

Gail brought up the subject of my business. She recounted the events that had taken place at Lola's house, and then turned to me to fill in the blanks. I told Sonya about my idea for a show in Pennsylvania to display Navajo weavings alongside Amish quilts. "Coool," was her response. She sat on the floor with her legs folded underneath her and became childlike and animated, giggling as I spoke. *Aoó* and a lot of head nodding interspersed my comments.

I used the time as an opportunity to find answers to the questions I'd formulated at Crow Canyon. When I asked about the spirit line, Sonya left the room and came back with a small weaving. "See the white thread at the top? That's spirit line. When I weaves, hair and oil from my fingers gets caught in the wool … that gives weavin' part of my gift. All my creative thoughts are in that rug, so I do a spirit line to let them out for the next weavin'."

"Lola Tsosie at Crow Canyon told me weaving was about *hózhó*," I said. "Does that have anything to do with the spirit line?"

"No." Sonya laughed. Over time I learned that Navajos loved to poke fun at the white man's ways, but I never felt offended; they enjoyed laughing at themselves equally as much. "Beauty is closest word you have to *hózhó*. When *Diné* speaks of beauty, we means all in balance and harmony … not just within, but with everythin' around us. When we say *hózhóní*, we tell you to *walk in beauty*."

"I didn't see any sandpainting weavings in your portfolio. Do you do them?"

"I go blind if I weaves a *Ye'ii* without ceremony." Sonya came and sat next to me on the couch. "Only when a woman is in *hózhó* is she ready to weave *Ye'ii*."

"Do you know Bertha Benally from Teec Nos Pos?" I waited for Sonya's response. When it didn't come, I pursued. "She's weaving a sandpainting for me."

"Has she had ceremony?"

"I don't know."

"You don't wants it if she hasn't."

A long silence fell over the room. It was taking time, but I was learning not to ask questions too eagerly. Sonya, when she was ready, would provide the answer. As we sat in silence, I reflected on how different doing business, or even talking with a friend, was in the Navajo culture. My tendency was to rush in with decisions or comments. As the cliché states, "time was money" in the business world, and on a social level, it was important to get your thoughts spoken before the interchange was concluded. The goal was to get the last word in. As hard as it was to refrain from my old habits, I liked this new way of conversing—a way that respected the other party and allowed for thoughtful responses.

"Sandpaintin' weavin's … they have pictures of *Ye'ii*. You know, deities. A weaver has to have a ceremony to put them in a rug, or bad things happen. Ceremony is called Beautyway. Tyler, he studies Beautyway. It teaches to put thoughts and heart in balance with body and spirit. That's how a woman comes to *hózhó*."

"That's a perfect way to describe what I witness in some Navajo women. I think I read somewhere that the Beautyway was also a puberty ceremony for young girls."

"That too."

In my thoughts it came to me that instead of striving to think with my heart, I would strive for *hózhó* … to walk in beauty. "Have you had the ceremony?" I asked Sonya. She shook her head. "So why doesn't Tyler do one for you?"

"*Hataalii* can't be in your family. So if I do sandpaintin', I'll go blind."

"Do you really believe that?"

"Maybe not right away … but sometime."

"The word starting with 'h' … what does it mean?"

"Medicine man, like Tyler," Sonya answered. "We calls them Singer or *Hataalii*."

The blindness thing was more than an idle superstition; Sonya was acknowledging repercussions from veering from what she knew to be right and wrong.

We discussed a weaving that I wanted her to do for me. I really liked the pictures she'd shown of her recent, prize-winning, raised outline rugs. She explained it was a technique, rather than a design, and that she was the only woman in the area doing the raised outline. She led me to her loom and showed how she used an edging weft of a different color that crossed two warps instead of the customary one. This produced an elevated design outline that was vibrant and three-dimensional in appearance. She called the raised outline weave *hoshtodi*, which she translated in visual meaning to the variegated feathers of the Bull Bat Owl.

We agreed on a tightly woven Two Grey Hills in the raised outline technique. Unlike Bertha, Sonya had a bank account. I wrote a check for fourteen hundred dollars, partial payment for a weaving that would measure approximately four feet by seven feet, and added another rule for doing business on the reservation to my project plan: *The women need money up front to buy their wool and for living expenses during the weaving process.*

As Gail and I were leaving, I gave Sonya my business card and explained that I would be moving to Durango, Colorado, but for the time being, she could always reach me at my toll-free number. She responded to the news of my move by explaining that she, too, was in the process of moving; she felt hemmed-in by Chinle's single stoplight and one strip mall. "An the trash. I hates all the trash." Sonya spoke of the town rubbish area just across the highway from her home. When the wind blew, the smell was bad and the roadside became littered with blue Wal-Mart plastic bags. She was moving back to Tachee, the place where she was born and where she could tend her sheep.

"My grazing land," she said proudly.

At Crow Canyon I learned the Navajos are a matrilineal society. The women own the homes, livestock and all the assets except the vehicles. Since reservation land belongs to the tribe and can not be purchased by an individual, people live on allotted land passed down for generations, from mothers to daughters.

"May I visit your place in Tachee someday?"

"Coool," was her response.

Woman Who Travels Alone

I could see Len standing inside the glassed boarding area as the twelve-passenger commuter flight taxied up to the gate. He was always there, waiting patiently for my arrival.

We'd been married for nine years, and for most of those I traveled extensively for my consulting business. When the Lancaster newspaper published an article highlighting the small airport that connected our community with the major hubs of Philadelphia, Baltimore, Pittsburgh, and Washington DC, I was pictured on the front page as a "regular" who routinely caught the 6:15 morning flight to Philly. The write-up focused on the busyness and efficiency of the US Airways commuter airport, but used me to spark interest with the fact that one of the regulars was a woman. In a predominantly Amish and Mennonite farming community, I was an anomaly because I traveled alone and operated in a male-dominated business world.

"So how did everything go?" Len asked when he leaned over to kiss me and take the bags from my shoulders.

"It was good," I said. "I definitely got my money's worth out of this trip. Crow Canyon was perfect. I learned a lot about weaving, and Jessie Begay gave me an entrée to the Navajo Reservation. I'm not sure I trust her, but that's another story. We went to Lola's house and …"

"Whoa. Slow down. Who are Jessie and Lola, and why don't you trust them?"

"They're sisters; well not really sisters but half-sisters. Jessie Begay and Lola Tsosie were the Navajo weaving instructors at Crow Canyon. I really liked Lola and trust her; it's Jessie I have problems with. But like I said, that's a whole other story. So Jessie took me to Lola's house, and there were at least a dozen Navajo women with rugs … they're in the duffel bags with my checked luggage … and I have ten orders for bed-size quilts that will be traded for more rugs. But the best news is that I met Sonya Bitsinnie. She's a master weaver … "

Len cut me off a second time. "Sharleen, I am really having difficulty following you." The baggage handlers had delivered my suitcase, two bags of quilt samples, and a new duffel bag stuffed with my rug purchases. "It's good to have you home, and I want to hear all your stories, but just not now. I thought we'd go to Reflections, order a bottle of Cabernet with dinner and you can tell me everything. I've also got some news."

At the restaurant I started over with my stories. I gave a detailed accounting of the Crow Canyon experience and the quilts for rugs exchange. Then I focused on Sonya Bitsinnie and managed to avoid any discussion about Bertha or the three thousand dollars. Once I wound down, Len shared his news. It was official. He had announced his retirement for April of 1994—less than a year and a half away.

I lay in bed awake that night, making lists: *finalize turning over consulting company to Janice; debut of my new business, Durango Trading Company, planned for October, '93; sell Pennsylvania house; prepare for upcoming holidays; find a place to live in Durango; and prepare for a cross-country move.*

In the months that followed, I poured all my resources, both time and money, into Durango Trading Company: brochures, a slide presentation, business cards, press releases, and magazine advertisements in <u>Southwest Art</u>, <u>Smithsonian</u> and <u>American Indian Art</u>. To my mind, there was no amount of money deemed too much to spend on making the Amish/Navajo exhibit enticing to my targeted, affluent customer market. Preparation for the event became an obsession—it was as though the last twenty years had been nothing more than a training ground for this new venture. I'd proven to the world, and myself, I could be successful in the computer industry, but I walked away from that lucrative business to start a new endeavor. Now I had to start again. The kickoff event became bigger than life, the defining moment in which I would show that doing things my way could prove to be wildly successful. Good intentions—learning to think with my heart and walking in beauty—fell by the wayside in a flurry of activity.

Obtaining quilts was the easy part. My Amish suppliers lived less than ten miles from my Lancaster County home, and the results of their craft were both predictable and reliable. The quilts of the Pennsylvania Dutch country were an expression of frugality. To people that call themselves "Plain," the quilts not only served a practical, functional purpose, but also were a form of entertainment. Many times groups of women gathered for a quilting bee to visit and "catch up" with one another once their household duties had been completed. I was able to purchase the quilts I'd contracted for at Lola's without any custom orders.

It was a Saturday when a midnight phone call came on my toll-free number. "Bertha's son, Charlie … he was hurt … real bad." Jessie's words were staccato bursts, interspersed with the crackling of a bad connection. "… needs money."

Two-thousand dollars, to be exact. Numerous questions and repeated answers revealed the story—Charlie had picked up a hitchhiker on his way to Albuquerque for a party. He was in the Critical Care unit of a hospital with over two-dozen knife wounds, and legs that had been crushed when his attacker tried to escape in his pickup truck. Not only was Charlie a deaf mute, he was also gay. Add that to being Indian and there was no limit to what the imagination could conjure as the reason behind the brutal attack.

"Western Union … to Safeway in Shiprock." Jessie assured me this was the easiest and fastest way to get money there. "Peoples do it all the time," she added to my protest over the uncertainty and charges. "'Sides, there ain't a better way." I tried to ask about my weaving, but Jessie's reply was indecipherable.

"What was that all about?" Len's voice was sluggish from a deep sleep.

"It was Jessie Begay. Bertha needs money for the sandpainting weaving."

His head cleared with the mention of money. "What sandpainting? Isn't Jessie the one you don't trust?"

"Bertha's got a family emergency and needs help. Go back to sleep. We can talk about this in the morning."

"Since we're talking money, when is the check from Janice going to come?"

Several months ago Janice and I signed the Letter of Intent; she promised the initial two-hundred-thousand-dollar payment after the first of the year, and I promised to help and support her through the transition period.

"In the morning … we'll talk about this in the morning."

Sunday dawned early for me. Unable to sleep, I crawled out of bed around three with a nagging memory of something I'd recently read. Laura Gilpin's book, The Enduring Navaho, gave insight to the request for money with these words: "Family bonds are very tight and demanding for the traditional Navajo. Culturally, material possessions are not to be hoarded but shared with those who are less fortunate. When a family member is in need, physically, spiritually, emotionally or socially, it is your responsibility to give, as you are able." I interpreted socially to be financially and ignored the requisite word "family."

After that I moved on to the Letter of Intent that formulated my buy-out agreement with Janice Gamblin. It was all there, the lump sum down payment of two-hundred-thousand due the first of the year and three subsequent payouts of one-hundred-thousand a year. There was also Janice's commitment to follow my clients through completion of their projects, and my willingness to be brought in, either on-site or via teleconferencing calls, as needed. It was mid-February and the initial check had not arrived.

I waited until a proper time and punched in Janice's telephone number.

"Janice Gamblin." Her tone was crisp and professional. There'd been a time I thought that trait appealing; this morning it was irritating.

"Good morning, Janice." I fought the tightness in my throat and tried to make my voice sound friendly. "I thought I'd call to see how things are going."

"It's awfully early. Why not get to the point and tell me why you called."

"I called about the money, but I also wanted to know how you are."

"Things are rather hectic here," Janice replied. "I can't afford the time to chat."

"Well then, what about the money? You do realize it's more than a month overdue. I thought we agreed if you needed help you'd call. I could come … give you a hand with some of the difficult clients."

"I really don't need any help right now. The only problem with the clients is they're not paying their bills."

"Janice, I got a call from Lisa and Christopher last week. They said you'd fired them." I clearly remembered Janice saying she was going to give several of my projects to Christopher. "I also received a call from John. He told me you're not working there. What's going on?"

"Why did they call you?" I could almost feel the receiver grow hot in my hand, as Janice's voice seethed over the phone line. "They had no right to call you."

"Oh, but you're wrong. They had every right. John isn't the first customer to tell me they terminated your contract. Janice, I'm concerned. If you need help with the business, I'll come. That aside, I need my money. Our buyout arrangement is my only source of income until I can get some sales going."

"I can't be concerned about your problems; I have enough of my own. I have to pay the taxes you know." Janice slammed down the receiver, and I listened to a dial tone. Previous calls had found her evasive, but never hostile.

"Who're you talking to this early in the morning?" Len groggily made his way into the kitchen in search of his first cup of coffee.

I hesitated briefly to determine what I would, and would not, tell him about the conversation. "Janice," I answered.

"She tell you about the check?"

"She said something about finishing the taxes and that she's having a few problems."

"What in the hell kind of problems?" Each day that went by without my check sounded another warning bell in Len's head. "You know I never have trusted her."

My financial situation was sound and, despite Len's concerns, I trusted Janice. The entire arrangement, with the initial payment and the annual installments over the next three years, was beneficial to both of us. It gave me some time to get my new business financially stable, and Janice didn't need to take out a loan to generate the cash.

Len sipped coffee in silence until he got up to refill his cup. "Are you going to tell me about the phone call that came in the middle of the night?"

The discussion about the three-thousand-dollar down payment on the sandpainting weaving could no longer be put off. I tried to step him through the sequence of events surrounding my exchange of money for Bertha's promise of a weaving.

"I've told you," Len interrupted. "You can't give them money up front."

"And I've told you … I'm doing this my way."

"Jesus, Sharleen. Just exactly what is your way?" I was grateful Len didn't wait for an answer—"my way" was in a real muddle. "So what was last night's phone call all about?"

"Bertha's deaf mute son was mugged and is in critical condition. She needs me to send two-thousand dollars."

"You're not really going to do it, are you?" He shook his head in disbelief when I nodded yes. "So you are going to send two-thousand dollars … to a person you don't trust … to add to the three-thousand dollars you've already paid … for a rug you still don't have."

His slow and deliberate words accentuated the ludicrousness of my decision. By Anglo standards, Jessie and Bertha were manipulating me— holding my sandpainting weaving as ransom to make me feel responsible for Bertha's personal tragedy. I chose to believe they were acting out of cultural mores. Those thoughts, coupled with the idea of not having the sandpainting weaving to secure the success of my event, outweighed Len's common sense.

"It's a family emergency. And it's not a rug. It's a weaving. A fine tapestry weaving."

"You know you need to stop buying inventory. No more trips to the reservation. And the Bertha thing … forget it. At least until you get some money." He was into his intimidating role; the harder he pushed, the more I resisted. We were in a full-blown battle of egos.

"Len, I can't … and won't just stop. I'm going to call 'crybaby' on this discussion."

When Len proposed marriage to me, my first response was no. I was determined never to follow in my mother's footsteps, and Len had a way about him, a look and tone of voice, that I found intimidating. It was as though he was trying to control my thoughts and actions. I knew a person couldn't be intimidated unless they allowed it, but warding it off took a toll on me, on my self-confidence and energy. I didn't want to be back to a situation where I would have to walk away in order to maintain my identity. We came up with a solution that we agreed to try for six months. Our signal was the word "crybaby," in honor of the way I felt when my father criticized or teased. I was unable to put words to the intimidating behavior; I only knew the feeling it brought within me, that pain of not being good enough. When we were alone, I simply stopped our conversation and announced the feeling. When we were in public, I fit "crybaby" into what I was saying. Whatever the situation, the signal brought an end to that exchange and gave time for introspection.

Monday morning I was at Western Union with two-thousand dollars.

Six months after my initial trip to the reservation, I was back on an airplane headed for Durango. I planned to finalize the trade of quilts for rugs and pick up my sandpainting weaving.

I was at Jessie's house promptly on the prearranged day with a duffel bag full of bed-size quilts. Although I'd sent her a letter stating the day and time, she was nowhere in sight. I sat on the steps of her front porch and made friends with an assortment of dogs that came to sniff the tires of the visitor. They all looked underfed and victims of neglect and abuse. I'd been there long enough to feed the strays a box of snack crackers and the leftover half of an egg croissant when an old yellow pickup truck pulled into Jessie's yard.

A traditionally dressed Navajo woman emerged from the vehicle. She appeared to be in her mid-sixties and walked with a cane, limping slightly. At first, I thought the stammer of her words indicated she didn't speak English well, but as she continued, I realized it was nervousness. Lucy Joe had heard of my pending arrival at Jessie's, and she had a rug to sell.

"I really didn't bring money to buy anything other than what I'm already committed to." That was a lie. I'd brought several thousand dollars above what I needed to pay Bertha, but I'd rehearsed the line for days as a way to avoid impulse buying. The battle with Len over the way I was spending money, Janice Gamblin's tardiness with the company buyout, and my growing anxiety over the success or failure of my new business venture was taking a toll. "Thinking with the heart" and "walking in beauty" were forgotten—I was back on the competitive streets of New York City.

Lucy unrolled her work and spread it on a blanket on the open tailgate of her truck. The piece was about four feet on each side and as tightly woven as anything I'd seen. A weaving is considered a tapestry when there are eighty or more weft cords to the inch—this was unquestionably a tapestry. "The wool," she said, "is from my own sheeps." Lucy told me she lived alone, over by Beclahbito, and tended a flock of forty-some sheep and goats. "I takes them up on the mountain everyday." I asked if she was married. "Men too much trouble," she answered. "All I needs are my sheeps."

The weaving had a background of brownish-gray wool, obviously handspun by the slight variations in the yarn's thickness; Lucy said she spun the wool ten times to get it fine enough for the tight weave. It was bordered with dark brown stair step designs that looked like mountains in the distant horizon. In the center was a delicate cornstalk, done in a muted olive green, which grew out of a woven basket; small brown birds sat on the branches. I'd seen this image in weavings called the Tree of Life, but they were typically done in bright colors with a white background. To the right and left of the cornstalk, four to a side, were identical figures woven with a lighter shade of gray wool. The figures lined up horizontally on the weaving with their heads pointed toward the cornstalk. They weren't *Ye'ii*, but the ornate feather and beaded adornments woven into the figures indicated they held some ceremonial significance. Lucy said they represented the Horned Toad, a powerful deity in Navajo culture.

"Is this a sandpainting?"

She was slow in her response, and a nod of the head was her answer.

"Have you had the ceremony?"

"I can't. Go to the same New Life Baptist Church as Bertha and Jessie. That's how I heard you were comin' to pick up Bertha's weavin'."

"What does the church have to do with the ceremony?"

"They says only one God. Not good to think about more. We has to give up all our old ways ... and that means ceremonies."

The image of the crucifixion hanging on Bertha's wall flashed. "Are you saying that if you join the church, you aren't considered Traditional?"

"*Aoó.*"

Laura Gilpin's phrase about responsibilities held among family members specified Traditional. "So Bertha isn't Traditional and hasn't had the ceremony. Is that right?"

Lucy didn't answer my question.

"I learned this design from Grandmother. When I starts to weave it, my mother says, '*Be careful ... powerful business in this design.*' I wants the ceremony so I won't go blind, but church says no."

Despite Sonya's words, "*You don't wants it if she hasn't,*" I counted out twenty hundred-dollar bills in exchange for Lucy's weaving. I put them in an envelope, along with my business card. This exquisite weaving I could see, touch, and take with me.

"You know what they calls you?" Lucy said as she tucked the envelope inside her handbag. "'*Asdzáán tá'dísbąąs t'áálah* ... that means 'woman who travels alone'."

"I don't understand."

"Ladies don't drive 'round without their man ... 'specially *bilagáana* or white women."

Tachee

Jessie arrived two hours late. My patience with Navajo time was running low. We drove to the quilt exchange in total silence.

Lola's house provided another lesson in doing business on the Navajo Reservation. One woman didn't show up to claim her quilt; another wasn't quite finished with her rug, but "Could she take the quilt anyway?" And two weavings were of such low quality that, even though I honored the exchange, I probably wouldn't include them with my inventory.

My newest Navajo business rule evolved: *Almost every event in the life of a Navajo took precedence over business matters.* There were tasks like hauling hay for the sheep and water for drinking, taking a granddaughter into town for a dental appointment, picking piñon nuts to roast and sell at the flea market, shearing the sheep or tending to a new lamb, attending a ceremony for an ailing uncle, or rounding up the cattle for branding. Priorities were determined by what is happening today; there was no time to plan or spend energy on something that is in the future.

As things were winding down, I presented Jessie with a quilt. "For your trouble." My previously thwarted stop at the trading post to "go it alone" with Bertha highlighted my need for a translator—Jessie would stay in the picture only until I had possession of the sandpainting.

"So, has Bertha finished my weaving?" I asked as we climbed into my rental car.

"Two more days ... says she needs two days."

"Okay. I'll pick you up Thursday at nine." The timing was good for me—I had arranged to meet Sonya in Chinle the following day; we were going to Tachee. "Tell Bertha I have the rest of her money."

Early the next morning I drove to Sonya's house in Chinle with a bag for an overnight stay. She was excited for me to meet her husband, Tyler, and he would be in Tachee for the day. A road project in the Red Valley area required that he rent a small apartment in Shiprock during the week and come home only on weekends. I left my rental jeep in her yard, and we climbed into the high seats of Sonya's robin-egg-blue Dodge Ram pickup truck. She was ready when I arrived; my new friend wasn't operating on Navajo time.

We drove south, out of Chinle, for about five miles and then turned west toward Piñon. The road was newly paved for the first twenty-or-so miles, turning to rough pavement as we approached a small community. A derelict platform, where gasoline pumps once stood, fronted a graffiti-covered building with the faded sign, Cottonwood Trading Post.

"Closed down years ago," Sonya commented without my asking. "There's a new one up a ways, in Blue Gap. Tyler wants to open a hardware store there."

She turned off the main road, onto a stretch that rivaled unimproved dirt for ease of travel—broken macadam dotted with potholes. Sonya laughed as she swerved from side to side, missing most. There were no fences along the sides of the road; herds of wild ponies and grazing cattle wandered close by. We crested a hill and came upon three anxious dogs barking and nipping at the heels of a flock of sheep and goats. Sonya braked heavily and honked the horn. The animals were not intimidated;

in fact, they stood and looked at us. Sonya shared my trait of impatience—she got out of the truck and tried to shoo the flock into action. The deeper my involvement with the Navajo culture, the more aware I became of their sense of humor. On the side of one particularly large ram—one that was slow and took up the rear guard—was painted in large red letters the word STOP.

We turned off the semblance of paved road at a cluster of whitewashed wooden buildings, a Mennonite boarding school and mission, Sonya said. We'd been climbing up the foothills of a mesa since we left Cottonwood, and now, on a steeply descending, washboard dirt trail, we headed back down into a grassy plateau riddled with dry washes and edged on two sides by flat-topped mountains.

"Fish Hook Point." Sonya tilted her chin toward a sharp rock protrusion on the southernmost edge of the ridge we circumvented. "A landmark out here." It looked appropriate to its name—a slender curving rock thrust skyward, ready to catch an unsuspecting cloud. Sonya's chin gesture was the same mannerism Jessie used. The tilt of a chin or the pursing of lips to the left or the right was the accepted Navajo way of directing someone's attention. I was in a culture that felt it rude to point with a finger.

The wild ponies increased in number as we made our way deep into what appeared to be a box canyon. They were smaller than the stocky plow-pulling horses of the Amish farm country and still wore their thick and shaggy winter coats. The further in, the closer the steep walls of the canyon became. And then we drove alongside a wall of white—large pillars of ivory-colored sandstone resembling human and animal-shaped figures clustered together to form a natural amphitheatre, open on one side. A strong sense of *déjà vu* brought the memory of that reservation trip with my father: *My double doll danced ... into a canyon filled with sandstone drip castles and monsters that look as if God formed them by squeezing wet sand through His fingers.*

When it appeared we could go no further, the road turned sharply to the left and snaked its way up the face of the ridge, behind and through the white rocks. "This is the road school bus takes, so they keeps it in good shape." I clutched the grab handle above my door—we were on nothing more than a steep, narrow trail. The sheer rock side of the mountain was close enough for me to touch out my side window, and the white rocks plunged several hundred feet on the driver's side. I looked ahead and prayed we wouldn't meet anyone coming down. At the top, the road made a horseshoe turn onto a flat mesa. A weathered board nailed to a post was propped against a rock with the word Tachee scrawled in dark blue paint; an arrow below pointed in the direction we were headed.

"The school buses drive that?"

Sonya laughed. "You haven't seen the other roads."

The landscape opened to a desert that received more rain than the Chinle area—small flowers bloomed purple and red mixed with the gray-green sagebrush. In the distance, clusters of buildings spread throughout the vast area, and flocks of sheep wandered aimlessly in search of food. At a place where a road intersected the one we were on, Sonya stopped the truck. "A short cut," she announced. "Saves time when you're coming from Durango." The road looked less improved than the one we were traveling on. "Goes west toward Black Mesa, and then, at the windmill, you turn north, up over the mountains." I pulled out my Indian Country map to make some notes. It was new (my father's map was sorely out-of-date) and still there was no road, not even a hiking trail, indicated on the map—just empty white space crossing Sastanha Mesa to the town of Rough Rock.

"I drives it all the time," Sonya said. "Exceptin' in rain. Then it gets real greasy."

We turned off the main road onto a tire-track trail that led to a solitary hogan with smoke circling skyward from the center of its roof. "This is it," Sonya announced. Off to the side stood a sheep pen, an outhouse, and a ramshackle storage building. A hundred-or-so paces away was a small wooden structure. "My sister, Thelma, lives there," Sonya said, "and Aunt Bessie up that way." There was a tilt of her chin toward the wooden house and another directed toward the mountains to the north. "Bessie took care of my sheeps till Tyler an I could be out here more. Now Thelma looks out for them."

Sonya nodded toward the sheep pen and told me Tyler was there. "He's waitin' for you," she said and jumped out of the cab. The pen was made of vertical log poles placed on an angle to support a conglomeration of different materials: sheets of corrugated metal, pieces of plywood, old discarded doors, and random patches of chicken wire—it reminded me of the shed at Lola's house. As I investigated, a dog hobbled toward me on a badly formed clubfoot. He was not threatening, only curious.

"More than twenty years old," a voice said, as I reached down to pat the dog's head. "Can't go out with the sheeps anymore, but checks them over comin' and goin'. Makes a heck of a racket if one gets lost."

"You mean the dog can count?" I looked up into dark twinkling eyes that were shaded by a wide-brimmed cowboy hat.

"Don't knows you'd call it countin'," he said and pulled a toothpick from his mouth. The man wore jeans, a snap-buttoned shirt, and boots that hadn't seen polish since the day they were purchased. The most striking thing, aside from his friendly eyes, was his jewelry—braided strips of rawhide held a huge chunk of turquoise around his neck, and a massive silver belt buckle peeked from under a slight paunch.

"*Yá'át'ééh*," he said, extending a hand that exposed even more blue-green stone. "You must be Sharleen."

"*Aoó.*" I smiled, an apology to my poor enunciation of the Navajo word.

"I'm Tyler." He didn't look at all like the college-educated civil engineer I'd expected. "Sheeps are lambin'. Needs lots of attention." He motioned for me to follow saying he'd show me around. When we passed by the outhouse, a large goose, wings spread and making a hissing sound, rushed toward me. "Don't pay attention to Matilda," he said. "She keeps snakes away."

At the door to the hogan Tyler stood aside and, with a flourish, gestured for me to enter through the small doorway. "Welcome to our home." I stepped over the frame, onto a floor of hard-packed dirt. The light was dim. An oil drum stood in the middle of a circular room; it had a pipe that protruded from the top and extended out a hole in the center of the roof. A square section was cut from the side of the drum, and a well-stoked fire burned hot.

When my eyes adjusted to the light, I scanned the room. I'd seen inside other hogans, even slept in one at Crow Canyon, but this was different; Sonya and Tyler were living here, and I would be a guest for the night. Curiosity took over thoughts that vacillated between excitement for the adventure and nervousness about my lack of privacy. It was at least twenty feet in diameter, but there were no walls dividing the space, and, with the furniture, it felt quite small. There was a two-burner gas stove with a large pot simmering; a propane tank sat next to the stove; and a bucket that served as a drain for the sink was inside a doorless kitchen cabinet. A washbowl and towel sat on a metal TV-tray to the right of the door. There was a wooden table with two mismatched chrome chairs, two single beds, and three aluminum lawn chairs with numerous plastic webs that hung loose. It was quite a contrast from Sonya's home in Chinle.

Tyler led the way around the center stove to the south side of the hogan. We'd only been there for a brief time, but Sonya was already immersed in her work. She sat at a metal loom stand that held an almost completed weaving. It was beautiful. On close examination I realized the weaving was the Two Grey Hills done in the raised outline technique that I had commissioned.

Tyler sat on his haunches next to her and motioned for me to join him. "When I was a boy, I would lie back here behind my mother's loom and play with my pet rabbit. That's how I learned of weavin'."

"Is it true she doesn't use a pattern?"

"It's in her heart ... in her spirit." His hands moved gracefully as though he was tracing the woven lines. "I haven't tried to weave, but designs are in my heart, too."

"Will be done tomorrow," Sonya said and turned to face me. "Alls we have to do is check on the sheeps, an then I can finish it."

"Perfect! This weaving will be perfect for the cover of the brochure for my business." Things were falling nicely into place. The graphic arts designer had been asking for professional photographs to put on the cover. "Let me take a photo of you at the loom; and then if you could send me home with the weaving and a couple of skeins of the natural colored yarn, I'll have what I need for my business brochure."

I watched Sonya at the loom. Like Lola's had been, her face was fixed in concentration. "Weavin' is the fabric of *Diné's* bein'," Tyler said. "It tells stories of Sacred Lands, animals and trees ... the whole *Diné* life." He rose slowly and motioned for me to follow. We sat in chairs at the wooden table, and he told of the Navajo Way. Often, when I asked a question, he responded with silence or "I really can't say." Then later, he would come back and give me an answer. I had the feeling he was testing the waters—making a determination of how I would react to his words.

We talked late into the day. At sunset a curtain was lowered over the window, and a lantern lit; Sonya no longer was at her loom. She brought each of us a bowl of mutton stew and a delectable pancake-shaped pastry that had been cooked in lard to a light and fluffy golden brown. She served it with honey and called it "fry bread."

"I understand you work for the BIA," I commented as we ate.

Tyler nodded, but then added that he didn't really work directly for the Bureau of Indian Affairs, he worked for the Navajo Roads Department which reported to the government agency. "You know what we calls the bureau?" There was a hint of mischief in his eyes. "BIA stands for Boss Indians Around." He talked freely of the difficulties of building roads across the Navajo Reservation. Much of the land was sacred to the *Diné,* and it was a cultural violation to scar it. And then there were the environmentalists. Tyler didn't think highly of them. He was currently embroiled in battles regarding protection of the natural habitat of the Great Horned Owl. At first this seemed like a contradiction until I learned that the owl plays a prominent role in Navajo superstition and witchcraft. Tyler never did tell me his official job title, but he appeared to be in a management role with many responsibilities.

"When we passed the old Cottonwood Trading Post, Sonya said you wanted to put a hardware store in there."

"*Neíyeeł,*" Tyler said with a broad grin. "Just dreamin'. It's hard for people around here to get supplies to fix up places. Nearest hardware store is in Gallup ... almost three hours away.

"Runnin' a business on the reservation is hard. Lotsa red tape. Get taxed by both governments ... Navajo and yours. And, since you can't buy property, the tribe can increase your lease whenever they want. There's some pretty crooked politicians out here."

Sonya was usually a bundle of talk, but this evening she said nothing, deferring to Tyler. He added more logs to the fire, packed tobacco in a long stemmed pipe and elaborated, almost ceremoniously, in lighting the pipe. Only then did he continue with lessons from the Navajo Creation Story. "We teach them again and again through the songs of the Navajos' traditional healin' ceremonies. They aren't magic. Our healin' ceremonies call upon the spirits of our ancestors ... to remind the People."

As Tyler talked there were many long lapses of silence. At one point he looked at me and asked, "What do you see when you look at a mountain?" I stammered and said something rather inane about its shape and the contrasting colors of the trees against the rocks. "That's *Bilagáana* way. They only think of mountains as a mass of earth and rock … a place to do mining, cut lumber, or build a fancy house. And when they take, they don't bless or give back. Power and strength is all around. Our people believe we don't need to take more than we can use. When you learn of Mountain Spirit, then you will understand about my people.

"It's our way. We believes that in the First World the Hero Twins killed monsters that threatened the People. And some turned into Holy People. These Holy People went to live in the mountains." Then he used a paper napkin and crayon to draw a strange picture with concentric circles. The smaller inside circle had an opening in which he inserted two parallel lines, making a corridor from one circle to the next, and then he colored a crude stick figure in the passage. "This is you, Sharleen," he said, and tapped the figure with the tip of his crayon. "You will be the eyes and ears to keep us in touch with the rest of the world."

He labeled the inner circle as *Diné* and the outer area as *Bilagáana*. "You come to us with thoughts and customs of White Man's world," he looked up from his drawing, "and you take back understandin' of our ways. This you will tell your people."

We sat in silence for what seemed like a long time—long enough that I determined Tyler would say no more. "But I don't have a voice in my world." The knowing way he stared, and now this message, frightened me. "Besides, how can I explain something I don't understand or believe in myself?"

He scratched a place on the back of his head and abruptly stood. "They'll help you."

"Does Matilda come out at night?" I whispered loudly.

"Only coyotes." Sonya handed me a flashlight and tilted her chin toward the outhouse. "Use it now."

"What in the hell kind of answer is that?" I muttered under my breath. I swung the beam of light wildly across the path and into a void of darkness. "Okay, Sharleen. What would you like best?" I talked in a strong, confident voice. "Will it be a poisonous snake, a vicious goose, or merely a docile coyote?" The outhouse door creaked as I inched it open to shine the flashlight beam across the rafters, into all the hidden corners, and down the black hole. Only then did I enter, and I didn't stay long.

I ran on my return from the outhouse, spurred on by thoughts of Matilda, snakes, coyotes, and the brisk chill of the night. I never enjoyed camping out; this was as close to the wilderness as I'd been in years. Sonya and I would sleep in the hogan; Tyler left after we'd talked to go back to Shiprock.

Warmth engulfed me the moment I stepped through the door. Sonya had added new logs to the fire that burned in the oil drum stove, and there was a stack of wood nearby. The two beds in the back of the hogan were piled high with blankets; Sonya's heavy breathing signaled she was already asleep in one of them. A washbasin of water, a kerosene lantern, and a selection of tea sat on a wooden table near the fire. A kettle steamed atop the stove. And there was quiet—intense quiet. The only sounds were Sonya's soft breathing, the crackle of the logs in the wood-burning stove, and an occasional howl of a distant coyote. All my concerns for sleeping in primitive conditions vanished.

I wanted to know more about Tyler's stories. I was fascinated by a comment he'd made about his people feeling safe only within the Four Sacred Mountains. I fixed a cup of tea and began to read <u>Navaho Religion: A Study of Symbolism</u> by Gladys A. Reichard. The book was my favorite of the several I'd purchased from the gift shop at the Thunderbird Lodge. It was all there, about the four mountains: Hesperus to the north, Blanco in the east, San Francisco Peak to the west, and Mt. Taylor in the south. There were beautiful, gothic stories of monster slayings and hero journeys. The victors become Gods or deities and lived on the mountaintops.

Just as Tyler had said, there were many sacred places, not just the four peaks that stood sentinel to the reservation boundaries. Traditional Navajos made journeys to these places to draw strength from their being. The mountains were considered either male or female—I liked that part, a creation story where the female stood as an equal beside the male—and designated as night, day, dawn or dusk. Tyler talked of them as an integral part in the Navajo's daily life. His phrase, "weaving is the fabric of the *Diné* being," certainly left no question as to the important role weaving played for the traditional Navajo.

Reichard's book spoke of a time when the People were all one with the creatures—with the spiders, with the grasshoppers, with the beavers, and with the bats. They lived together during that time, all could communicate, and all were considered equal. The animals and the insects were able to teach the People how to live, how to make a living. The Spider People are the deities who taught about weaving. Spider Man showed how to build the loom, and Spider Woman taught the people to weave. "So weaving is a ceremony," Tyler had said. "It's not just an artwork. It belongs to Beautyway ceremony."

It had been a long day. My eyes burned with weariness, but I knew sleep wouldn't come easily. My mind was full with all Tyler had told me. And the picture of the circles with me in the center had been disturbing. It was as though Tyler knew something that I did not. I pulled out my journal and began to write: *Today has been extraordinary. I learned another valuable lesson about life: Navajos believe as people we shouldn't take more than we need. I'll add that to my lessons about "thinking with the heart instead of the head" and "walking in beauty means all parts of life in balance and harmony." I find that I'm beginning to draw calm within myself by just being on the reservation. There is no question that Sonya Bitsinnie is a Master Weaver. Now that I've met her, my dilemma deepens, however. I can see no way to bring these masterpieces of art to the public without the women being there. The women and the place are such an integral part. And then there's Tyler Bitsinnie, a very strange man. He seems to know what will happen before it does. The way he watches me—it's as though he's looking inside my head. (Tyler would say my heart.) So far my experiences on the reservation are very disparate. Some of the people appear aloof and untrustworthy; others embrace me with familiarity and intimacy. Tyler says I'm called to tell of Navajo ways. And then he said "They" would help me. Tomorrow I'll ask Sonya if she knows who "They" are.*

When I did fall asleep, Tyler appeared in a dream. He walked slowly away from me, waving turquoise and white scarves and beckoning me to follow. I tried. But men, their hands arm-locked together into a barricade, encircled me. I ran and thrust my body against their arms, only to be hurled back into the center of the circle. The harder I tried, the louder their jeers and laughter. One figure grew larger than the rest, his body huge, ugly, and misshapen. At first it was a coyote, then it became the man at the trading post, and finally, my father. The changing faces taunted, *"you're just a girl, and you don't belong."* I struggled harder. And the words turned physical. The circle of men began to pinch and slap and shove. They pushed me from one side of the circle to the next, until finally, defeated and crying, I fell to the ground.

Skinwalker

T he next morning there were sheep to tend, water to haul, and countless other chores to be performed before Sonya could get back to her loom. It made me realize how much I take for granted with my indoor plumbing, telephone, electricity, and modern kitchen conveniences. My questions about Tyler's prophecy went unasked, and the dream was forgotten. When chores were done Sonya finished the top edge of the Two Grey Hills weaving; that left only the arduous task of taking it off the loom stand. We worked well together—Sonya with her engaging laughter and the fumbling *bilagáana* eager to learn.

"Would you consider flying with me to Pennsylvania for the debut of my company?" The words were out of my mouth before I'd considered all the ramifications. "It would be great if you could be there to demonstrate."

"Coool," Sonya replied.

Our drive from Tachee back to her Chinle house was filled with excited chatter. I told her everything I could think of pertinent to the trip, and she asked a million questions about the event. The sun was setting when we pulled into the yard of Sonya's house.

I didn't like driving the reservation at night, but I had a three-and-a-half hour trek back to the motel in Durango and an appointment the next day with Bertha and Jessie to pick up my sandpainting weaving. By the time I reached the paved highway a blanket of darkness had lowered over the desert floor. I flipped my headlights to high beam and scanned the sides of the road for stray dogs or sheep that hadn't made it back to the safety of their pens. Last week, in the <u>Navajo Times</u>, I'd read about an elderly man headed home after a drinking binge in Gallup. On foot, he'd followed the highway markings and was struck and killed by an oncoming vehicle.

The darkness swallowed me in loneliness. Off in the distance, caught by the edge of my headlight beam, I saw a flash of movement. A large shape was crossing the road. I pressed hard on the brake pedal. At first, all I could see were two large eyes, and then the shape of a coyote took form. It stood motionless in the center of the highway and stared directly at me through the windshield. The reflection of my headlights made its eyes look like two chunks of coal, burning yellow-orange—like the eyes of the coyote in my dream. After several long minutes, the creature turned and ran into the darkness. My hands gripped the steering wheel, and my body was covered in a clammy sweat.

It was yet another anxiety-ridden night of little sleep, and I did not welcome the six o'clock alarm. Once again, Jessie was late for our departure to the meeting with Bertha. I felt the discomfort my body experiences when my blood pressure is high; I felt jittery, agenda driven, impatient. I had difficulty in focusing, my chest was tight, and there was an ache in my throat—the kind one gets when trying to suppress tears.

"So where were you? I've been waiting over an hour."

I started the engine of my Jeep rental before Jessie completed her climb into the passenger seat. Jammed the vehicle into reverse and then slammed on the brakes—just missing a pickup truck that was pulling into the parking lot of the Teec Nos Pos Trading Post.

"We were supposed to be at Bertha's by now."

"You're a grump."

"I'm sorry. I'm just anxious about picking up my weaving. And I didn't sleep well."

"How's come?"

"Nervous, I guess. I saw a coyote on the road last night."

Jessie turned in her seat to face me directly. "He runnin' away?"

"More like running toward me. I had to stop in the middle of the highway. He stared at me for two or three minutes."

Jessie gave a low keening moan and started to rock in her seat. "Ya needs ceremony … maybe seen a skinwalker."

"What are you talking about?"

"Bad spirits or bad people, either one. They come wearin' animal skins. Mostly coyote. Try to steal your spirit by lookin' at ya. That's how comes we cover the windows when the sun goes down."

"I think my spirit is just fine."

"Ya needs ceremony to get spirit back."

"Well, I can't take the time to worry about it now. Besides, your church doesn't even believe in the ceremonies."

"Can't not."

We continued on in silence.

"The Beautyway ceremony," I said, needing to change the subject, "… the one women have to allow them to weave the sandpainting weavings … has Bertha had it?"

"Costs too much. 'Sides church says we cain't."

"But doesn't your culture tell you to have the ceremony?"

Silence.

"Why does she weave sandpaintings?"

"Okay since we born-again. Had to gives up all that, how you say, 'stitious stuff."

"Superstitious. You had to give up your superstitious beliefs. But you didn't. You still believe in skinwalkers."

142

It all came down to money. Bertha had a skill that brought her more money than the average weaver. When we arrived at her house Jessie got out of the jeep to open the gate of a chain-link fence that enclosed the yard and driveway. It was a new fence, I was certain of it. This visit, after my travels with other Navajo women, I saw the dwelling through different eyes. They would have called it a "bad place" because there was nowhere to keep the sheep, and the front door didn't face to the east. I did take note, however, there was no outhouse, and Bertha's was one of the nicer homes in the government-built housing development. But I couldn't help wondering if the fence had been paid for with my money.

Jessie was knocking on the front door by the time I came to a complete stop. As before, it was a child in diapers who opened the door. The scene was almost identical to my first visit. The same elderly couple sat on the couch, a muted television played cartoons to an audience of children sprawled on the floor, and Bertha sat in the chair by the stove. Only Charlie was missing, and there were no greetings.

We sat in silence. As the others stared at the screen, I fixed my attention on the crucifixion plaque that hung on the wall—it verified that Bertha, like Jessie, was a born-again and had not experienced the Beautyway. "*Weaving won't be good,*" Sonya and Lucy had both told me. "*If a woman did a sandpainting without a ceremony, bad things would happen.*" I remembered Sonya's warning: "*You don't wants it if she hasn't had the Beautyway.*"

I waited in the silence as long as my patience allowed before I spoke. "So how is Charlie doing?" I directed my question to Bertha who simply looked at me with a blank stare.

"Moved him last week to hospital in Shiprock," Jessie answered. "Still bad."

Six weeks had passed since I'd wired the two thousand dollars via Western Union. "Tell Bertha I've got the rest of her money." I still owed a thousand dollars.

A verbal exchange, all in Navajo, took place. It contained far more words than I thought necessary. I cursed my dependency on Jessie as a translator and wanted to shake her into telling me what was going on. Finally, she turned and said, "She sold yer rug yesterday."

It took several replays in my mind before her words registered. "What do you mean, sold it?" I looked back and forth, between Jessie and Bertha, pleading for a shred of understanding. Bertha's head was down; she stared intently at the cheap shag carpeting on the floor.

"Trader comes by an asks what you pay for rug. Says he'll give two-hundred dollars more. She needed money real bad."

"Bertha can't do that. I've paid her five-thousand dollars. That's stealing." As though in slow motion, I rose from the couch and headed down the hallway to the spare bedroom where Bertha did her weaving. The loom stand was stripped. My chest constricted, and tears welled in my eyes.

"Which trader?" I shouted on my way back to the living room. "Which trader took my rug?" I knew it was the one who'd said, *"Ya' know, Lil' Lady … these Injun's, they'll cheat ya' every chance they get,"* the one who appeared with the coyote in my dream—he was the trader who had bought my rug. I held the tears inside and forced myself to speak. "Don't tell me she really needed the money." My voice came high and shrill. "That's a brand new chain-link fence around her house." I was at a loss for what to say or do. "Does she plan to weave another one for me?"

No one spoke. My questions reverberated through the solemn quiet. I looked briefly at the faces of the elderly couple sitting quietly on the couch—a hint of sorrow showed in the woman's expression, but when our eyes met, she quickly looked at the floor. And then I ran, out of the darkness of Bertha's living room and into the brilliant sunlight. Hardpacked dirt and a wheel of the jeep became my support for letting the tears flow; I sat mired in the betrayal I'd felt in Bertha's dark, crowded living room.

Sonya and Lucy both told me that if a woman did a sandpainting without a ceremony, bad things would happen. But the bad things were happening to me. And then I remembered Sonya's warning: *You don't wants it if she hasn't.* All the forewarnings were right, and the dream I had in the Bitsinnie's hogan unfurled in front of my eyes: the coyote in the road, the crucifixion plaque hanging on the wall of Bertha's home, the truth in the trader's warning *they'll cheat ya every time*, and my father's crybaby taunts followed by ... *only a girl, you don't belong.* On the hard-packed dirt of Bertha's yard, the last part of the dream played out; I fell to the ground, defeated and crying.

It was a long time before Jessie came out and we climbed back in the jeep. "You wanta know what bothers me?" Jessie didn't wait for my response. "It's that coyote. If it was a skinwalker, then somethin's out to get ya."

The last thing I wanted was advice from Jessie. "Well, I don't believe in skinwalkers," I told her. "All I know is, I've given away a lot of money and have nothing to show for it."

We drove on in silence.

I dropped Jessie off at her house and started the two-hour drive back to Durango. My mind replayed nonstop the treachery I'd been through in Bertha's dark, crowded living room and the events leading up to it. Tyler had said that weaving is the fabric of the *Diné* being. The prophetic poetry in his words spoke to the vision I'd created for what my company could become. I dreamed of a business that reached international acclaim with masterpiece weavings that captured the essence of a richly spiritual culture and were acknowledged for artistic excellence. I hoped for a business that showed the heart of the Navajo people.

My intense emotional response was all balled up in discordant concerns—was it about the lost money, the sandpainting weaving that would not be available for my exhibit, or having to admit that I was wrong and needed to give up my dream? It had been almost a year since I walked out of a half-million-dollar contract with the New York Stock Exchange to pursue that dream. I was smart, experienced and worldly-wise. I'd owned a computer consulting business that catered to Fortune 100 companies and provided me with a six-figure annual income.

Being swindled out of five-thousand dollars by a "floor-starer" was insignificant when I thought of the thousands of dollars I'd spent on marketing brochures, business cards, press releases, magazine and television advertisements, and venue rental for the debut of my new business—an event scheduled to happen in less than six months. An event that was dependent upon a sandpainting weaving. Then there was the stress put on my marriage. There'd been countless warnings from, and arguments with, my husband about the manner in which I was spending money and the way I was proceeding recklessly in a market and culture I knew very little about. And my arrogant responses about following my heart and doing things my way.

How did I come to this place? I really had to explain that to myself.

In the days after the Bertha incident, before I was scheduled to fly home to Pennsylvania, I contacted several attorneys in Durango. They were unanimous with their counsel. They told me I had no recourse if I paid money without a product or some written guarantee of a product. It was the same message I'd gotten from Len. I spent the long hours in airports and planes trying to script what I would say to my husband.

Len was at the airport, waiting, when I landed. "We're going out to celebrate," he said and gave me a big hug. "I've got some great news."

Thank God, I thought, *I could use some good news right now.*

"The check from Janice came." He pulled a deposit slip from his pocket and handed it to me. "Only three months late, but it's here. I went ahead and deposited it into your account. Wanted to make sure it didn't bounce."

Discussions at the restaurant and at home focused on Janice's tardy check and meetings I'd had with the architect and contractor for the building of our dream house. Almost a week passed before Len asked, "So when are you going to show me the rug?"

I tried to avoid his question by showing off Sonya and Lucy's weavings, along with the ones I'd obtained in the quilt exchange. But he didn't buy it. "Where's the one you paid six thousand for?"

"There's a problem with that one."

"And?"

"When I got to Bertha's to pick it up, she'd sold it to someone else."

"You told me you'd paid for all but the last thousand."

"I had. A trader came by and offered her more money. She sold it."

"Sold it twice, you mean." Len stood from the table and began to pace. "So what're you going to do?"

"What can I do?" I chose not to follow Len's pacing with my eyes, but stared intently into my wine glass, swirling the deep bluish-purple fluid around the sides. "We didn't have any kind of written contract."

"Sharleen, I've told you this before." He stopped long enough to take a finishing gulp of wine. "You can't be paying them money before the rugs are done."

I set my glass down and looked directly at him. Len was expressing the same rage I'd felt at Bertha's; why couldn't I just acknowledge it and agree with him? Instead, I began to defend Bertha. "There were extenuating circumstances you don't understand. Charlie was mugged. She needed to be with him. And then ...."

"She's a thief. And that Jessie who drives you around isn't any better. Following your heart doesn't make good business sense. That's for the philanthropists."

"I'm sorry Len, I don't agree with you."

What I felt was difficult enough to explain to myself. My ego would not allow me to reveal the "meltdown" I experienced in Bertha's front yard. I wasn't ready to admit to Len that the sandpainting fiasco had happened because I'd used poor judgment in my business practices. And my defense of Bertha was nothing more than a distraction to avoid admitting he had been right. I was a smart business woman, but I couldn't explain why I had walked into this situation so naïvely. I did know it had something to do with the transition from my old world to a new place—a place where I didn't yet know the rules. My defensive responses were cover-ups for massive feelings of uncertainty and insecurity. I'd put myself under enormous pressure to perform … and to perform well.

My throat tightened, and I held the tears in check. I ended discussions with Len when tears came. Years of being taunted by my father taught me that tears were a sign of weakness and the male world used any and every opportunity to prove their superiority over women. I'd taught myself not to give them that advantage.

"The Bertha incident is an isolated situation. Besides, it's my money."

"Yes. It is your money."

In the following weeks I spent countless hours poring over my business plan. When I began this venture I vowed to run the Durango Trading Company with compassion, to give up those tried-and-true men's rules that only looked to the bottom line. But this betrayal by Bertha only served to highlight my stupid business decisions. The belief that I could prove myself successful doing things "my way" was so strong it had not allowed me to see, let alone admit, my faults. Now I was left to redefine "my way."

I started with the section titled INVENTORY and reread the underlined statement: *Buy directly from the weavers.* This prompted a complete rewrite of the guidelines to follow in making new acquisitions. From there, I moved to the plans for my company's opening event. A lot needed to change. Drafts of press releases and advertising propaganda needed the name of the sandpainting weaver changed from Bertha Benally to Lucy Joe. References to a master weaver now named Sonya Bitsinnie. And my Two Grey Hills weaving needed to be professionally photographed for the cover of my brochure. Brief biographies and pictures of Sonya at her loom and Lucy Joe with her fine tapestry were added to the list of brochure content. And now, with my hasty invitation to bring Sonya to Pennsylvania, the entire venue of the company debut needed to be revamped.

All of the changes meant money, lots of money. I poured over my financial plan, shifting money on paper from one category to another and spacing out my cash flow. It all worked, but was heavily dependent upon the annual influx of cash from the sale of my consulting business. If Janice Gamblin was three months behind in making the initial payment, there was no telling how late the subsequent payments would be. It might be necessary to take out a short-term business loan.

And then the phone call came.

"I just can't manage the business by myself. You'll get the letter from my attorney. I'm filing for bankruptcy."

The voice at the other end of the line trailed off as I tried to comprehend the words. I think I asked some questions, but it's all a blur. Janice owed me three-hundred-thousand dollars. With a few papers filed her debt was gone and, for the second time in less than a month, my dreams for the business came crashing down.

The letter arrived the following morning by express mail; the eggshell color of the expensive paper and the austere formality of the law firm's name gave it an ominous look.

Dear Ms. Daugherty:

Please be advised that Janice K. Gamblin, sole owner of Business Systems, Inc. has filed for Bankruptcy under Ohio Code #743.

This act renders the Daugherty/Gamblin Buyout Agreement dated July 6, 1992 null and void.

We regret if this action causes you any undo hardship.

Respectfully,
James K. Williams
Attorney at Law

After reading the letter, I went for a long walk to be alone with my thoughts. Our suburban Lancaster home was situated in the midst of Amish farm country. I could walk a circular route of less than three miles that took me across two covered bridges and several large fields. It was May and the seedling tobacco plants were big enough to begin transplanting. I found a low stone wall that I sat on to watch this fascinating process. A strange-looking device, pulled by two mules, made a furrow in the dark soil of the field. The machine carried a large water tank and two young girls—they couldn't have been more than seven or eight years of age—who sat on a back platform, low to the ground, and dropped the plants into the soil. I'd read that the planting is staggered, so that all the tobacco does not mature at once. This way they could harvest the mature plants at their prime. My company debut was carefully scheduled for mid-October, after the labor-intensive cutting of the tobacco in August and September.

The impact of Janice's bankruptcy on my company was enormous, but the biggest blow was to me. The money represented my financial independence for many years to come. More than that, the money represented who I was. Walking with my thoughts, I realized the yardstick by which I measured my worth was coming up zero.

That night, when Len and I sat down with our wine to discuss the events of the day, the words came in a rush. "I need to tell you something, Len. I think … I think this is more than I can handle by myself."

"Sharleen, what is it?" He rose from his chair, came to me and cradled my head against his chest. I'd spent the afternoon in the throes of emotions that swung violently between rage and despair and thought all the possible tears were gone. Not so. It took time, and several Kleenex, before I was able to speak. I told him about the phone call and handed him the letter. His jaw clenched, eyes narrowed into steely slits, and his body turned rigid.

"I want you to know … I want you to know, that I'm sorry for the way I discounted your concerns about Janice Gamblin. I've been flippant. I don't know why. God knows I didn't feel that way." And the tears began again.

"We'll make it work, Sharleen." His body and face softened. "If you need money to make things happen, it will be there."

Shiprock

"**H**-h-hello, my name is Crystal. Crystal Redshirt." There was a long pause and the telephone connection crackled. "M-m-my mother weaves rugs just like Bertha's." I could hear voices speaking Navajo in the background. "C-c-can you visit us in Shiprock?"

Len was adamant that I continue with my plans for the business. I still had money of my own to invest in its success, and he assured me there was family money that could back me up. I was making monthly trips to the reservation. I gave an approximate time frame for my next visit, and we arranged a day and time.

"Damn washboards," I muttered. "This better not be another wild goose chase." Getting to Shiprock was no problem, and following Crystal's directions to the dirt road just past the hospital with a red-painted wooden sign had been easy. But as soon as I made the turn, I faced a wye with three branches. Through my travels with Sonya I'd learned, when the rains come and the roads are bogged down with mud, drivers simply circle around, across the desert, to avoid getting stuck. My directions said nothing about three roads, so I took the one in the middle. That's when my vehicle started the wild shimmy.

Just as I thought it was time to turn back, I saw a house trailer that fit the description—two shades of brown aluminum siding with a shed attached to one end and steps up to the front door. I pulled to a stop and honked the horn to announce my arrival—the way I'd learned from reading a Hillerman novel. I waited, what seemed to be a very long time, until I felt foolish and concluded that this courtesy must not apply when the person lived in a town. I approached the front door and knocked, waited, and then knocked again, this time louder.

A faint message, "Come in," came from inside. The first door led me into a storage area. It was a wooden structure, built as an attachment to the front of the trailer, and looked like it was designed to give added space while keeping the cold air from coming into the main living area. My stomach did some flutters, and I felt the muscles in my throat tighten. This was my first visit in a Navajo home without a friend or interpreter. Coming from the bright mid-morning sun made it difficult to see clearly in the darkened place. I rounded the corner and faced another door; this one stood open.

Three Navajo women sat on the sofa facing me, lined up like an audience with me at center stage. The eldest was on the left. She sat in a very stately regal way, leaving no question that she was the matriarch. Next to her was a woman who appeared to be in her sixties with a smile that lifted my spirits. On the end of the couch was a younger woman. From her dress, stretch-cotton leggings with a long tunic top, I guessed her to be in her mid-thirties.

"Y-y-you must be Sharleen," the young woman said, as she stood and offered her hand. "I'm Crystal Redshirt." She had a friendly look. She was a bit overweight, with eyes that sparkled, pudgy cheeks and long, black hair that curled softly around her face. Her feet and legs seemed inappropriately small to carry such a heavy torso, and her shoulders rolled forward as though to protect a concave chest.

"Th-th-this is *shimasání*," she said softly and led me to the eldest woman, "my grandmother, Anna Mae Hoskie." The old woman had wrinkles that cut deeply into skin marked with dark brown moles, and her gray thinning hair was pulled back into a bun and bobby-pinned to her head, exposing the scalp. She extended her hand and responded to my greeting with "*Aoó.*" When our eyes met, I recognized her; she was the one who sat with the elderly man on the couch at Bertha's. My heart gave a lurch when I made the connection, and my face must have shown the reaction.

"M-m-mother an Bertha are sisters. We were 'fraid, if you knew, you wouldn't come."

I didn't say the words, but her fears were correct. I wouldn't have.

"An this is my mother, Grace Yazzie." The woman with the broad smile reached out to clasp my hand in a soft, gentle grip. "*Yá'át'ééh,*" she said and beamed. "We glads you here." With her words came a schoolgirl giggle that she covered with a hand cupped over her mouth. "English not good." The words, the shy laugh—they were identical to Lola's at Crow Canyon.

The difference in appearance and mannerisms of the two sisters was startling. Grace's face was full with joy and love; there was no pinched mouth or beady eyes. Crystal gestured toward a chair for me to sit and went back to her place on the couch. The three women watched me in silence.

I was inclined to leave; I needed more time to deal with the blow of learning this woman was Bertha's sister. But instead, I stared back, looking closely at the way the women were dressed. Anna Mae wore a long-sleeved velvet blouse of a rich, midnight blue. Her skirt was three tiers of ruffled cotton in a bright turquoise color that matched many of the stones she wore. Both wrists were encircled with large cuff bracelets— tied on with cotton string—each containing at least thirty small chips of turquoise. At her neck, a large pin of sky-blue fastened the collar of her blouse together; it was a centerpiece for multiple strands of turquoise that held a pendant made from swirls of coral beads. Grace was every bit as resplendent in her dress, but with Grace, it was the smile that caught my attention.

After examining the women, I scanned the surroundings. This home was different from Bertha's. The room was bright and cheerful and there was a television in the corner, but it sat quiet. From the back of the trailer, I could hear the low buzz of a radio; the voices spoke in Navajo. The most prominent object in the room was a large metal-pipe loom stand. It took up one complete side of the living area. A sheet was draped over the metal pipes, hiding all but the bottom portion of a rug. From what I could see, it looked about the same size as Bertha's.

"Do you all live here?" I finally asked.

"J-j-just me an' the boys," Crystal responded. "Mostly, Mom stays here to help out." My question seemed welcome; I decided they were waiting for me. "My mother an grandmother both have homes close to Red Valley."

"Their grazing land?"

Crystal nodded. "We calls it Sheep Ranch.

"*Shimasání's* mother came there after *hweeldi*, the place of sufferin'. Your peoples call it Bosque Redondo. She got grazin' rights then." Crystal spoke of the place near Fort Sumner, New Mexico, where, after a war of legendary horror, Kit Carson led the Navajo people to a four-year incarceration.

"Come look." Crystal stood and motioned for me to follow her to a wall of photographs and memorabilia. "Barboncito," she said, and pointed to a large, framed picture of a stately looking man—he was bare-chested, draped with a striped blanket over one shoulder, and held a long pipe in his lap. "In 1868, he led *Diné* home, what your people call Long Walk."

Later I would read of Barboncito in Raymond Friday Locke's <u>The Book of the Navajo</u>. He was the leader who, when the confinement at

Bosque Redondo had failed miserably, and government officials offered Cherokee country as a place to relocate the Navajos, replied: *"When the Navajos were first created, four mountains and four rivers were pointed out to us, inside of which we should live. That was to be our country … I hope you will not ask me to go to any other country except my own."*

We continued to look at the wall of photographs. Crystal had a story to tell with each one. "That's Peter MacDonald," she said and pointed to a picture of a handsome man dressed in a velveteen shirt with an impressive coral and turquoise strand necklace. In my readings, I'd learned that Peter MacDonald was an illustrious leader who had spent an unprecedented four terms as Chairman of the Navajo Tribal Council. He was now incarcerated in a Federal prison. Over time, I would learn that MacDonald's biggest mistake was going to battle against Barry Goldwater. Navajo opinion and support is divided against the charges that resulted in MacDonald's prison term—opponents say he committed fraud against the people; proponents contend he was set up by the Goldwater political machine. Ultimately, Peter MacDonald became one of the controversial prison inmates pardoned at the end of Bill Clinton's presidential term.

"A-a-an, Thomas Atcitty, Grandmother's nephew." Crystal pointed to another photograph of an equally distinguished looking man. "He is Vice President now."

As we continued to talk, Grace stood and moved across the room to her loom. She removed the rug's protective cover and positioned herself to begin work. This was Crystal's cue to start the business part of the conversation. She turned from the wall of photographs and directed my attention to the loom. And then she spoke in Navajo to the older women. I watched the faces of the three generations and listened to the soft exchange of words—they were punctuated with gentle bursts of laughter against a background of thuds made by the wooden comb as Grace beat down the weft yarns.

"Mom can weave rug for you, just like Bertha's." As Crystal became comfortable, her stuttering decreased.

I hesitated. I wasn't certain I wanted to involve myself with this family. "What about this one?" I was struck with how similar the weaving was to the one Bertha had done. Without waiting for Crystal's translation, Grace flashed a smile and spoke. "This for trader."

"She needs to pay down credit." Crystal explained that the traders let them take food, gasoline, and other necessities on a line of credit. Once their debt reached a certain level they paid it off by weaving a rug. "But Trader marks up food prices, so she just weaves fast an makes lotsa mistakes."

"So why don't you just take the rugs somewhere for the cash?" I asked. "Why bother with the credit?"

"It's how we've lived for long time. We needs food before a weavin's done, an when we needs cash real bad, Trader gives us money for our jewelry."

It was the hopeless cycle of the company town. This morning I'd driven into the reservation by heading south of Durango to Farmington— called a border town because it sits close to the eastern edge of the Navajo Reservation—and then west to Shiprock. The highway from Farmington is a constant stream of pawnshops, mobile home sales, and used car lots. I knew this to be the strip where Navajos could get quick cash for family treasures, short-term payday loans, or drive away in an automobile financed with a plan they could never pay off.

"I do good one for you," Grace said.

"You don't even know me."

"Do now," she didn't pause with her work. "They tells me you comin'."

My eyes went first to Crystal, and then to Grace, with my question, "Who?"

"M-m-my mother is younger than Bertha. Peoples think Bertha weaves best. Mom dreamed long time ago that *bilagáana* comes to find her. To be her, how you say ... patron."

Crystal spoke in Navajo, addressing both Anna Mae and Grace. The old woman simply nodded, adding *Aoó* from time to time. Grace responded often, smiling and glancing my way when she spoke. "Mother wants me to tell you, since she was young girl, spirits come, an they speak to her. They say, you're comin'."

Maybe 'they' were the same ones Tyler said would help me.

Crystal talked and Anna Mae struggled to pull herself up from the low couch. She walked with a cane, unsteady as she moved across the floor to where Grace sat. From between the warp cords of the loom, Anna Mae pulled a flat stick worn smooth. Crystal explained that what she held was a batten, and it was used to separate the warp cords. "It's marriage gift. She gots it when she married Little Man's son." The old woman watched for my reactions; then she spoke—her voice musical, and her expressions animated. She paused only for Crystal to translate.

"*Shimasání* taught Mom an' Bertha to weave. This was her batten, but she gives it to Mom." Anna Mae handed the long stick to me. It was slick and cool in my hands, reminding me of the worry stones that people set on their desk to stroke in times of stress. "When Grandma was young girl, she wants to learn to weave. In summer, when they takes sheeps to mountain, she'd watch Little Man's wife. Other women, when they took rugs to Trader, got 'bout ten dollars of credit. But Little Man's wife gots as much as one-hundred dollars."

I handed the batten back to Anna Mae. On one long edge were small indentations that she gently ran her fingers across. "See notches," Crystal said. "Tension from yarn over lots a time made those." Anna Mae gave the stick to Grace and returned to the couch, talking as she walked. "She wants to tell you *Diné* are like batten—shaped an' smoothed by Old Ways."

Crystal was finishing her story when I heard the front door open; two young boys, accompanied by a man in his mid-to-late sixties, appeared.

In the customary fashion, the boys came directly to greet me, but the man quietly slipped through the living room and headed for the back of the trailer. "My sons, Naalzheí an' Little Eagle. An' that was my father, Thomas Yazzie. In Old Ways, a man an' his mother-in-law can't be in room together. We have Navajo word, *naadaaní*, means "your in-laws." Family members shout to warn a husband his mother-in-law is comin'. Most don't follow that anymore, but Grandma … she's old."

I stayed through the afternoon, talking and watching Grace weave. Anna Mae stretched out on the couch for a nap, and Crystal prepared lunch for everyone. At one point I asked Grace if she'd had a ceremony to allow her to weave the sandpainting. Her face lit up, and she nodded yes. Grace shared with Tyler Bitsinnie an inner peace that permeated her being. And when she spoke about a dream telling her that I was coming, I was reminded of the strange dreams that had been coming to me and, seemingly, predicting my fate. I was comfortable in this home. It was a place that honored the value of money and worth, not for power or control, but for how it fed the necessities and dignity of life. A special bond was being formed, a tapestry of friendship woven among four very unlikely women.

The violation of Bertha's deceit vanished as I watched the image of a *Ye'ii* appear in Grace's weaving. We discussed what she needed in order to weave a sandpainting for me; the fifty-percent-down payment was similar to Bertha's, but the price of five thousand instead of six agreed with my estimates. I talked about my business and the Pennsylvania exhibit I planned for October. The more I talked, the more I was reminded of the time at Crow Canyon when I watched the face of Lola Tsosie at the loom, and the visit with Sonya and Tyler that made me wonder: *How could I ever convey to a collector or buyer the <u>real</u> significance of a weaving.*

"Grace, I want to know if you would come to Pennsylvania with me, to be in a show with some Amish women." *I'd already invited Sonya; why not one more?* "I would travel with you, and you could stay at my house." Grace's magic smile gave me her answer.

There was a flurry of Navajo exchanged between Grace and Crystal, with more gestures and laughter in their speech than normal. And then Crystal turned toward me and in a quiet voice asked, "C-c-could I come, too? My mother would not want to go without me. I needs to translate an do her hair. You know, things like that." She paused for just a second, and before I could respond, she began again. "I know how to spin wool an 'bout plants to use for dye. I could show how to do that as Mom is weavin'. An I could help you set things up. Lots of hard work. Too much for Mom."

PART THREE

Footprints in the Sand

Late on the evening before I was to meet Sonya, the telephone in my hotel room rang. I'd written to her about making another trip to the reservation, and that I would be staying in Durango at the Jarvis Suite Hotel.

"Can ya hear me?" It was Sonya.

"Barely."

"Won't be home tomorrow. We gots to go to Whippoorwill Springs," A loud roar cut off her words.

"Sonya, are you there?"

"Big truck just passed," she said and laughed. "I'm in front of tradin' post. Come to Tachee day after tomorrow. Shortcut I showed you. Take that."

"Why?"

"Tyler an me have to go to his mother's." Balancing the phone between my chin and shoulder, I reached for my Indian Country map. "Head toward Bears Ears ... each fork in road till you gets to big windmill, then go other way, not towards Piñon." I could see her large almond-shaped eyes as she scrunched up her mouth to point the way. "Then you gets to my place. We're livin' there now." I spread out the well-used map and located the scribbled-in windmill.

"Sonya, the last time you gave directions, I ended up in someone's front yard."

"That's cause you turned after little wash instead of big one."

"I'm used to highway signs and roads that are on a map. Any idea how far?"

"Long ways. More than Tachee to Piñon. Once you pass second windmill, you go little bit an then pass pile of old tires. Road's right after that."

"Second windmill?" My fingers drummed the map.

"Don't worry. Just be coool. Remember, two windmills an then tires."

"Put some red yarn on a bush at the turn to your place." I located Whippoorwill Springs, where Sonya and Tyler were headed. It was about midway between Cottonwood and Piñon, off the road Sonya and I took on the way to the white rocks. Blue Gap and Tachee were north; I would be headed into the white void on the map—nothing was there but a large landmass called Sastanha Mesa. "I'll be there by noon."

"Navajo time?" Sonya chimed. It had become a joke between us. Sonya loved to tease me about my obsession with time. She encouraged me to take note of how many Navajo homes I saw with clocks or people wearing wristwatches. Aside from the digital displays on the infrequent coffeemaker, there were none.

"Just be home at twelve o'clock. Okay?"

"*Hágoshíí.*"

Coool was her favorite English word, but in Navajo it was *hágoshíí*, which meant, "everything is settled." Nothing ever felt settled to me: questions went unanswered, concerns ignored, and, for me, noon was twelve o'clock, not give or take an hour or two. In the world I'd come from, planning was the key. I'd spent endless hours alone, or in tedious meetings, mapping out every possible scenario and developing a contingency plan—insurance that guaranteed I was always in control.

Now I was being forced to operate without those defenses, to use that hated phrase of the younger generation, "Go with the flow." Going with the flow only added to my stress and blood pressure problems. For me, time was still money, and money was running low.

Sonya's situation gave me an extra day. A visit with Lucy Joe in Beclabito seemed in order. I pulled out the directions she gave me when we met at Jessie's. Unlike most of the women I dealt with, Lucy had a telephone. A quick call confirmed she was home and would welcome a visit. I started the trip with a stop at the grocery store. One of the items that seemed in short supply when I visited people on the reservation was fresh fruit, so I gathered up a bag filled with oranges, apples, grapes, melons and peaches. Out of Durango, I headed southwest through Cortez and Four Corners—the geographical location where Utah, Colorado, Arizona and New Mexico come together—into Teec Nos Pos, a small community in the northern part of the reservation. Beclahbito was an easy five miles east on US 64.

Lucy described her house as simple to find: "Turn at the top of the hill, before you get to the trading post. You'll go across a cattle guard, and there are four roads, take the one closest to you." My questions regarding the one closest to me revealed that I was to veer to the right. I was dodging boulders and driving through soft sand when I realized the wash I crossed was the other end of the road I had tried to take months back, on my way to the quilt exchange. Lucy was true to her words—I could see her house from the road, but between it and the wash was a maze of tire ruts, formed when the rains made the road a soft muck, enlarged by erosion when the rains came again. Some were almost a foot deep. I was in a Jeep Wrangler—a plentiful rental option in Durango—and didn't know the width of my wheelbase, so I zigzagged up the bank, taking the ruts at an angle instead of parallel.

Lucy's sheep and goats roamed freely around her house. The pen was about fifty feet off to the side, but the animals were quite at home on her front porch. She saw me arrive and came outside to greet me. The house was old and small—two bedrooms, a living room/kitchen combination, and a bathroom. It smelled of Lysol cleaner, and the furniture was free of dust and clutter. Like the hogans I'd been inside, Lucy's house had a wood-burning stove in the center that burned hot. She was dressed in a housecoat, a Wal-Mart special, and apologized because she didn't look very good. Lucy had only one photograph displayed on the wall, the same picture of Peter MacDonald I'd seen on the wall of Crystal Redshirt's trailer. It hung next to a large calendar issued by the Navajo Nation Museum.

I presented my bag of fruit, and she put a small saucepan of water on the stove for tea. "I pick this when I take sheeps up to the mountain," she said, and dropped a bundle of stick-like herbs tied with cotton string into the boiling water. "Good if you have a stomachache." Lucy could only tell me the name of the plant in Navajo. Later, when I expressed my liking for the tea, she filled a plastic baggie with bundles that she kept in an empty Folgers coffee tin, and gave it to me.

"I'm real mad at Jessie," she said at one point in our discussion. "You 'member day I came, an you bought my weavin'? Well, Jessie, she comes after an tells me I have to pay her 'cause we met at her house." Lucy continued with a story that was difficult to believe. She'd been to Wal-Mart to buy some new clothing and came home to face Jessie on her door stoop. They argued. After Jessie left, Lucy realized she had taken her bag of new purchases. "She's *wooshch'íid* ... envious of my money."

Lucy's revelation prompted me to tell her of Bertha and the thievery that had taken place there. She was as appalled by my story as I was of hers. Slowly, my sensibilities toward the Navajo were changing. Rather than accepting them as all good, or all bad, or all victims, I could recognize them as individuals making choices according to their own beliefs and needs.

When the time came for me to leave, Lucy stood and asked that I wait as she retrieved something from her bedroom. "Okay for you to take gift?" she asked on her return, obviously hiding something behind her back.

At first I didn't understand. Then I nodded and said, "I'd be honored."

She smiled and held out a beautifully crafted squash blossom necklace. It was strung on white cotton twine, meaning it was old— newer pieces were on a stronger plastic fishing line. "It was *shimá's*. I wants you to have it."

I stared in disbelief. "I can't take this." Earlier that morning, I'd learned that Lucy's mother had recently passed away; they had been very close. Lucy's smile faded, and her eyes dropped to the floor. "I mean ... it's wonderful." I cupped her hands in mine. "But it is worth too much, lots of money."

"Not 'bout money," she smiled. "We have same heart. An it's our way ... Old Way. Don't tell Jessie."

The heart word again. Tears filled my eyes as I zigzagged my way back across the tire-rutted road to the main highway. Like Lola and Grace, Lucy had not gone to boarding school. Jessie's words, about the grandmothers holding back the best children from the White Mans' school, played through my thoughts.

Early the next morning I headed for Tachee. I estimated it to be a four-and-a-half hour drive, but I'd never taken Sonya's shortcut, so I didn't know what to expect. From Durango to Rough Rock the paved-highway portion of the trip was easy; it provided plenty of time to feel nervous tension about traveling an unfamiliar route. After Rough Rock the road became slow and difficult; it was dirt and turned narrow and steep as it switchbacked up the face of the mesa. On the top there was a pullover, a place to take in the view and a few deep breaths.

I grabbed my camera and headed for a large outcropping of rock that hung off the edge of the ridge, hundreds of feet to the desert below. From this vantage point I could see the red Mesozoic cliffs the geologist called Chinle and the distinctive rock formations of Monument Valley. As I sat, enthralled in beauty, the wind circled through the pines carrying memories of a time long ago. Unconsciously, I reached for the thunderbird pinned to my shirt. It had been a long time since I'd thought of my childhood friend, Nanabah; I wondered if she still lived on the reservation. Sonya Bitsinnie had the same shy laugh and long shiny black hair, but Nanabah had been my age—Sonya was too young, by at least ten years.

I slid behind the steering wheel of the Jeep and eased my way back onto the rutted dirt road. Deep cuts formed by runoff from the ridge could bury a tire. The twisting, steep road would not be a good place to get hung up on a boulder or in a ditch. I'd passed through Rough Rock an hour ago and hadn't seen a single person or vehicle—it might be days before help came. I shifted into four-wheel low gear.

As I left the ridge and snaked through the heart of Sastanha Mesa, the terrain flattened. The road, no longer full of rocks, was covered with several inches of fine silt sand that would turn into a thick mire of mud with the next heavy rain. I remembered Sonya's words about the roads getting real greasy and checked the sky.

The view out my window was constantly changing. The road wound itself among tall, jagged rock formations—in and out of washes that would run swift at the next heavy rain. I only turned around three times in someone's yard before I learned to watch for the tires, piles of rocks, or wooden posts that indicated a private drive. Two windmills followed by a really big wash and I found the sagebrush with bow-tied red yarn on top.

Sonya was outside, under a structure that had four vertical poles supporting a pseudo-roof made of aspen logs lashed together in a square with small branches across the top. She sat in an aluminum lawn chair that faced a stone fire-pit and patted clumps of bread dough into a pancake shape and placed them on a griddle to cook.

"*Yá'át'ééh*," she said. "I'd greet you properly but my hands are full of flour."

"Are you making fry bread?"

She nodded yes and indicated the shade structure was called a summer hogan; it was used for cooking during the hot summer months. Sonya finished her bread making, and we headed inside. Tyler sat at the table with a cup of coffee. He greeted me with a handclasp and motioned for me to sit down. I allowed time for courteous chitchat: "How many lambs this month? Will the summer be unusually dry? Where are the road crews working?" And then I broached a question about the piles of cinderblock I'd seen when I drove into the yard.

"For my new house," Sonya answered proudly. "The money I got from you pays for those." Each rug she sold meant they could make the drive to Gallup or Farmington and pick up another load of cinderblock. When she had enough, construction would begin on her home.

We'd finished the mid-afternoon meal when Tyler said he had a story to tell. Sonya stood from the table and went to her loom to weave. "*Amá sání*, my mother, and my niece, Carlesha, live together over in Whippoorwill Springs." He spoke in hushed tones. "Mother had a stroke years ago. It left her unable to speak. So Carlesha looks after her, fixes meals, and tends the sheeps, things like that."

"Last week *nílch'i* came to *amá sání*."

"Who?" I asked.

"*Nílch'i* … Spirits.

"Carlesha tells that Mother started hollerin' in the middle of night. '*Get ready. They're comin'.*' Carlesha didn't know what was happenin'. *Amá sání* hasn't spoken for years an usually needs help gettin' out of bed. Here she was, standin' in middle of the room."

169

"Then she hears a whooshin' noise." Sonya spoke from where she sat at the loom.

"More like high-speed whinin'." Tyler gave a look telling her not to interrupt. "Mother headed out the door with Carlesha behind. They stopped right outside the door." Tyler titled his chin toward the door of the hogan. "*Nílch'í* stood ten or so paces away.

"Like both women were frozen; they couldn't move. *Nílch'í* were over there in front of hogan ... two of 'em." Tyler continued to describe two iridescent blue pillars that were like dust devils on a hot summer day, whirring as they glided toward the hogan. Abruptly the pillars stopped, and the sound ceased. "Like time stopped, it was so quiet," he said. Out of the whirling lights two men emerged; one was dressed in soft buckskin and wore a necklace of blue-green that danced like a flame in a fire. He glowed white from the long hair that streamed down his back to the moccasins on his feet. The other figure was the color of turquoise—intense shades of swirling green—and adorned with strands of coral and white shell. Tyler's description was surreal. "Women tells me they were 'fraid to look at 'em an mostly kept eyes down."

My strong Southern Baptist upbringing left little room for anyone but God to appear in the form of whirling sand or burning bushes, and what Tyler described didn't come close to my Sunday school image of God. I wanted to pass off the apparitions as nothing more than a beautiful dream.

"They left message," he said. "One of *nílch'í* raised his arm, pointed a finger to *Amá*, an warned her *Diné* were divided ... not following old ways."

Then Tyler looked at me. "For you, Sharleen, it starts already."

"What?"

"Things we speak of when you visited us last."

Like the picture of the two circles he'd drawn on a napkin, Tyler drew another sketch. This time it was a teardrop with a spiral that started at the tip and circled many times around the fullness. "Many don't understand things that direct their journey."

"Tyler, I don't mean to be disrespectful of your ways. I just have a lot of trouble believing this. As for what you said about me being a spokesperson or something …" I shook my head. "I don't see it happening. But some very strange and bad things have been happening. You've been in dreams I've had lately … always before something bad." I told him of seeing the coyote in the road right before Bertha's betrayal and of my business partner filing for bankruptcy to avoid paying the money she owed me.

Tyler only nodded and continued with his story. He told of two sets of perfectly formed footprints twenty paces or so from where his mother had stood. There was a thin outline of corn pollen, from the tassels of the white corn plant, around the footprints. "*Nílch'í* message says that many *Diné* forget Old Ways … forget to give respect." The reason Tyler and Sonya had gone to Whippoorwill Springs was to witness the footprints. Evidently, medicine men and spiritual leaders from across the reservation were making treks to Tyler's mother's hogan.

"*Amá* able to speak now. An she can walk on her own."

There was a silence—a Navajo silence.

Today the quiet gave me time to absorb Tyler's words. The constant chatter and noise of my world kept out the inner voices and forced my mind to race ahead without giving proper respect to what had been said. What did Tyler mean by saying, for me it starts already? And what was the teardrop drawing all about? Faith healings take place all the time. That could explain the miracle that occurred for Tyler's mother, but there was no logical answer to how the footprints came to be.

Tyler continued. "*Nílch'í* come to help us remember. If *Diné* forget Old Ways, we have no face. Many people today, they go way of modern world … *Bilagáana* world … they forget."

So soon the lesson of silence forgotten, I rushed in with a question. "What did they mean about the people being divided?"

Tyler smiled. "You hear about the new church?"

"If you mean the Native American Church, I've done a little bit of reading about it. I read that it was a combination of Christianity and traditional Indian beliefs. And Native American Church members are the ones who use peyote as part of their ceremonies."

"*Diné* are divided. Just like *nílch'í* say. There's Born Agains … they have to give up all Old Ways." *Like Jessie and Bertha.* "Then Traditional, like Sonya an me. And then the Peyotists. They're new. Plains Indians come to Reservation from Oklahoma in fifties. They come with teachin's from *bilagáana* missionaries all mixed up with Old Ways, an calls it Native American Church. If you ask me, I say they lost point of both. Peyote is big part of way they do things. Family in Tachee stays high on drugs all the time. I sometimes think those Native American churchers are so hard into their peyote they forget they're *Diné*."

"What do you think are approximate percentages of Navajos in each group?" I'd been exposed to the Born Agains and the Traditional; I wondered how many Native American Church goers I'd met.

"Peyotists are most," Tyler answered. "That's why the *nílch'í* message."

A Bag of Bluebird Flour

The busyness of the summer of '93 rivaled anything I'd experienced with my consulting company. In Lancaster my time went to the commercial art designers who were producing my marketing materials. Sonya's weaving went on the cover of the brochure. I deliberated over copy proofs, press releases, biographies of the women and two men from whom I'd purchased rugs. There were pamphlets that described vegetal dyes and the process of coloring the wool, complete with sample pieces of yarn in an array of colors. I approved postcards that advertised the Navajo/Amish event, pricing sheets for making custom orders, gift certificates to enable future purchases and poster-sized photographs of the areas on the reservation where the weavers lived.

Monthly trips to Durango were woven into the event planning. We had decided to build a home to live in after we moved, so there were meetings with the architect who was drawing plans for our home, business with the downtown quilt shop interested in displaying the Amish samples as a means to custom orders, sessions with a realtor to line up a place to rent until the house was completed, and the ongoing search for an inventory of Navajo weavings. I always included a stop at Grace and Lucy's, just to check on things and to say hello. Sonya joined me on some of my trips—her aunts and nieces were supplying most of my new acquisitions. But mostly, I traveled alone. By mid-September I called a halt to the reservation trips and returned home to wait until it was time to escort the Navajo women to Pennsylvania.

The telephone call came after I had gone to bed; a hollow and lifeless voice spoke from the other end of the line. "C-c-can you come, Sharleen?" The only way to identify the caller as Crystal was the stutter. "Mom needs to see you."

"What's wrong?"

"Just come."

Sleep evaded me for the rest of the night, as my imagination swung wildly through all the possible reasons for the call. Images played nonstop through my mind: the coyote standing in the middle of the road, a rabbit dangling from the talons of the hawk, the scene when the trader called me Little Lady, footprints outlined with corn pollen, and the most prevalent, the empty loom in Bertha's bedroom. Earlier that day I'd finalized travel arrangements for the Navajo women to come east—the trip was only three weeks away. My plan was to fly to Albuquerque, rent a car, and pick the women up at their homes. I contacted the airlines sometime between three and four in the morning and, for a nominal fee, they moved up my departure date.

There was an unfamiliar vehicle parked in front of Crystal's trailer, and the gray Ford pickup truck the family drove was nowhere in sight. I jumped out of my rental car and made my way to the front door, impatiently turning the doorknob, as I knocked. The door was locked, and today the trailer looked as though it was abandoned. I knocked a second time, loudly enough to rouse Crystal's dog, Brandy, from a deep sleep.

"Y-y-you gots here fast." Crystal didn't smile as she pulled the door open for me to enter. "We didn't expect you for couple of days."

My heartbeat quickened as I hurried through the dark storage area into the living room, but there was Grace facing the loom of an almost finished weaving. On the sofa sat a man whose presence seemed to overwhelm the small space of the living area. He sat cross-legged with his right leg forming a large open triangle that positioned a polished snakeskin cowboy boot to be the focus of attention. Arms were splayed across the back of the couch, and he wore an expensive-looking cowboy hat pulled low over hard, brown eyes. Even sitting down, as he was, I knew he swaggered.

"Th-th-this is Lewis McGuire," Crystal said.

I held out my hand for the customary greeting, but he did not return the courtesy. A long silence followed. With effort I was gaining comfort with Navajo silences, but this one felt different. Lewis stared at me with eyes that bore deep—not the gentle look that I'd experienced with Tyler.

"I'm Grace's brother," he said, breaking the uncomfortable silence. A long pause accentuated his words. I certainly knew about Grace's sister, but I'd heard nothing about a brother. "You plan to take them to Pennsylvania? What is your agenda?"

His abrupt manner thrust me back into the boardrooms of countless companies; a familiar tight constriction began in my chest and crept up to my throat. Grace momentarily glanced my way and turned back to her weaving. Crystal's head was bowed. Caught off-guard and feeling betrayed by Grace and Crystal, I stumbled through the itinerary.

"Three shows are planned," I told him. "The first one will be with the Amish women in the large community room of a department store in Lancaster, Pennsylvania. The second is scheduled for a Native American museum in Ephrata, and the last one will be in Philadelphia, at a place that specializes in handmade textiles. After the work is over, I plan to take them to Cape May, New Jersey for a look at the Atlantic Ocean and then to Washington, D.C." I had saved for last what I thought the best part. "We have an appointment at the Smithsonian Institution."

An audible "humph" was his only reply.

Then I handed Lewis a copy of the freshly printed brochure—Grace and Crystal had not seen one. On the inside center page and billed as "four generations of Navajo weavers," stood Anna Mae, Grace, Crystal and Crystal's two sons. While Lewis studied the colored document, I averted my attention to the wall of family photographs. Hung to the far left was a picture of Lewis with the same steely eyes as his sister, Bertha, staring at the camera from under the bill of a military cap. I vaguely remembered seeing the picture on my first visit, but no mention was made, and I passed over it.

"What do you plan to gain from their presence?" Lewis' voice grew louder with each word, and his face turned red; both boots were squarely on the floor now, and he leaned forward to stare directly at me.

His gaze sparked an old memory—I couldn't have been more than three—of a tent revival meeting. The preacher's eyes were aflame with a message of Satan, Hell, fire and damnation as small rivulets of sweat streamed down the sides of his face. "*Repent and be born again,*" he shouted, waving the Bible in the air with his outstretched arm. "*Swine, worthless swine, all of you. Come down the aisle and accept Jesus Christ as your Savior or burn in the fires of Hell for all eternity.*" People around me swooned and cried out, "*Save me, save me,*" before they crumbled to a mass on the floor. I curled up at my mother's feet and cried softly.

"Did you pay them for using this photograph?"

It never occurred to me to pay them. I smarted at the implied exploitation and called upon learned defenses, those intimidate-back techniques that for many years in the business world had enabled me to stand up to arrogant men. I pulled a copy of my business plan from my case and handed it to Lewis. "That document will tell you everything you need to know. You may keep it if you like." In the plan I had detailed the manner in which I would pay the women: prices to the consumer were marked twenty percent above what I paid for a rug; in the case of custom orders, once the weavers determined their price, I marked it up to retail price, and required a fifty percent pre-payment to cover expenses during the weaving process. When the women were present during an exhibit, profits of the day would be equally divided between me and the weavers. The plan was more than generous. I knew the traders marked their weavings up more than 100%, but they didn't pay the women a fair price.

It was Lewis' turn to be caught off guard. I smiled inwardly as he fumbled with the plan. As though on cue, Grace's husband, Thomas, entered the trailer. He hung his hat on the coat rack near the door and approached me with a broad smile and an outstretched hand. "*Yá'át'ééh*." His greeting was soft spoken, and his handshake a gentle clasp. "We glad you here." He shook hands with Lewis, sat next to him on the sofa, and embarked in a lengthy discussion in Navajo.

I'd heard much about Thomas and saw him briefly that day when Anna Mae was there, but this was my first opportunity to observe him. He was the type of man that many women would look at twice in passing: lean, rugged, a man who spent his days with outside work. His dress of worn Levis, a long-sleeved plaid shirt, and unpolished leather boots fit his role until you got to the jewelry. Around his neck hung a massive stone of turquoise rimmed in silver. It resembled the typical bolo tie, but the size and intricacy of the silverwork set it apart from anything I'd seen. He wore rings, cuff bracelets, and a large silver buckle strung on a leather belt. Thomas was a man's man, and yet his mannerisms were gentle and his eyes sparkled with friendliness when he glanced in my direction.

As the two men talked, I reflected on Lewis' accusations. My company's mission statement was to promote the arts and the artisans, but it wasn't a nonprofit organization. I stood to make a lot of money if the business was run properly, and the presence of the women gave me the credibility for that to happen. There were opportunities for the women also. If all went as I planned, they could separate themselves from the scams of the traders. I rationalized that I could teach these women a lot and help them gain some financial independence.

The discussion ended abruptly. Heads nodded, and Lewis stormed out the front door without any goodbyes. Grace stopped weaving when he left and smiled at me. "He be okay. Just angry 'cause he not goin'." And she began to laugh—the schoolgirl giggle that gripped my heart. Soon we all were laughing.

When Thomas left the room, I knew it was back to work. Men were never present when discussions of the business side of weaving took place. A lengthy exchange in Navajo ensued between Crystal and Grace. "Something you must know," Grace said.

Silence.

"Crystal is answer to highest wishes. Thomas an I lived in Shiprock. He work for uranium mill over by river."

There was a time when I would have considered the long periods of quiet between Grace's statements to be her struggle to find the right words, but I was learning that long pauses were really a courtesy to me— time for me to grasp the significance of her words.

"We build hogan close … very good for us. Could throw rock from house to yard of mill. We use mill's empty metal drums to store drinkin' water. You know, couldn't take from river, mill put bad stuff in river." At this point Grace lowered her head and twisted a piece of her skirt between her fingers. "I try to have baby, always somethin' wrong, an lose baby." When she looked up I could see tears in her eyes.

"We have many ceremony. They not work."

I wanted to embrace this beautiful woman and allow the tears to flow from both of us, but instead I choked back the lump that welled in my throat and said, "Grace, did the doctors ever tell you it could have been the uranium waste from the mill that kept you from having a baby?"

"No, but they tell me bad stuff cause big pain in belly. Many people have big pain if they lived by mill. Big lawsuit—they try to get money for us. Not right for mill boss to keep secret 'bout big pain. Crystal come, an I forget 'bout havin' baby. Like Crystal come out of my belly."

Grace turned back to her weaving. Crystal continued. "M-m-my uncle is also my father." Crystal stopped to give me time to absorb her last words and watched intently for my reaction. I was stunned. I replayed the scenario of Lewis' visit. The information I had just learned helped me to understand more about the hold Lewis had over these women. It explained why they allowed him to confront me as he did.

"My brother make wrong." Grace set aside her weaving tools and continued with the story. "He gots out of beauty, an Crystal born. Nobody want Crystal, so I took her. Thomas an I love her like own ever since. Only problem—we not bury baby cord." I wanted to ask why Crystal wasn't with her birth mother, but I was learning that all things would be revealed when the time was right. "In our way, when baby born, cord to mother buried near hogan. This ties baby to land. If boy, it goes near sheep pen. If girl, near loom stand. I not do that for Crystal. That's why so many troubles learnin' to weave."

And once again, Grace turned back to her weaving.

"So is Lewis what you called about?" I blurted out. Other than the Lewis thing, I really couldn't see how Grace's story of Crystal affected me, and my anxiety was building over the telephone call.

Crystal looked puzzled; it was as though she had forgotten that I came two weeks early at her request. "*Sh-Sh-Shimá* doesn't think she can finish weavin' in time. An she's 'fraid we can't go if it's not done." Grace turned toward me, fiddling nervously with her weaving comb.

"Is that all? Is that the reason for your telephone call?"

"You not angry?" Grace's face showed anxiety until I shook my head no, and then it lit up with one of her dazzling smiles.

I didn't know whether to laugh or to cry. My first emotion was overwhelming relief, followed quickly with the disappointment of not having the weaving for my show. "There's still time. You weave fast, and we've got two weeks." The five-foot-square tapestry was well over halfway completed. The design would have four *Ye'ii* or deity figures, just like Bertha's, with feet pointing toward the center of the rug, and their bodies forming a cross. The background was gray; the figures were brownish gold, adorned with colorful beads and feathers. Grace had completed three of them.

"In Old Ways it shows disrespect to weave after sundown."

"Why sundown? You have electricity. You could weave when it's dark."

"Not good," Grace continued. "Spider Woman … Old Ways … says not good to weave after dark. Bertha weaves after sun go down, that's why she gots so many troubles." Crystal nodded her agreement. "That an 'cause she not have ceremony." The more I learned about their beliefs, the more I realized how strongly this belief system shaped their daily life.

"Of course, you both can still go. We just won't take the weaving." I tried to temper my letdown with the thought that it was really having the women at the show that was important, but all the while, my mind raced with changes that must be made to the press release and display layout. Grace flashed her magic smile and turned back to her work.

Driving to Shiprock the morning before our flight to Pennsylvania, I said a few prayers that today we would not be operating on Navajo time. I planned to pick up Crystal and Grace—Tyler was bringing Sonya—and we would all meet in Albuquerque at a prearranged motel. It promised to be a long day.

When I entered Crystal's trailer, I noticed an odd assortment of bags—mainly of the fifties vintage—neatly piled beside the door. "Well, this won't be stolen." I looked down at a huge orange-vinyl suitcase. "No one would want to be seen with it."

Grace giggled while Crystal explained that she'd tried to talk her mom out of taking it, but they didn't have a good replacement. Off to the side, away from the other luggage, I saw a large black duffel bag. "What's in this one?" I asked, as I tried to pick it up. "It weighs a ton."

Crystal gave me an embarrassed grin. "B-b-bluebird flour. She needs it for Amish." Grace had spoken with me about serving a traditional Navajo meal to the families of the women. With the naïve assumption that the ingredients could be purchased in Pennsylvania, I'd agreed.

"You're kidding." I unzipped the bag and found, wrapped in some old towels, a twenty-five-pound cloth sack of special grind flour, the type used for making Navajo fry bread. "Who's going to stay home so we can put this in the seat of the airplane?" I quickly followed up with "just teasing" when I saw the terror-stricken look on Grace's face. "Seriously. It's too heavy. We'll be over our allotted weight."

We had already shipped two large crates to Pennsylvania. Sonya and Grace needed loom stands that could be taken apart for shipping and then reassembled for the exhibit. Crystal had the paraphernalia necessary to demonstrate the spinning and dying of the wool, and there were display items that Tyler had built out of aspen log poles. Most of our allotted weight on the airlines would be taken up by the many weavings we needed to carry back for the show.

"I needs to tell you about *metate*."

"*Metate*?"

"Grinding stone." Grace was on her knees next to the orange suitcase. With a lot of effort, she laid the bag down and opened it. Crystal went to her side and pulled the clothing away from a large flat rock. It was the size of a garden stepping stone, only much thicker, with a smooth indentation on one surface.

"W-w-we use it to grind the corn into meal for *atolé*." She unwrapped a smaller stone, one you could hold in your hand, and showed me how it fit perfectly within the shallow bowl of the larger rock.

"Can't you use that flour?" I nodded toward the black bag with the flour.

"Not for *atolé*." Grace was up and headed to the kitchen. She returned with a grin on her face, holding a bag of blue cornmeal. "Has to be like this." I learned that blue corn was considered special, and that the *metate* was the traditional way of grinding the kernels into meal—the meal was then stirred, with the special prayer sticks, into boiling water until it reached the consistency of Cream of Wheat cereal.

Negotiations ensued. The sack of Bluebird Flour would be shipped two-day express mail from Albuquerque, and we would take with us the small bag of already-ground blue cornmeal. That, along with additional clothing, would fill the gaping hole left by a *metate* that stayed in Shiprock. I conceded that Grace could carry on the bundle of prayer sticks. They were approximately three feet in length and were tied together in the center by a strip of rawhide. She explained that the sticks were necessary for the *atolé* preparation. I was too exasperated to argue any further.

It was close to midnight when Sonya and Tyler arrived at the motel; our flight departed at 6:15 the next morning. I'd left two large canvas duffel bags with Sonya for the rugs that hadn't been finished in time for early shipment—we would check them through with our luggage. Sonya had taken over one bag and insisted she must carry it on the plane with her.

"Sonya, it's too big."

"I know 'bout flyin'," Sonya said. "You gets two carry-on bags. My purse an' this one; that's my carry-on."

"I don't think you do know about flying." The bag in question was unwieldy, like a huge beanbag chair, and very heavy. I unzipped the duffel and began to pull out its contents. "So where did all these rugs come from, anyway? I don't recognize a single one."

"Sharleen, you're messin' up my packin'."

"Who did them? I didn't contract for any of these."

"Grandmas, aunts … I got lotsa grandmas an' aunts."

"So where are we going to display them, Sonya? Have you taken over the exhibit arrangement in addition to weaving?"

"You said bring as much as we could, so I'm takin' lots."

"Sonya, I've spent weeks photographing and documenting our inventory for the advertising and insurance. What if something happens and this bag is lost?"

"Now you knows why I hafta carry it on."

"This whole thing is absurd. What if someone wants to know about one of these rugs? I don't even know the weaver's name or how much they cost."

"Just come asks me, I'll tell you what to say."

"Sonya, it's late, and I'm too tired for this. You'll have to argue with the ticket agent when we get to the airport."

"*Hágoshíí.*"

Buggies and Frybread

We were at the airport at five the next morning. I wanted plenty of time for checking in. We found a cart for all the bags, except the one duffel that Sonya insisted on managing herself. "Both of these women want windows," I said to the ticket agent and nodded toward Crystal and Sonya. "And I need to be seated beside this woman." I pointed to Grace's ticket. "She's a little nervous."

"Have any of them flown before?" the agent asked.

"Sonya Bitsinnie. But that was a long time ago."

I held my breath when he asked for photo IDs. I hadn't thought about that as an issue. Fortunately, Sonya and Crystal could produce a driver's license. Grace smiled and handed the young man her documents of Navajo authenticity—a paper issued by the tribe to verify Navajo blood for selling items that claim to be handmade by a Native American. It took two co-workers and a supervisor to resolve the issue, but eventually the ticket agent inserted a comment in the computer that Grace was traveling without a photo ID.

"You carrying your grandmas in the black bags?" the ticket agent quipped.

It was early, and coming on the heels of our previous dilemma, his remark took a few seconds to register. "They're almost big enough, aren't they?" The young man tagged one of the duffel bags and motioned for Sonya to put the second one on the scale.

"This one's part of my carry-on," Sonya said.

"You gotta be kidding." The agent pointed to a small aluminum stand to the side of the counter. "All carry-on bags must fit inside that square frame."

Sonya argued that there were things in the bag she had to have with her. Exasperation showed on the ticket agent's face, and he motioned for us to step aside so he could help the next person in line.

"I hope you believe me now. You can't take this bag onto the plane with you. So what is so important it must be hand-carried?"

Sonya was accustomed to having her own way. Angrily she rummaged through the bag and pulled out a rolled-up-fringed blanket that she used as a cushion. "My grandma's batten," she said, as she laid the bundle down and unrolled it. "An my loom." Inside the blanket were the long slender stick she used to separate the warp cords and a partially woven loom that was rolled around the supporting dowels. The dowels were about four feet, too long to fit in her suitcase. "Too much chance for breakin' if bag is checked."

It was Grace who came to the rescue. She dropped to her knees and rolled the loom and the batten back inside the blanket, giving instructions to Crystal in Navajo. A few moments later Crystal and a baggage handler arrived with silver duct tape and some twine. When Grace finished the bundle was transformed into something that looked like an arrow quiver.

"Coool," Sonya said and slung it over her shoulder.

Weavings were put back inside the duffel bag, checked with the rest of our luggage, and the agent wrote out our boarding passes. "I want my ticket," Sonya demanded, as I was putting the papers in my briefcase.

"It would be easier if I just carried all of them; no chance of one getting lost."

185

"I'm not a child, you know." She assumed a petulant stance until I complied. The strong, independent woman, who had become my friend, and I were in the midst of a major struggle for control. Ticket in her purse, Sonya headed off toward the boarding gate.

I heard her voice before I saw her. "I gots pictures in there." She was arguing with security about her camera. "Step aside," the guard said to Sonya, as I approached.

"What's the problem?" I said.

"They wants me to put my camera on that belt. It ruins pictures."

"Have you taken any?"

"No, but I'm gonna."

"It'll be fine. Just finish the roll, and rewind the film before we fly home."

The line of people waiting to pass carry-on bags through the x-ray grew. I handed boarding passes to Grace and Crystal, walked through the metal detector, and watched from the other side as the two women shed their jewelry. I'd cautioned them not to pack any of their valuables in suitcases that were being checked. Instead they wore the jewelry or carried it in their purse. Sonya was delayed for the second time. "Give them my boardin' pass, Sharleen," she shouted from the other side of the security barrier.

"I don't have it. Remember, you insisted on carrying your ticket and your boarding pass." Sonya dug through the pocketbook she'd just emptied of jewelry, but could only retrieve her ticket. I tried to dampen a slow building rage. The security guard was trying to explain that the boarding pass should be inside the folder along with the ticket. They asked her to step aside.

"Here it is," she said indignantly and pulled a wadded ball of paper from her coat pocket. "They didn't used to do it this way."

I sighed with relief when we were all seated on the airplane. Sonya was in the back; her voice carried over the din made by the other passengers.

She was telling those around her about the important business she had in Pennsylvania. Crystal sat quietly at her window seat across the aisle from where her mother and I sat.

We were in the critical part of take-off. "Lift up your feet, Grace," I said. She looked at me with wide eyes. "Helps the plane get off the ground."

Grace complied and then giggled. "You teasin' me."

Our flight went from Albuquerque to Chicago and on to Philadelphia. From there we would have a two-hour drive to Lancaster. In Chicago we rode an airport train to change terminals, and then onto a moving sidewalk that carried us through the bowels of O'Hare. The corridor was narrow with room for two moving walkways going opposite directions and a stationary sidewalk in between. An impressive display of laser lights played nonstop fireworks over our heads, bouncing the light off the ceiling and walls. "This is sooo coool!" Sonya shouted, bringing stares from the people around us. Grace even let go of her shyness and laughed along with Crystal.

I resisted any attempts at shopping or food purchases until we reached our departure gate. "I'll only be gone a few minutes." Sonya was adamant about looking for coffee mugs; she collected one from every place she traveled. She had no idea what her antics back in Albuquerque had done to my blood pressure, but I was too worn down to argue.

"Do you know where the gate is?" I hollered after her. There was no reply. Grace insisted on clutching my hand, and Crystal wanted to browse through the airport gift shops. I agreed to stay with Grace so Crystal could catch up with Sonya.

And now they were missing. The boarding process was almost complete, and there was still no sign of my Navajo charges. Grace was in tears. Minutes that seemed like hours passed. The agent made a final boarding call. And then I saw them. Sonya and Crystal both carried packages and were laughing. There wasn't time to ask questions. The flight attendant rushed us down the boarding ramp and into a fully loaded airplane of impatient people.

The following day we were expected at the home of Rebecca and Amos Stoltzfus. Sonya was quiet on the drive into the heart of Lancaster County Amish country, and all three women were hushed as we made our way up the lane to a sprawling three-story farmhouse. "It so green," Grace said as we got out of the car. "An' huge." Her eyes were wide like a child's in a toy store. "Looks like hotel in Albuquerque."

"The Amish are like the Navajos," I said, "only with their sons. When a boy marries he brings his wife to his parent's house. They just add a few more rooms."

"Coool." Sonya pointed her chin at a buggy that stood next to the barn, "It's like ones we passed on the road." The Amish farm was like a picture with fences freshly painted white, manicured lawns and sparkling windows in the house and barn.

"How comes ..." Sonya stopped mid-sentence. Rebecca was coming down the porch steps leading a small army of children. I counted nine—ranging in age from about three to sixteen. They were look-alikes in their dress and appearance. The youngest peeked from behind Rebecca's skirt.

"Welcome. Welcome." Her voice was high and shrill. "We're excited about you coming." Out of the corner of my eye, I noticed her husband, Amos. He and two older boys stood watching from the entrance to the barn. "I let the children go late to school so they could meet you awhile." She put a hand on the shoulder of the oldest, "John, Jacob, Sarah, Matthew, Ruth, Esther, Joshua, Mary ...." After their name was mentioned, she gave each a little push to send them on their way, "and Rachael." Rebecca had to pull the child from behind her skirt.

Rachael tugged at her mother's arm, coaxing her down so she could whisper something in her ear. Rebecca gave a hearty laugh and said, "Rachael wants to know if you're going to scalp her." Sonya stooped to the child's level, handed her a piece of hard candy from her pocket and said, "Not if you gives me a ride in your buggy."

In her all-work-no-play fashion, Rebecca said something about forgetting her manners, and wouldn't we all come in. A huge platter of homemade donuts and cake sat atop a table that would easily seat sixteen— long benches lined each side. As the women exchanged amenities, Amos and the two older boys come in from the barn and poured themselves a cup of coffee before they sat down at the table.

At first there were furtive glances and hesitant smiles, but slowly the conversation began. "How ya say 'nice day' in Navajo?" Amos asked, focusing his attention on Crystal. A friendly banter took place between the two, interrupted by Rebecca when Amos wanted to know how to say "pretty legs."

"We'll have thirty for dinner," Rebecca said. "More with the children."

I volunteered to make a grocery list and do the shopping. "How many pounds of hamburger do we need for thirty Navajo tacos?"

Rebecca was on her feet opening cupboards to expose huge kettles and other equipment to cook for crowds. "We take turns having church," she explained, making it sound like feeding thirty adults plus children was an everyday occurrence.

Armed with the grocery list, Crystal and I headed for the store. When we returned Grace was in a conversation with Rebecca. "Not little one," Grace insisted.

"I think she wants to butcher a sheep." Rebecca looked horrified. "Something about mutton stew."

It was hard not to laugh. "*Ndaga',*" I said to Grace and shook my head. "No time."

"Where's Sonya?"

"The barn."

I had visions of her up to her elbows in the blood of a fatted calf. There were voices when I rounded the corner of the barn; Sonya was not alone. A group of teenage boys surrounded her. "Men wear these?" she asked as she examined their Old Order Amish dress of black suits and hats. They seemed fascinated by her colorful speech and clothing. The boys passed a wooden box between them, and one held up a large turquoise and silver bracelet.

"Sonya." I tilted my chin Navajo fashion to call her over. "What's going on?"

"They wants to buy."

All three of the Navajo women had brought boxes full of jewelry in the hopes of making some extra money. "Do you realize that's against their religion? They'd be shunned from the church and their families."

"Don't know why," she responded. "'Sides, I already sold a bolo tie to Amos. He just stuffed it under his shirt sayin' somethin' about not lettin' Rebecca see it."

The rest of the afternoon was a blur of activity. Fortunately the kitchen was large—children and women from surrounding farms came to watch the excitement of real Indians in Rebecca's home. Sonya and Crystal set up an assembly line to produce the fry bread; they gave lessons in patting out the balls of dough to laughing Amish women. Grace stood at the stove using her bundle of sticks—the sticks that had hung on the wall in the Shiprock trailer—to stir the blue cornmeal as it boiled. She had Crystal explain to the Amish women that the sticks had been blessed by a medicine man and were used for a variety of things: to lay next to an infant in the cradleboard as protection, to comb a young girl's hair during her *kinaaldá yik'aas* or puberty ceremony, and to stir the sacred *atolé* for special occasions such as this.

There were laughter and wide eyes from the Navajo women as Rebecca's daughters' added leaf after leaf to a dining room table that would accommodate thirty adults comfortably, and we all stood in amazement as the girls brought out perfectly matched bone china place settings for each person. Later, I explained that even though the Amish are considered "Plain People," when an item is a necessity, rather than a luxury or convenience, they allow themselves to be elaborate.

Sonya was giddy with excitement when the buggies arrived and the horses were unharnessed and led into the barn. Families filled Rebecca's dining area; the atmosphere was one of hushed expectancy. The meal began with prayers, first by the Amish delivered by Amos in a dialect that combined German with Pennsylvania Dutch. Grace followed, speaking in Navajo. In no time, the room filled with talk and laughter.

The day of the big event arrived; the process of getting dressed in traditional garb took longer than usual. The women took turns tying each other's hair into buns and ironing, for the second or third time, their velveteen blouses. As they prepared themselves, I ran a taxi service delivering Rebecca, her mother-in-law, and two other Amish women to the site of the event. Amos and the children would come by bus.

"What's gonna happen at this show?" Sonya asked, as she stared out the passenger window of my car. Grace and Crystal sat quietly in the back seat.

"Your displays will be set up, and there will be pictures and information about how making quilts and rugs fit into your lifestyles. I have a slide presentation about similarities and differences between the two cultures. And you'll be there for people to ask questions."

Sonya turned away from the window and faced me. "How are we alike?"

"Obvious things. You both live a traditional lifestyle, you live off the land, and you learn your art from the grandmothers who came before you. Things like that."

Silence.

"Differences are a little more subtle. The sale of quilts is a big part of the Amish family's income, just like weavings are to the Navajo, but making a quilt means something different. Rebecca told me that quilting was her way of expressing love for her family."

"Does she just give them to her kids?"

I took a deep breath, not sure how to explain what I was trying to say. I'd found that my visits among the Navajo left me exhausted, beyond a normal tired. It was the energy I spent holding back my typical behavior in an effort not to make a cultural *faux pas*. This was one of those situations: I did not want my words to offend. "The Amish people believe it's wrong for somebody to try to be better than their neighbor. They think that's prideful."

Silence.

"So they all do things the same way," I continued. "They dress alike, they wear their hair alike, and their houses look alike—everything is the same. That way no one thinks one person is better than anyone else. And the quilt patterns don't change. They're old designs taught by their grandmothers."

"That's like us," Sonya interrupted.

"That's right. But they don't make new designs like you do." I saw a slight smile cross Sonya's face with my compliment. Throughout the trip I'd noticed a type of competitiveness from Sonya toward Grace. She liked to be "top dog."

"So why aren't we gonna sell?"

"This show won't be the right time or place for selling. That'll come later."

"So that's how ya do business." Sonya was quiet for the rest of the trip.

The entire fourth floor of a downtown department store had been made available for our event. The large room was a blaze of color and activity. One end was set up with chairs and a slide screen for viewing pictures that contrasted and compared the Amish culture with the Navajo. The other end of the cavernous space had tables set with a variety of Amish-baked delicacies, punch and coffee. In the center were three large quilting racks surrounded by Amish women, two Navajo looms attended by Sonya and Grace, and an area where Crystal demonstrated the spinning and dying of the sheep's wool. The press were everywhere with television crews and blinding flash bulbs.

"Just trying to get the little girl sitting next to the loom." A burly man with a Nikon camera was elbowing his way through the crowd, looking for the perfect angle.

"You can't get her face," I insisted. "You know the Amish don't believe in having their pictures taken." Rachael had attached herself like glue to Grace, and the crowd loved it. Grace, resplendent in her brightly colored velvet dress and turquoise jewelry, spent the entire morning guiding the three-year-old hands through the motions of the weaving process.

Grace and Rachael stole the show.

We had a day to rest after the first show closed. All Sonya and Crystal wanted to do was shop. We arrived at the shopping mall, one of the biggest in the area. Sonya and Crystal headed off with instructions to meet at the mall's center at three o'clock. Grace hadn't been eating properly and she tired quickly. We stayed behind and had a leisurely lunch. It was during these alone moments with Grace that our friendship grew. I saw in her quiet, gentle ways a strength and serenity that I longed for. I tried to emulate her grace, to slow down my typical frenetic pace and accept the beauty of the moments as they occurred. Grace didn't confront people; she had no need to defend or prove herself to anyone. Grace Yazzie knew and liked who she was.

The shows in Pennsylvania were wildly successful and, at the same time, financial disasters. Those who came to see the events loved them;

the newspaper and television coverage was extensive, but the expenses piled up, and there were only a handful of rug and quilt orders. My company's debut brought results in unexpected ways. The International Contemporary Furniture Fair held at the Javits Center in New York City invited us to attend, and a home furnishing show in Boston wanted an exhibit that included Navajo weavers.

The timing of the New York show was difficult. It was scheduled for March of the following year, only a month before our move. The event came in the midst of preparing for Len's April retirement, the selling of our Pennsylvania home, and our subsequent move to Durango, Colorado. In the flurry of activity, I lost sight of my lessons from Grace, and, once again, the recognition and opportunities spurred my need to prove I could be successful. The anticipated cost and effort of the show paled, in my mind, to the publicity and exposure. Len tried to be supportive but couldn't help reminding me of my new financial situation. Despite his admonishments, I forged ahead.

To cut back on expenses, I did the Javits Center event by myself. It was a real learning experience in what a trade show was all about. Rental on the least expensive, ten-foot-square booth with only side walls and no accoutrements ran a thousand dollars. All the setup, hanging of posters and weavings, had to be performed by unionized laborers for an exorbitant hourly rate. The nightly vacuuming and cleaning of each booth was a required item on the final bill. And, due to the value of my display, I felt it necessary to pay for additional travel and exhibition insurance, beyond the standard coverage on my inventory. Added to these expenses were the costs of shipping the inventory back and forth between Pennsylvania and New York, food and lodging for a four day stay in the heart of Manhattan, and train and cab fares in the City. The event was exhausting. I had one small weaving stolen, gave a second one to the woman who worked the booth next to mine who had spelled me for breaks during the long ten-hour days, and sold three quilts to other exhibitors.

But like the Pennsylvania shows, the furniture fair spawned other events: We received invitations to the Surfaces/World Floor Covering Expo in Las Vegas, Nevada; the San Francisco Furniture Mart; and the Oasis Gift Show in Phoenix—always focused on Navajo weavings, never quilts. I was forced to make the decision to give up quilts as part of the business.

I returned from my failed endeavors in New York to face the task of packing a houseful of belongings for a cross-country move. Len's last working day was the fifteenth of April, and we were anxious to be in Durango as soon after that as possible.

The Old Ways

Less than a month after we moved to Colorado, Grace was diagnosed with stomach cancer.

Crystal called to tell me the sandpainting weaving was finished and could the family bring it to Durango. They arrived in Thomas' black pickup truck, Crystal and her two sons, Naalzheí and Little Eagle, along with Grace and Thomas. It was a glorious June Sunday—blooms of the high country's prolific wildflowers shouted their color under a cloudless sky.

Yá'át'ééh, Grace hollered and flashed a smile. "We bring gift for you." She tilted her chin over a shoulder, pointing to Thomas who struggled to remove a large bundle from the laps of the backseat passengers.

"No need for a gift," I said and gave her a hug as she stepped out of the truck, "it's just good to see you."

"Welcome to our home." Len swung open the front door and went to help Thomas.

"Oh, but you like. Very special gift."

Len and Thomas whisked the bundle into the house, and I greeted Crystal and the boys. "Needs to talk," Crystal said. "But be with *Shimá* first."

When I entered the living room Len and Thomas were standing on chairs, each holding a corner, to extend a finished sandpainting weaving for full viewing. It was over five feet on a side and every bit as magnificent as anticipated. "Get the camera, Sharleen," Len hollered. "And Grace, you need to stand in front so we can take a picture of you with your beautiful creation."

There was laughter and oohs and aahs. All the while Grace stood nearby and smiled. She'd dressed carefully for the day. I knew her royal purple velvet blouse and squash blossom necklace to be what she wore for special occasions. As the excitement wore down, Len announced he would take Thomas and the boys to a nearby lake.

"It's time us fellows earn our keep around here ... we're going to catch some trout."

The men headed off, and Crystal guided Grace to a bedroom so she could lie down. Her look was solemn when she returned. "We been to doctor. He says Mom has cancer."

Silence.

All the joviality of moments before left, like a popped balloon in its erratic flight as it expelled all the air. "But ... she looks so well. Do they know for certain?" I knew she'd tired easily during our travels back east, but passed it off as excitement of the trip.

"Doctors say it in stomach and needs to be cut out. We go next week."

Grace underwent surgery, and the doctors believed the cancer had been removed. In keeping with Navajo traditions, the family held "sings" or ceremonies to purge her body of any evil spirits that might have invaded her being during the hospital stay. Grace spent most of her days resting at Crystal's trailer in Shiprock and caring for her preteen grandsons while Crystal attended classes at Fort Lewis College in Durango.

Every Monday, Wednesday and Friday, Crystal made the two-hour drive for her economics, statistics and computer science classes. She had set a goal to become an accountant. It was her habit to come to my house for lunch between her classes and her lab workshops.

"Mom wants you and Len to come to Sheep Ranch on Sunday," Crystal announced one afternoon. "Wants to fix a special meal for you."

"That sounds nice. Is there some occasion?"

"Not really ... Well, sort of ... You'll see."

The dining room table was set beautifully with a freshly ironed tablecloth, special china that was obtained as a trade for a weaving and a glass centerpiece that held tall, white candles. "I gots it at a flea market," Grace said when I commented. The three women wore their best garments and were draped in strands of coral, turquoise and alabaster beads. Even Grandpa was adorned with a bolo tie and cuff bracelets that displayed large chunks of the blue-green stone. There were place settings for six: Len, Anna Mae, Roy, Grace, Crystal, and me.

"Will Thomas be here?" I asked after counting heads.

"He eat in other room." Grace tilted her chin to point the direction. Then a hand went up to cover a shy giggle. "You knows, that in-law taboo thing."

"Boys will be at the coffee table in livin' room," Crystal added. "Not room enough here." She was busy placing glasses with a small portion of water in front of every place setting. "Come to table now. *Shimasání* will say prayer before we eats."

Anna Mae began to speak in Navajo. Out of respect for her prayer, Len and I bowed our heads even though we couldn't understand a word she was saying. As her prayer became lengthy, my eyes roamed across the table, over the once steaming bowls of squash and cornmeal mush and platters of roasted mutton and fry bread that were growing cold. I thought I could even see the bananas in the fruit salad begin to turn brown. My gaze left the food and found their way to Len, whose eyes were also wandering. When our eyes met, and he rolled his to the back of his head, I had to hold my breath to keep from laughing. It was then I noticed no one else's heads were bowed; instead they looked intently at the elderly woman as she spoke.

Anna Mae continued to drone on in her singsong manner. I'd found Navajo to be a beautiful sounding language, but rarely was it delivered with any inflections or facial gestures. She spoke for what seemed like an endless amount of time; others at the table frequently punctuated her words with *Aoó* and head nodding. Then, rather abruptly, everyone picked up their glasses of water and took a sip. The prayer was over. Len and I followed suit.

I've since learned that because water is believed to be the giver of all life, it is customary to conclude a prayer by honoring it with the sacred water. It still wasn't time to eat. Anna Mae reached under her chair to pull out an item concealed in a flour bag. "*Shiach'é'é*," the old woman said. She smiled broadly and passed the bag down the table to where I sat.

"She calls you daughter." Crystal spoke with gravity and sincerity; it was obvious that this was an important event. "The prayer was 'bout adoptin' you." Crystal paused, giving me time to absorb her words. Every eye was on my face, waiting for a reaction. And then, after long moments of silence, Crystal continued. "Grandma gives you name 'Yahnahbah.' In our culture we don't tell our *Diné* name, it gives our power away."

I was totally unprepared and clueless about how to act. "But, but ... what does it mean that she adopted me?" Being surprised by someone's comments or actions wasn't that unusual; I was good at drawing upon my experience-base and formulating a verbal response—the emotional reaction could come later. But this! I had no framework to operate from. My face must have flushed; I suddenly felt quite hot. I grabbed my almost-empty water glass and drained the last few swallows. "What does it mean; you know ... why did she give me that name? And what must I do now that I am adopted?"

My discomposure must have shown. Grace giggled behind her hand and Grandpa loudly cleared his throat. "Your name is: She Faces Her Enemy Directly," Crystal spoke as she stood to pour more water in my glass. "This is what took Grandma so long to explain. She tells that you are to be trusted. You walk squarely an face your problems or enemies directly. You don't circle or hide behind things. You stood up to Lewis when he questioned you. An she knows that my mother has grown to love you." Grace nodded her head and smiled. "Now that you are adopted, our family must respect you, treat you as one of our own."

"Does this mean Lewis, too?"

"Grandma won't tell Lewis. He wouldn't approve. An adoption means an exchange of gifts. Grandma's is in the bag."

I pulled a course-textured weaving from the bag. It was small, approximately eighteen by thirty inches, and beautifully crafted. Two *Ye'ii* stood on either side of a cornstalk surrounded on three sides by Rainbow Woman. The rough texture indicated that Anna Mae had done her own spinning; the soft, muted colors were a result of vegetal dyes. I was struck by the amount of time she must have spent in creating her gift.

"*Shimasání* wants to teach you to weave," Crystal said. There was head nodding, laughter and *Aoós*. "Now you must return a gift. Give Grandma somethin' special to you … you knows, from your heart."

Len and I sat up late that night talking about the events of the day.

"I don't know whether to be happy or upset. On the one hand, I've grown to care a great deal for Anna Mae, but what does all this really mean? It's pretty overwhelming."

Len was quiet, a trait I have learned to respect. His opinions are only voiced after thoughtful contemplation, never spontaneously. "Didn't it bother you that they did not even ask if you wanted to be adopted? You know, Sharleen, these people live in pretty desperate circumstances. You have come along and provided them with a whole new world. Maybe they see you as a golden ring. And the cancer thing with Grace … maybe you are being asked to help out with that. "

"Oh, Len, you make it sound so unfeeling. Isn't there ever room for genuine caring? What if Anna Mae really likes me? What if it doesn't have anything at all to do with money?" *What if this is God's answer to my prayer to turn me upside down and make me an Indian?* I thought. "And as far as Grace is concerned, the doctors think she is going to be fine."

"You can believe whatever you like, but Anna Mae didn't give you that Indian name for nothing. Trust me. She's a crafty old woman, and I think she's setting you up to fight her battles. And now it's late. Let's go to bed."

Len's logical approach to questionable situations proves right more often than not, but tonight I didn't want to agree with him; tonight I wanted to bask in the warmth of being accepted and loved for who I was—not for what I should or could be. But then, as so often happens, that inner critic's voice took over: *Why that name? She Faces Her Enemy Directly must portend something. And whose battle will I face … Anna Mae's, Grace's, Crystal's, my own … perhaps all?*

Grace grew stronger as the days progressed. It was summer and Crystal's boys had no school, so they spent much of the time at the sheep ranch. Early one Sunday morning I headed to Red Valley. My habit was to stop in Shiprock at the KFC and buy a bucket of chicken.

Anna Mae was on the front porch when I arrived. She waved her cane in the air and shouted angrily at Crystal, who was in the yard beside her grandfather, Roy. The old man stood and tapped his cane in front of him— into the uneven sandy ground to identify anything that would impede his step—and, satisfied the way was clear, he bent forward, leaned heavily against his cane, and continued his forward shuffle. A small dog called Puppee that Roy had taken from the litter of a stray nipped at his heels.

Crystal said Roy suffered from Alzheimer's disease—some days he knew me, and other days, I was a total stranger. *"Bik'ee neeshchééł … yishnááh."* His voice was frail. It matched a thin bent body that had seen over ninety summers. Roy, like Anna Mae and many others in his generation, could not speak English.

"Doochool," Anna Mae hollered and continued to rant in Navajo.

"She calls him foolish. He lives in Old Ways with his horses and sheep. Last night he tried to crawl in bed with her. She put saddle outside the door." Crystal tilted her chin toward the nearby hogan. "Stays there now." By placing her husband's saddle next to the door, Anna Mae announced she wanted a divorce; it was time for the old man to leave. "She's upset 'cause summer or winter, my *hacheii* builds a fire to stay warm. He adds too many logs; sparks come out and burn holes in her wooden floor."

I walked with them as Crystal supported her grandfather. I doubted he understood what Crystal was saying, but he acknowledged her words with an occasional *Aoó*. "He forgets house is not a hogan. If coffee is left after drinking a cup, he tosses it on the floor. *Shínálí* thinks it's his time to lie down up in the mountains." We left Roy in the hogan adding logs to an already adequate fire.

"Some days he thinks he's back to when he was young and courting Grandma. And he's taken to heading out across the desert. He looks for his horse, Pinto. It's been dead for more than sixty years now. When he goes out like he did today, he searches for the Old Ways. You heard him say *yishnááh*. That's 'bout Old Ways being gone. He doesn't understand why things aren't the way they used to be."

Roy searched for the Old Ways as I strove to forget my past. My days spent wandering the Navajo Reservation were the most satisfying I could remember ever having. No television, no telephones, no horns honking, no appointment calendars, no waiting in airports or train stations, and no alarm clocks waking me at 5 AM—just raw, unspoiled beauty and quiet. There was no need to perform, no expectations. But then I would remind myself there was also no six-figure income. Finances would be very tight if I hadn't married a man well versed in money management. My business was both a grand success and a major failure—successful in finding and engaging talented weavers; a failure in securing a market for the collectible masterpieces.

Every now and then my name, She Who Faces Her Enemy Directly, came to mind; I knew there were battles looming, but for now all was quiet. I began to wear the Thunderbird pendant from the double doll when I made my reservation trips. The doll was in such poor condition it couldn't make the trips. Its remembered Indian face embodied all my memories of Nanabah, combined with the beauty and strength of my Indian friends: Lucy, Lola, Sonya and Tyler, Crystal, Anna Mae and Roy, and especially Grace. During my travels I often sat at a favorite roadside overlook and mused as I danced the remembered Anglo face across the distant landscape, just as I had done over forty years ago. Then it was the brown face, but the white girl was at home here now.

I sat on the couch in Anna Mae's living room and watched the design of her weaving emerge from the loom. She wove a *Ye'ii* rug: four deities faced forward, two on a side, with a cornstalk between them. Rainbow god formed a U-shaped border under their feet. It was similar to my gift, but much larger and more finely woven. The background was gray, and the figures were adorned in shades of brown, gold, green, and white. Anna Mae's fingers were gnarled, yet they had a graceful, knowing way. The wooden comb she used to beat down the weft made a rhythmic thud, reminding me of my time with Lola at Crow Canyon.

Intermittently, Grace, Crystal and Anna Mae talked in the lulling singsong language with many more words than ever were translated. Today's banter was sprinkled with laughter—Anna Mae's wizened chuckle, Grace's shy schoolgirl giggle, and Crystal's loud throaty laugh. I often felt excluded in the talk: the absence of facial expression, gestures, or emotion-caused inflections made it impossible to guess the subject matter. The only telling thing was the laughter; I sometimes wondered if that was directed at my strange *bilagáana* ways and me.

"Grandma wants to make trade with you. She wants to know if rug she is weavin' would be worth a new front door." Crystal stood and motioned for me to follow. "Locks on this wooden door don't hold tight anymore. She's 'fraid someone will break in while she's gone. She wants a new steel door."

"It's so remote out here. Is robbery really a concern?"

"Peoples who need money come lookin' for jewelry, old baskets or rugs—anythin' they can take to pawnshop for a few dollars. You know how old women are about wearin' so much jewelry? *Shínálí* is the same. When she goes out she puts all her jewelry on, or carries it in her purse. So it won't be stolen."

Anna Mae stopped her weaving and watched as we examined the door. She spoke again to Crystal, this time in a very animated fashion, using her cane for emphasis. "It's also to keep Grandpa away. She's 'fraid he forgets an tries to come back in middle of night."

Anna Mae and Roy lived in a very remote and desolate area of the reservation. Their home was built in 1968 through a Navajo Work Program under which the recipient paid for materials, and the labor was provided by the government. It may have been free, but twenty-six years of wear on a poorly constructed home had taken quite a toll. It needed a lot more work than just a new front door. As I examined the frame of the existing door, I knew that replacement would not be a simple process.

"And what else would she like fixed, besides the front door?" I went to the loom to study the piece more carefully. It was about five feet wide and masterfully crafted in the style that was distinctly Anna Mae's—the

204

same designs and shapes she had taught her daughters, Grace and Bertha. Colors were muted, and there was intricate detailing in the adornments of the *Ye'ii* figures. Crystal told me the weaving was not as fine as Anna Mae could do in her younger days, but nonetheless, this piece would bring at least three-thousand dollars in the marketplace.

"How much does she want for her weaving?"

My questions brought another interchange between the women; talk was punctuated by the thud, thud of Grandma's comb as she pounded the weft yarns tightly in place. "Three years ago *Shínáli* gave Lewis six-hundred dollars to fix things up. He bought some paints with money but never did the work. Maybe you could use paint on livin' room or kitchen.

"She doesn't want to set a price on weavin', just whatever you think."

I smiled inwardly. Len had said it; Anna Mae was a shrewd old woman. I scanned the room, the disrepair left little doubt she would come out ahead in any trade we arranged.

It was two weeks before Len and I returned to the sheep ranch. I tried to explain the condition of the house and the expectations, but Len was reluctant to commit to anything without assessing the situation for himself. A conservative and cautious man, he succeeded in what he did because of methodical, thoughtful planning.

When we pulled into the yard his demeanor changed. He scowled, gave an imperceptible gasp, and shook his head, as he scanned the house. His eyes came to rest on a large picture window to the right of the front door. It had two long cracks, each covered with silver duct tape that ran the width of the window. "I wonder if that's to hold the window in place, or just to keep the dust out of the house," he muttered. Freeze and thaw of sub-zero nights had crumbled the corners of concrete steps. They pulled away from the porch with large cracks at the seams. And one of the four-by-four supports to the porch roof dangled uselessly off the edge of the concrete.

"I think what she wants done is on the inside," I said.

Upon entering we made the customary greetings. For this special visit Roy was granted the privilege of coming into the house. He sat in a broken recliner chair with Puppee lying at his feet; a bright magenta Pendleton blanket with bold stripes in turquoise and yellow was draped over his shoulders, and an unlit pipe was in his mouth.

When the greetings were over, Crystal and I headed to the kitchen to prepare lunch. Len, with his tape measure and clipboard, made notes to himself. The vinyl-tiled wooden floor had a large buckle, rising in some places at least four inches. The tiles had cracked, and large patches peeled away, leaving raw wood flooring that accumulated dirt.

"Crystal, do you know anything about the cause of this buckle? I don't think I've ever seen anything quite like it." Len stepped out the length of the problem and looked for where it began and ended.

"Grandpa did most of the building on the house. After the crews came and put in the foundation, he thought the empty space needed to be filled … so he just put all the dirt back."

"You mean he filled the crawl space under the floor?" Crystal nodded yes.

The plastered walls had large cracks running throughout—in some places they were a quarter of an inch wide. And the walls were heavily stained with years of smoke buildup from the coal and wood-burning fireplace. "I don't think painting will work in here," Len announced. "We'll need to do some type of paneling, you know, the four-by-eight sheets. And the bathroom, that's a whole different matter."

Crystal explained that the plumbing was put in the house when it was originally built, but ten years passed before there was money to buy fixtures. And then there was the issue of water. I knew drinking water was hauled in from Shiprock—there were two ten-gallon containers in the kitchen—but general household water came from a well half-a-mile from their home. The kitchen sink had water from the tap; it drained into a bucket that sat under the sink and was emptied onto the plants in an outside garden.

"Grandpa laid the pipe to bring in the water himself. You know how at my house the tank sits on a platform outside our bathroom window? That's how it used to be here. When Grandpa fixed the water they got the washing machine."

In my travels, throughout the reservation, I noticed that many of the homes had a washing machine sitting outside; at least Anna Mae had hers in the house. The problem Len was addressing had to do with where her machine sat. The bathroom door was placed on the far left side of a wall with the flush toilet positioned to the right of the door, next to the bathtub. Water and drain pipes for the sink were three feet from the door's opening—on the wall that ran perpendicular—and the washing machine was placed here. The door was blocked from swinging wide, and made it difficult to negotiate the narrow opening between the washer and the toilet. A washbowl sat on a cabinet next to the bathtub with the intent that water was drawn from the faucets in the tub and carried to the washbowl. When you were through, the water was emptied into the tub.

"Grandma wanted Lewis to add more pipes so the washing machine could be moved to the corner, and the washstand hooked up, but he says, not now."

We'd finished eating lunch when Lewis unexpectedly arrived. He avoided the customary greetings and, lacking tact, plunged right into his typical interrogation mode. "Why are you here? What are you doin'? Did Anna Mae know you were comin'?"

"Hello, you must be Lewis." Len stood from the table and thrust his hand out for a proper introduction. "I'm Sharleen's husband, Len, and have heard a great deal about you. Now what is it you want to know?" The room suddenly became very quiet, and Lewis fidgeted uneasily under Len's intense scrutiny. Over six feet tall, slender, with shocking white hair, and a finely chiseled facial structure, Len conveyed a sophistication that contrasted sharply with Lewis' cowboy appearance.

Len managed to move their discussions into the living room, but I could hear the conversation clearly. He was using an intimidating voice, and it was clearly working. "So where are the rest of the supplies that you bought with the six hundred dollars? We found paint, but there's less than fifty dollars' worth of that."

Lewis spoke slowly—no more arrogance—just a controlled rage. "My parents are old. There's no tellin' how much longer they will be here. I don't see the sense in spending the time or money to fix up this house. Did Crystal ask you to do this?" With the last question Lewis was gaining strength in his voice, and I saw Crystal flinch.

"It doesn't really matter who did or didn't ask us. We're here and plan to do some work for Anna Mae and Roy." Len responded in his calm, in-control voice. "I'm asking you if there are any more supplies and, if not, where the rest of the money went."

"There is no money left," Lewis said. "So how much are you chargin' Anna Mae to do her work? You know they don't have any money, an you won't get any from me."

I turned my attention away from the conversation and busied myself with the kitchen cleanup. Earlier I was concerned that Len would throw up his hands in total dismay and walk away from the project, but Lewis' visit guaranteed that Grandma would have her way.

"Nothing in that house is square," Len complained. "Two-by-fours aren't where they're supposed to be, and the electrical wiring defies all reasonable logic. It's a nightmare. Standard length screws, fasteners, everything for that matter, are an anomaly." His challenge was heightened by the fact that the nearest hardware store was seventeen miles on dirt washboard and another seventy on paved road. "And furthermore, Lewis is a thief. He's worse than Bertha. It's one thing to steal from a white woman. It's a whole different thing to rob your parents."

Rarely did I see the anger that Len was showing. The fixing up of Anna Mae's house became a matter of principle for him. That afternoon as we drove home, Len and I discussed ways the work could be done. The job required tools and a skill level that neither of us possessed. Trade was the device Anna Mae used to meet her needs, and trade seemed to be the answer for us. The contractor, Martin, who was building our home in Durango had expressed an interest in securing a Navajo weaving, but did not have the cash. I decided to contact him to see if we could work out a trade.

Len began the work slowly. The first few trips he did nothing more than replace bare light bulbs with fixtures, put on switch plates to cover exposed wires, and take measurements to buy supplies for the work that he and Martin would tackle. Successful with those endeavors, he moved on to the bigger task of replacing the front door and the broken living room window. All the jobs that required special carpentry skills or tools were reserved for Martin. The bargain we struck was for three full days of his time and the use of his mobile truck of tools. We believed it to be a fair trade for the weaving.

Most workdays Len and I stopped in Shiprock and picked up Crystal before continuing on to the sheep ranch. Crystal acted as a translator for Anna Mae and Roy while I prepared food for everyone, helped with the painting or basic cleanup and provided moral support to Len. Some days Crystal and I left, in search of weavers. Plans were still in place to do the show in Boston.

No one could explain Anna Mae's fondness for Len, especially when you considered the taboo; by Grandma's tradition, once she adopted me, he was her son-in-law. One afternoon, while Len worked on the Hoskie house, Crystal and I returned from running errands to find the old woman out walking in the desert. I stopped my vehicle and Crystal walked out to retrieve Anna Mae. When they returned the old woman looked grave, but Crystal was laughing. "She's 'fraid Len not have enough to eat ... out searchin' for sheep to butcher for mutton stew."

That afternoon Crystal and I worked together to clean the walls of the kitchen in preparation for painting. "I'm puzzled by Lewis' neglect of his parents," I said. "I read that, unlike our culture, being a Grandmother in the Navajo community is a venerable role, you know, very special." Grandma was at her loom as Crystal and I spoke. She seemed to know we were talking about her. I decided, like Grace, she understood more English than she professed.

"Traditionally that's how it is. But Lewis was in the army and learned to think like a White Man. He gave up most traditional ways."

"He still lives on the reservation. So what kinds of things did he give up?"

Crystal looked to Anna Mae, and the two women talked. "*Shínálí* says you must know about Old Ways before you can understand what some *Diné* give up. Back in eighteen hundreds," Crystal continued, "when Kit Carson came lookin' for all *Diné*, people hid everywhere ... lots in Cañon de Chelly. But soldiers burned all fruit trees and corn. People starved. They finally gave up, and soldiers took them to Fort Sumner in eastern New Mexico."

"Is that the place you call *hwééldi*?" I interrupted.

Crystal nodded and continued. "People were there four years ... many died. When they finally let go, they just walked home. They call that Long Walk. *Shínálí's* mother was born at *hwééldi* an just a baby durin' Long Walk."

Crystal spoke with Anna Mae and then resumed the story. "*Shínálí* wants me to tell you that she was taught troubles make people strong.

When she was little and gots hungry, her *shínálí* would say, 'This is good, now you able to stand tall.' And it was bad if she lost sheeps. She'd only seen six summers when she an her brother had to stay out all night lookin' for a baby lamb." Anna Mae began to shake her head and make a clucking noise with her tongue. "She thinks today young ones don't understand this is how it should be. She thinks they are too lazy. *Shínálí* tried to teach Old Ways to her children. She says Lewis always wanted to be in charge. He wouldn't take time to learn where the grasses were good for sheeps or what place to take sheeps to mountains for summer. He didn't sit by fire in winter when *Hacheii* told stories of old ways.

"Bertha always jealous of her brother an sister. When buses come to take children to boardin' school, both Bertha an Lewis wants to go. My grandparents were afraid to let them all go. There is much work to do with sheeps. And *Shínálí* would miss my mother. So they hid my mother. That's why Grace learned Old Ways."

As Crystal spoke, Roy shuffled into the house and claimed his favorite chair. A truce had been formed in which he slept the night and took naps in the hogan, but was allowed into the house during the day.

"Grandma says parents need to teach children to be *Diné*. They need to teach them the language, how to care an butcher sheeps, about clans an ways families hold together … an they needs to tell them stories of Old Ways … when every day is in *hózhóní*. It's cookin', watchin' sheeps, watchin' children … everythin' *hózhóní*."

Roy started pounding his cane on the floor; he wanted to say something. The old man spoke at some length in Navajo. "*Hacheii* wants me to tell you how he walks in beauty. Every mornin' when sun is ready to come up, he takes his bag of *tádíníín*, that's corn pollen, an goes to stand out there," Crystal nodded toward the front door, which faced the east, "to look at face of Gods. He says his prayers an sprinkles *tádíníín* in all four directions, then up to sky an down to ground. In his prayers he asks to do right for just this day ... that he will know who he is an act right.

"An he does," Crystal said with a chuckle. "He's out there every mornin', is facin' the sun as it climbs into the sky. When I was young an would get discouraged, my *hacheii* told me to get out of bed an say my prayers. Most of the time I was too tired, but when I did, whole day seemed to be better."

There was a long silence, and Roy began again. This time he was animated and waved his cane toward the loom stand where Anna Mae worked. "He says it's just like that weavin'. When my *shínálí* first started doing it, loom stand was important. It held things up an helped her get perfect amount of tension on all cords. That's important ... if one is looser than others, rug won't be *yá'ánísht'ééh*, or how do you say it? Rug won't lie flat. When she's done, loom stand's not needed. *Hacheii* says place where he grew up is his loom stand. It kept all those yarn cords tight while he learned 'bout what was right an *doo ákót'ée da*. Now it's up to him to just follow those patterns for life, that's where corn pollen comes in.

"Pollen reminds him of ceremonies, all that teachin' of how our peoples came to be. In some rugs you can see stair-step designs leadin' to center of that rug. Well, designs from bottom are our young years, the growin' ones. Then when we reach center—oh, 'bout fifty-years-old, then we start comin' down those steps. But you look, in a good rug, the up an down match perfect. That's way it's s'posed to be when you're 'walkin' in beauty.' It means *hózhóní* is still there even when loom stand is taken away."

There was a long silence—a Navajo silence. Finally I spoke. "*Ahéhee'*, Roy." I took care to use the Navajo word for thank you. I turned to Crystal and said, "Tell Grandfather that was beautiful ... that he has given me a very special gift." As Crystal translated my words, a broad grin crossed his aged face.

The restoration project took longer than we anticipated. Several weeks into the work, Lewis' son, Raymond Hoskie, visited us. When he arrived he extended his hand, and there was a genuine friendliness to his firm grip. Raymond was in his mid-thirties and had the handsome features of many Navajo men—high cheekbones, long shimmering black hair which he wore in a single braid, narrow hips, and a strongly muscled upper body. His hands and wrists were slender, the hands of an artist, and adorned with massive turquoise and silver jewelry.

He told us that he followed the dancers' circuit, competing throughout the United States in Native American dance competitions. When he wasn't dancing, Raymond worked as a backup surgeon's assistant in emergency rooms; he moved across the country from one hospital job to the next to allow the assigned personnel vacation or leave time.

"I'm home for a few weeks," he said, "and I would like to help out."

"We would welcome your help," I replied. "Your father isn't pleased that we are out here doing this. How will he feel about your being here?"

"He means well." Raymond picked up a scrub brush and joined in with the kitchen restoration. Years of chimney smoke and kitchen grease needed to be removed before we could cover the walls and cabinet doors with a coat of paint. "He had a difficult time when he was in the service. He fought in Korea and hasn't let go of the things that happened to him."

"Did he see a lot of combat?"

"It wasn't the fightin' so much as the way he was treated. Indians were thought to be 'ignorant savages' and always given jobs no one else wanted. Dad changed his name. He thought his troubles were made worse by being a Hoskie. And then he gave up more than just his name. He tried to become manlier, like other soldiers."

"Are you saying he gave up the Navajo ways to be more macho?" I asked.

"To understand you must know about our people. In the old days, men and women were equal. Each of us has a male part and a female part.

Our culture reveres the femaleness and maleness of each person ... each part has a special role. The *bilagáana* world has difficulty understandin' this. During the war my father felt he must give up his femaleness to fit in, just like he gave up his Indian name. But it didn't work. He was still rejected. He is unable to forgive your people for the way they treated him. Our people have a ceremony for soldiers after they return home ... a kind of cleansin' of the bad memories. Dad won't have it."

"And you? You seem very comfortable with your Indianness." Unlike his father, Raymond stood tall with an air of self-confidence and pride. There was no arrogant swagger in his walk or surliness in his speech.

"I am successful in White Man's world. I make good money and command respect from those with whom I work. This makes my father proud. I am his son, so he ignores the fact that I am a dancer and keep my Indian name."

"Does that bother you? You know ... the fact that he ignores who you really are."

"It used to, but not anymore. When I was young, I would get very confused. My grandparents helped to grow the part of me that loved the land and animals, the gentle side."

"You're fortunate to have your grandparents. When I was born my father had wanted a son ... he never did accept me as the person I was. For a long time I was insecure about that. It hurts to feel not good enough."

"So what did you do about that?"

What did I do? I walked away. "Same thing you did in my world. I worked hard, earned a lot of money, all those things that my people feel makes a person successful."

"And then your father accepted you?"

"Well, no. You see, he wanted me to be a boy, but when I turned out to be a girl he wanted me to act like a girl. At least act the way he thought girls ought to act."

"I know what actin' like a girl means to the *bilagáana*. I was a weaver, like Bertha's son, Charlie. But when the missionaries came on the reservation, they taught us that men and women have different roles to play. Men were supposed to work outside, weavin' was women's work. Well, some of my friends just kept on weavin' and people called them unnatural, you know gay. That's what happened to Charlie. He got beat up because he was gay. So I studied to work in the hospital."

"I understand what you are saying," I said. "I gave up the female part of me, thinking if I were more like a boy my father would love and accept me. By the time I discovered that didn't work, I had developed a disdain for many women and all things female. I didn't have any close women friends until I got to know Grace. She's very different than your father."

"Grace stayed with her culture. Indian people who stay in their traditional beliefs have a love of the sights and sounds of nature. That's why there are so many artists among us. But then Dad would say I was becomin' a sissy. He said I would never be able to survive if I didn't become tough and take control of situations. Now I know better. I play the game to be accepted in the *bilagáana* world, and then come to visit my grandparents to regain the strength and calm of my world."

Play the game. The phrase repeated through my mind. It was exactly what I had done. I'd given up my femaleness in order to be accepted in a world that was out of balance, tilted in favor of men. I'd been driven to make money as a measure of my worth. And now here I was, just like Raymond, coming to the reservation to get things back in harmony.

One morning when we pulled up in front of the house, I noticed a strange absence. Puppee did not come to greet us. Last week the dog got in a fight with a rattlesnake and could no longer be petted or touched; there was a fear the animal would act as a conduit for the snake's evil. I adopted circuitous ways to pet the starved-for-attention Puppee.

"Maybe Grandpa is out searching for his horse again," I said to Len, as we entered Anna Mae's house. But there was Roy, smiling at us from his favorite rocking chair. Greetings were made, and I was finally able to pull Crystal aside and broach the subject. "Has Puppee run away? He isn't out on the front porch."

"*Aoó*," Crystal responded and motioned for me to follow her outside. "*Shínálí* did away with him."

"What do you mean 'did away with him?'"

"She was frightened ... ever since rattlesnake. An Grandpa was takin' Puppee into hogan with him to sleep at night. So she fed him antifreeze."

"Antifreeze? My god! Grandpa loved that dog. *I loved that dog. Whatever happened to the Navajo belief that all living things are sacred? How is he reacting?*"

The day I'd shown up at Sonya's hogan with my Polish Lowland Sheepdog, Farley, and she refused to let him come inside, I learned from Tyler the traditional Navajo story about dogs. "*During the time this world was first created, Dog took First Man and First Woman to all the significant parts of the reservation. When they arrived at White House in Canyon de Chelly the man and woman were instructed to go inside, but Dog sat outside by the door.*" Tyler told me that the dog was considered a very powerful and sacred part of their culture, but it had its place and that would not change. It was beyond my comprehension. Roy had violated customs by allowing the puppy inside the home, and then there was the snake.

"She told him Puppee ran away. So now when he goes off to desert, some days he looks for Puppee ... other days, Pinto."

After many trips and many hours, the work Len planned for Anna Mae and Roy's house was finished. The ceilings and kitchen were painted a bright white and a light gray paneling covered the walls in the living room. Len had installed a new picture window and a steel front door with a deadbolt. Slipcovers renewed the tattered furniture, wall-to-wall carpeting covered the living area, and indoor/outdoor covering was on the floor of the kitchen. Len apologized that he could do nothing about the floor buckle—it was beyond his abilities or finances—and the new bathroom pipes would be left for another day.

I hung the pictures of the family back on the wall. The fifteen framed photographs, all hung perfectly, except for the picture of Lewis. I couldn't seem get it to stay straight. "He is out of balance in life," Crystal said and laughed. "Why not picture, too." The day we were packing tools to leave, Roy spoke at some length to Crystal. "He says he doesn't know who you nice people are, but you do good work."

We'd spent almost a month working on Anna Mae's house. Much more needed to be done, but it would have taken a professional contractor and special equipment. The daily drive to the sheep ranch was long, and I was anxious to get on with my planning for the trip to Boston. Lewis refused to acknowledge that we did anything and even stopped coming by to visit when he thought we might be there. Anna Mae smiled happily because someone had paid attention to her need for the house to look nice, and Roy—perpetually happy because of his Alzheimer's disease— probably noticed very little, except what was missing.

A Midnight Blue Sweater

The Boston show was scheduled for the second week of October. Grace had recovered from her surgery, and in an effort to contain expenses, I chose her as my traveling companion. Sonya was still in a pout over the lack of sales in Pennsylvania, and Crystal was busy with her college classes. Grace taught me to put her long graying hair into the traditional Navajo style—pulled back and folded into a rectangular bun wrapped in white yarn at the nape of her neck. This was a job typically reserved only for Crystal, but as Grace and I traveled together, I was her helpmate.

Sales were brisk in Boston, and I was imbued with a sense of success. My business plan might actually work. The day after the show closed, Grace and I were tourists, seeing the sights of Boston. The water shuttle taxi to Logan airport and back was a favorite. "Never been in boat," she said and giggled every time the waves caused rocking. "Never sees one, 'cept in pictures."

Faneuil Hall was her "best favorite," however. She bought gifts for everyone. In the courtyard, at a street-vendor's insistence, she tried on a midnight-blue angora sweater with beadwork and sequins and preened at the image she saw reflected in a small hand-held mirror.

"It's beautiful, Grace. The color is perfect for you."

"But so many dollars. For gift maybe, not for me."

"How often have you bought something for yourself just because you liked it?" I knew the answer was never. The price was $79.95, not exorbitant by my standards. "Besides, the show was good. You worked very hard and sold three weavings. You can do this for yourself."

I resisted my urge to buy it for her; it seemed important that she do this for herself. My thoughts were vindicated with the care and pride in which Grace wore the sweater for the remainder of our trip.

October crept by in slow motion, as though each day struggled to begin and end. The cancer had come back and taken hold of Grace's body. The dark mass growing in her stomach became relentless. Crystal's studies at Fort Lewis dictated she make the two-hour drive from Shiprock to Durango three times a week. Grace's dream was for her daughter to have an education, so, even as her energy waned, she made the long trip, staying with me while Crystal attended classes. Thomas waited in Shiprock for Crystal's boys to come home from school.

As women have always done, we sat at the kitchen table and shared memories of a time past, Grace with her cup of tea, and me with my coffee. I'd traveled hundreds of miles with this woman I had come to love, shared hotel rooms, and stood next to her in the kitchen as we prepared countless meals, yet there was so much I did not know about her.

There was a day toward the end of Grace's struggle, an unusually warm day for so late in the season, with a sky of cloudless turquoise. It was a day to be melancholy. "Tell me about when you were young and first met Thomas."

Grace smiled shyly. "His people from White Mesa area. Long time ago closest tradin' post was Red Rock, near my home. He come with family—a very long wagon trip. They always stay two or three nights. People 'round know when trader buys rugs and sheeps. Then we all come.

We have powwows, you know, get-togethers, or how you say, party ... That's way Thomas an I meet." She put her hand up over her mouth and covered a schoolgirl giggle. "He prettiest boy I ever seen. I watch him lots before, dancin' with others, but never knew he would pick me. Then one night he did. I was so, how you say, unsettled. But did right. I took his hat an gave to *Shimá*. Then we danced all night."

"What do you mean 'took his hat?'"

"It's Old Ways. Boy has to pay to dance with girl. Big skirts *Shimá* an I wear," she stood and twirled in the middle of the kitchen floor, catching her broomstick skirt with both hands to spread it out and show the size, "they hide things. When boy pay money for dance, then he gets hat back. When Thomas askes me to dance, I take hat an give to *Shimá* to hide."

We laughed. It sounded like a very reasonable plan to me. I stood and went to the stove to refill our cups while Grace continued her story. "Back, long time ago, no money. Some boys pay nickel or penny for dance. Three days pass, then Thomas comes with two sheeps in wagon. Come to get hat. That's when I know I marry Thomas."

"I guess two sheep were worth a lot in those days."

"*Aoó*, sheeps always worth lots to my people. That's why it so bad when Washington men come to take them away. They say they eats too much grasses."

She spoke of the Livestock Reduction Act. Books documented our government's decision that the Navajos were overgrazing their land, and decreed that all forms of reservation livestock be reduced in numbers.

"Do you remember much about that time?"

Grace became very solemn and her body took on the sadness. "*Shimá* tells me. There were people who owned many sheeps then, maybe two or three hundreds." She continued to tell of the Navajo belief that "sheep is life": food for the family, wool for making rugs, and hard cash when sold. In those days a family defined their wealth by the size of their flocks.

It was common to take the sheep to the trading post to be dipped in a pesticide to rid them of bugs. One year the word was spread throughout the reservation that the dipping would be free. "Then talk changed," Grace said. "When peoples took sheeps for free dip, came home with only two hands of sheeps. Everyone confused. They not understand. Men rode horses to trading posts to find out."

Her head lowered, and we sat in silence as she twisted the cup between her hands. Then she took a deep breath, straightened her body, and continued with her story. "What men found was washes full of dead sheep, cattle, an horses. They hides at night, back in bushes behind tradin' posts, an watch. Next day government men led sheeps into wash ... men stand on top with shotguns. Shoot them. No take meat or hides, just kills them an leaves for coyotes."

Grace didn't appear to be complaining; she seemed to accept that this was the way it had to be. I didn't know how to respond. "So what did the men do?"

"They didn't take sheeps for dippin'." She continued with the story of Navajos throughout the reservation refusing to take their flocks to the trading posts, and the government trucks that came in the night and emptied the pens. "Washington men very angry; they take horses, too. That's when Pinto taken."

I choked back the large lump that welled inside my throat. When I'd first read of the Livestock Reduction Act, I was appalled at the insensitive way in which it had been carried out. Now I was seeing the real effect on the people. I reached across the table and covered Grace's hand with mine. "Let's go back to talking of happy times." Grace flashed her joyful smile. "So after Thomas came with the sheep, did you marry then?"

"We wait for Thomas to get weddin' price, how you say, dowry? When he come my heart got big. Come with two tall horses, two goats, three blankets, all 'cause of me. Highly good price."

"It was payment for a queen. He knew how special you are. What about the wedding? Did you have a traditional Navajo wedding?"

"They say only weddin' in White Man's court is good. Judge comes to tradin' post every month. He marry us. When Crystal gots married she got both kinds of ceremony, *Diné* and White Man's."

Crystal had married a Navajo man who was an abusive alcoholic. He abandoned her with two young sons, six-year-old Naalzheí and four-year-old Little Eagle. That was when Grace and Thomas began to spend time in Shiprock, helping Crystal and caring for their two grandsons.

I could see Grace grow tired. I helped her out of the chair to the sofa in the living room where her sandpainting weaving hung over a gas-fed fireplace. Despite the warmth of the day, Grace pulled her sweater—the vibrant blue mohair purchased in Boston—tighter around her body and asked that I turn on the fire. The blue sweater, the symbol of Grace gifting herself, became like a hallmark for her. She wore it everywhere, as though she knew her time was close and the sweater represented all that was good and nurturing about how she cared for herself.

Three weeks after we returned from Boston, I sat with Grace and Crystal in an examining room of the San Juan Regional Cancer Center. Crystal twisted a frayed tissue between her fingers, and Grace, just back from a barrage of tests, lay on the stretcher; a white sheet covered an engorged belly that protruded from her otherwise frail body. The doctor's voice was strong, necessary to reinforce the gravity of his words, with only the slightest hint of the sorrow that surrounded his message: "An aggressive stomach cancer ... It will soon be time to bring in hospice."

A dark silence hung over the room. I turned to the doctor and asked, "Is there a hospice service to the Shiprock area?"

"I don't know about Shiprock, but we could certainly arrange for them to come from Farmington," he responded. "Let me ask my nurse to check it out." The quiet in the sterile, chrome-appointed room was palpable, punctuated only with the receding footsteps of the doctor as he searched for availability of health services to a trailer on the Navajo Reservation.

It was Grace who broke the silence. "Not *Diné* way," she said. And then with slow and cautious movements, she pushed her upper body from the stretcher, twisted slightly to face her daughter, and rested the weight of her shoulders and head on one bent arm. As Grace spoke to Crystal in Navajo, there was much head nodding and long pauses. Crystal's only response was *Aoó*.

"She can't go to next world from home," Crystal said, her eyes never leaving her mother. "I would have to board up trailer an leave. You knows, just like Washington D.C.."

After the weaving exhibitions in Pennsylvania, the women and I visited the nation's capital, complete with a sightseeing tour on an open-air bus. Everything went fine until Arlington Cemetery. Sonya, Grace and Crystal, all three, covered their heads with scarves and insisted the bus driver take us back to the entrance, away from the gravesites. "Bad spirits," Crystal had explained. "When peoples leave their body, good an bad spirits stay behind. If we sees or get near them, they can make us sick."

Grace's words came in a whisper: "Can I come to your house? For hospice, I means."

The simple question tumbled and raged through me. Two years earlier my mother died at home of pancreatic cancer. Her death took a slow, painful six months, and even though I wasn't her primary caregiver, the memory was still raw and ragged. It was too soon for me to make this journey with Grace. Up until now I had been the Anglo woman who befriended someone of another race and culture. Grace, with her question, invited me to come into her most intimate world, and her request went unanswered.

The door swung open, and the small examining room filled with the presence of the doctor. "I've learned there are no hospice services available on the reservation. Give me a couple of days and, when the time is right, I will arrange a private room at the hospital here in Farmington." As quickly as the doctor arrived, he was gone.

Mother's time at home after they did exploratory surgery to discover her cancer was not easy. My sister carried the main burden, but I remembered the morphine drips, the diapers, the hallucinations, and the agony—most of all the agony. Fears for my own discomfort took hold; I had failed my first real test as an adopted daughter and sister.

A Deposition

Sarah Dent and I watched from the motel lobby as the Dodge Ram pickup truck pulled into the parking lot. Crystal was the first to step out of the vehicle. She dressed as an Anglo: stretch-cotton leggings with a tunic top and long black hair that curled fashionably to frame her face. The only mark of her culture was the strand of coral and silver beads around her neck. She held open the passenger door for Grace. Her mother was dressed for the early morning cold in a three-tiered ruffled skirt made of turquoise taffeta, a thickly-padded hot-pink ski jacket and, folded in a triangle and tied under the chin, an orange and green paisley scarf. Recently polished cowboy boots were the first thing seen as Thomas climbed out of the driver's seat. He wore a fleece-lined canvas jacket over a pearl-buttoned shirt and newly purchased blue jeans.

"Would you take a look at that?" A group of pin-stripe-suited attorneys stood alongside Sarah. "I really like the footwear." The men snickered and nodded at Grace's slip-on black loafers and white ankle socks.

"Have a little respect," Sarah chided. "She's dying of stomach cancer."

Crystal nodded to the waiting group and said, "M-m-my name is Crystal Redshirt." Then she extended her hand to each—it was not a firm handshake, but a soft, gentle grip accompanied by the word *yá'át'ééh*.

"M-m-means hello," she said with a laugh. "And these are my parents ... Thomas and Grace Yazzie."

When Thomas removed his jacket he exposed several large chunks of turquoise in a bolo tie and belt buckle, and even more of the blue-green stone was visible as he moved through the group, gripping each person's hand in both of his and saying *yá'át'ééh*. Grace stood waiting behind her husband, resplendent with bracelets that encircled both wrists, a large brooch of turquoise chips at the collar of her sky-blue velvet blouse, and a squash blossom necklace.

Sarah, the only female among the attorneys, stepped forward and, rather than extend her hand, gave Grace a hug. "I'm very glad you were able to come."

"Me happy, too." Grace flashed one of her dazzling smiles and then, as was her habit, covered it shyly with her cupped hand. "Sorry. English not good. Crystal mostly talks."

Grace was the one who found Sarah and asked for her help. It had been announced that $100,000 Compassion Payments would be made available under RECA, The Radiation Exposure Compensation Act, to Navajos diagnosed with cancer or other respiratory ailments linked to uranium mining. Thomas had been a miller instead of a miner. He didn't qualify. Sarah rallied the families of all the Shiprock millers and filed a separate suit directly against their employer. Problem was, they were dying faster than Sarah could get to court.

"Thanks for coming," Sarah said to Crystal. "Will your mother object to a video camera?" Crystal shook her head.

"Then let's get started."

"For the record, today's date is November 6, 1994, and the place is the Iron Horse Inn, Durango, Colorado. The firms present are: Strand Considine & Hall of Los Angeles and Bernstein Newton & Grossman of New York City, both representing Kerr-McGee, and Dent & Associates of Tuba City, Arizona, representing the Shiprock Millers. Sharleen Daugherty of Durango, a friend of the Yazzie family, is here to take part in our proceedings." A faint clicking from the stenotype and whirring of the video camera competed with the droning voice.

"Due to her diagnosis of a fatal illness, we convene for a Deposition to Perpetuate the Testimony of Grace Yazzie, wife of Thomas Kee Yazzie. Ms. Dent, representative for the plaintiff, will begin the questioning."

"Please tell us, Grace, where you and Thomas currently reside?"

"M-m-my parents live at sheep ranch near Red Valley." Crystal looked at puzzled faces across the table. "Thirty miles southwest of Shiprock, New Mexico."

"Let the record show that although the Yazzies understand English, they do not speak it well. Their daughter, Crystal Redshirt, will be their spokesperson." Sarah turned to Crystal and asked, "Can you explain to these gentlemen about the sheep ranch?"

"Where M-m-mom has grazing rights. Over in Mitten Rock area."

"Mrs. Yazzie ... Grace. We'd like Crystal to tell us, as much as you can remember, the places and dates your husband worked for the uranium industry."

Crystal and Grace had a brief exchange of words in Navajo. Crystal began with the mid-thirties, methodically recounting the places, making a broad circle beginning in southern Colorado and Utah, going through northern Arizona and New Mexico—the area known as Four Corners. "Last place was Shiprock, Kerr-McKee Mill."

"How long?"

"Nineteen-sixty-seven through seventy-four. S-s-seven years."

"What were the family's living conditions while your father worked at the mill?" Sarah looked at Thomas when she asked the question and then turned to Crystal.

"We l-l-lived few hundred yards from plant ... next to r-r-river." Crystal twisted a strand of hair and her eyes darted from the tabletop to the man who sat across from her. His name was Joe Styvick and his eyes focused only on her.

"That close?" Joe interrupted. "It must have been very convenient ... living nearby."

Grace placed her hand over Crystal's and whispered something in Navajo before she responded. "Hogan already there. Plant built next to it."

"Hogan?" Joe looked to Sarah. "I don't know this word."

"The Navajo's traditional home. Hexagonal, octagonal or round, made of logs or mud, dirt floor, no electricity or running water."

Joe Styvick returned to his line of questioning. "That was good of your employer ... to make a home available to you."

"Real good," Grace nodded and lowered her eyes to the table.

Crystal exchanged words with her mother in Navajo and then turned to face the men across the table. "Sh-sh-she wants you to know we couldn't drink river water, only collect in barrels mill gave us ... you knows, for washin' clothes an stuff."

"How old were you when your parents moved to Shiprock?"

"Four."

"Tell us what you remember about living there."

"I liked to draw p-p-pictures in yellow dust on kitchen table. Mom scolded 'bout that." Still pencils suddenly took notes.

"Can your parents understand what you're telling us?" Grace and Thomas nodded. "Let the record show that Crystal's testimony is confirmed by the Yazzies."

Joe Styvick was unlike the other men at the table; he had removed his jacket and loosened his tie as soon as he'd come into the room. Now he made a show of taking out gold cuff links and rolling up his shirtsleeves. "Mrs. Redshirt ... it is Mrs.?"

"I'm d-d-divorced."

"Do you live with your parents now?"

"Some. Boys an me g-g-go between trailer in Shiprock an Sheep Ranch."

"Any of you have jobs?"

"Mom an Dad gets social security, b-b-but mostly we live on money from Mom's weavin'. I'm t-t-takin' classes at Fort Lewis College."

"Guess it would be pretty nice to get a big handout from your dad's uranium work." Joe feigned a laugh and then shuffled through some papers.

Silence.

"It says here that because you are Native American you get free tuition at the college."

Sarah Dent squirmed in her seat. "I'll take over from here," she said and turned her attention to me. "Ms. Daugherty. Please tell us about your association with the Yazzie family."

"I've known them for a year-and-a-half. Grace travels with me. I have a business buying and selling collectible art … primarily Navajo weavings."

"Does Grace Yazzie weave for you?"

"Yes. Exceptional pieces. And when we go to shows, the people love her." I glanced at Grace; her head was shyly bent forward.

"And you? How do you feel about Grace Yazzie?"

"She has a quality. A quiet dignity that speaks from her heart."

Joe Styvick cleared his throat and one of the other men unbuttoned his vest. "It's warm in here," Joe said and stood up. "Let's take five minutes."

When the group reconvened, Joe took charge again. "Ms. Yazzie, Grace … do I understand correctly that your complaints against Kerr-McKee were filed in April of 1993?"

"Aoó."

"Crystal stated earlier that your husband worked the uranium mines as early as 1934. By my calculation, that comes to thirty-three years in the mines before he came to Kerr-McKee. Why not go after the government money from RECA?"

There was an Exchange of words in Navajo. Crystal was the one to answer. "W-w-we can't prove he worked at mines."

"Are you telling us your father worked for over thirty years and there is no accountability for his labors?" Joe leaned across the table and stared into Crystal's face. "You can't even prove he worked for the mill … can you?"

Sarah held up her hand indicating for Crystal not to answer.

"Joe, you're out of line again. It clearly states in the briefs you were given that the typical method of payment to Navajos was cash. Companies didn't put them on the books, didn't collect social security. There are no records. In fact, if you read over the previously documented depositions, when the inspectors were scheduled at Kerr-McKee, Thomas, along with the other Navajo workers, was told to stay home."

An awkward quiet fell over the room.

Joe straightened his back and, in a slow methodical way, unrolled his sleeves and put the cuff links back in place. "Assuming we do believe on blind faith and the good word of these people that Thomas Yazzie was, in fact, in the employ of Kerr-McKee for the alleged seven years, how do we know that uranium, and specifically the uranium milled at the Shiprock plant, is responsible for the illnesses in his family? There are no medical records."

I was at the sheep ranch when Grace sat patiently on the edge of the couch as Crystal opened the letter with *Dent & Associates* engraved in black on the ivory colored envelope. "The subject is Kerr-McKee Corporation versus Thomas K. Yazzie." Crystal's voice was strong and confident when she read. "It's addressed to you, *Amá*. We regret…" her words trailed into silence. At the bottom was a scrawled note from Sarah, *I'm sorry.*

Crystal handed the letter to her mother; Grace stared at the paper she could not read.

"Money isn't comin'." Crystal's words slipped into Navajo and she explained that the court hadn't heard sufficient proof that her father actually worked at the uranium mill or that his death was due to uranium exposure. Grace quietly stood and crossed the living room to sit in front of an unfinished weaving on a loom.

The Ceremony

Crystal's invitation for "doin's" came ten days later. "A Blessingway," she repeated over a telephone connection that rasped and crackled. "Mom wants you to come."

I'd only read about traditional Navajo ceremonies and had no idea what I was bargaining for. Visions that ranged from cultist voodoo happenings to deep spiritual encounters raced through my mind. "What should I bring?" A myriad of other questions: *What do I wear? Where is it? What will happen? …* went unspoken.

"You don't needs to be here whole time. It's five-day ceremony…" A roar of background noise cut off her words. "Come Saturday morning … plan to stay all night."

"Where are you?" I shouted into the telephone.

"Pay phone at tradin' post in Red Valley. We needs food for Sunday. Fifty people … at Sheep Ranch."

Fifty people. Where would everyone stay? "Do I bring a sleeping bag?"

"Have mattresses in hogan. But with peoples for five days, we do lots of cookin'. Sunday is a feast. Bring food for that."

"Give me some hints on the food?"

"Jell-O salad, cookies, maybe some muffins for breakfast. We butcher a sheep an make lots of fry bread."

"For the ceremony? What can I bring for that? Maybe something for Grace?"

"Bring a blanket. I means a shawl. The *hataalii* is a woman."

"The medicine man is a woman?"

"*Aoó*. We gives *hataalii* five-hundred-dollars, a deerskin, two baskets, an a blanket. Can you bring blanket? Mom would like that."

A cotton thermal from Sears … "What kind of blanket?"

"A Pendleton Chief's blanket … one with fringe, since it's for a woman. Go to the tradin' post, they know the right kind. Oh … an bring somethin' special you wants blessed."

Finding the right Pendleton blanket was an experience in itself. The only thing I knew about the Pendletons was something I'd read in National Geographic magazine. There'd been an article that traced the "trade blanket" back to the original Hudson Bay Company. European trappers used the blankets to trade with the Blackfoot and Northern Plains Indians. The article went on to tout a quality wool blanket as an invaluable trading commodity for trappers and explorers. Then in the late 1800's, Pendleton Woolen Mills became the only mill founded specifically to produce trade blankets. Since that time the blanket's popularity had increased; it was a staple garment and trade item at powwows and other Indian gatherings.

I started my search in Durango, which was clearly a mistake. The shop owners there knew of the blankets only from a tourist's point of view. I eventually followed Crystal's instructions and went to a trading post on the reservation. From a particularly helpful young Navajo woman, I learned that the box the blanket came in was more important than the blanket itself. And it had to be a Pendleton, the smooth-wool, bold-patterned, bright-colored blanket made in Oregon. Nothing else would do. A blanket—or in this case a shawl because it had fringe—was payment for services. More times than not, the medicine man brought the newly acquired blanket, in the box, back to the trading post for pawn. The saleswoman had rarely seen a blanket being used. It was for bartering.

I shifted my Range Rover into low gear and turned from the gravel road to creep along the rutted, rock-embedded trail that stretched arrow-straight as far as my eye could see. The sun, more than halfway into its daily climb, had taken the chill from the December air. Snow was forecast in Durango, but here—less than sixty miles as the crow flies, on the high desert country of the Navajo Reservation—the horizon was cloudless. I lowered my window and gulped the pungent sage-infused air to fortify myself for the approaching day.

I'd driven on this road dozens of times and had been to countless clusters of dwellings where Navajo families lived, but today everything seemed foreign and surreal. There was the sheep pen, fenced by an odd assortment of vertically-placed aspen logs, previously used timbers, plywood, cinder blocks and corrugated metal, and the small shed-like structure off to the side of the pen where Keith, the sheepherder, lived. Then the wooden, flat-roofed garage that housed a derelict black pickup truck propped on blocks because there were no wheels, came into sight. And finally, arranged in triangular fashion, each about fifty yards apart, two pitched-roof cinderblock houses and the family hogan. Traditional in its eight-sided shape, the hogan had been modernized. Instead of being constructed by stacked logs chinked with mud, this one had plaster-covered plywood walls washed pink and the roof was shingled in silver-gray asphalt. White smoke billowed skyward from a stovepipe that extended out of a cupola erected in the center of the hogan's pyramid-shaped roof.

Pickup trucks were scattered haphazardly in the yard, and people milled about. A group of elderly men crouched in a circle under the shade of a lone tree. Young men and children chopped wood and stacked it near the entrance to the hogan. It seemed as if every eye was on my box-shaped burgundy vehicle that was far too new and clean to belong in this place. I parked as close to Crystal's truck as possible and climbed out, scanning the area in hopes of seeing a familiar face. Three dogs of a nondescript rez variety sniffed the tires and then, each in turn, lifted a leg to mark his territory.

"*Yá'át'ééh*," Crystal hollered as she came from Anna Mae's house. "You're late."

"You just said morning ... I wasn't sure." There was no excuse for my tardiness. I'd left home in plenty of time. "I stopped at the KFC in Shiprock for some coffee." I couldn't explain to myself, let alone Crystal, why I'd eaten a full breakfast, drunk four cups of coffee, and obsessed over what there would be to eat, if I'd worn the right clothes, would I be able to stay awake all night, and most of all, what the bathroom situation would be. "So what did I miss?"

"Part where *Hataalii* does sandpaintin' like your rug."

My heart sank as I realized it was the opportunity of a lifetime. "I didn't know." I'd gotten so caught up in my own stuff that I lost track of the important things.

"There's still tonight. Did you bring blanket?"

I pulled the box out of the back of the Rover, and Crystal guided me toward the hogan. "When we go in, just do what I do. I'll explain what everythin' means." We walked past the group of men and boys that chopped wood. Eyes watched from under the brims of cowboy hats and ball caps. Those I knew—Grace's husband, Thomas, and Crystal's sons, Naalzheí and Little Eagle—gave a slight nod of acknowledgement. All but Lewis, his gaze was intent and direct.

"He thinks you don't belong here," Crystal whispered and placed her hand on my arm. "But Mom an I both want you."

Crystal pulled aside a blanket, a temporary door that hung from the inside of the doorframe, and nodded for me to enter. I stepped over the threshold, onto a floor of hard-packed dirt, and into a darkened enclosure. The only daylight came from two small windows and the hole in the cupola in the roof. I'd been inside the hogan before, but today everything looked different. A fire burned hot in an oil-drum stove with a square section cut from its side for inserting logs. It sat in the center of the room; a pipe protruded from the top of the drum and extended up to a hole in the roof. The heat was oppressive, and the smoke-filled room carried a faint odor of bodies mingled with the sweet pungency of cedar and sage.

When my eyes adjusted to the dim light, shapes began to form. I saw dozens of mattresses lining the side walls of the circular enclosure, and, to my right, I saw a makeshift curtained area. I later learned it was the dressing room and bathroom accommodations for Grace. Along the west wall, directly opposite the door we'd entered, was an upholstered couch mounded with blankets.

Crystal guided me in a clockwise direction while admonishing that one must always move in the path of the sun when coming into or going out of a hogan. She led me to a woman who sat cross-legged on a mattress next to the couch. They exchanged Navajo words.

"This is our *hataalii*," Crystal said. Unlike other introductions to Navajo people, there was no handshake or formal greeting. The medicine woman merely gave a nod and uttered the word *hágoshíí*.

"She says okay you're here."

Crystal took the Pendleton box from me and laid it on the blanket alongside a Navajo ceremonial basket and a deer hide. "All part of payment for ceremony," she explained, and motioned for me to follow her to sit on the mattress on the other side of the couch from the *hataalii*. It was then I saw Grace under the mound of blankets. "She sleeps," Crystal said, "makes ready."

Crystal took several deep breaths and began to explain the rituals of the medicine woman. "Sandpaintin' was there," Crystal said, tilting her chin to point toward the dirt floor in front of the couch where her mother slept. I leaned back against the wall and closed my eyes while Crystal described the ceremony; the images appeared in my mind. She told of a sandpainting that resembled a large wagon wheel with a square center hub and spokes that radiated out to the edges. A U-shaped rainbow surrounded three sides of the wheel; the spokes of the wheel were ornately detailed figures—with their feet toward the center hub and heads pointed north, south, east and west—and four colored branches: blue, yellow, white and black, separated the figures. The four figures were the Holy Ones, and the branches represented the sacred herbs used in the healing ceremony. White Guard and Black Guard, two figures at the north and south end of the rainbow, kept the good spirits inside the rainbow while the opening let the bad spirits out. She told of a sandpainting like the one that hung over my fireplace.

And she told of the ritual transformation: the painting of designs on Grace's face and chest, and the pine boughs woven through her hair. The transformation turned Grace to the likeness of a Navajo deity. The image of Grace's being was powerful and it wrapped me in a warm blanket of love. I must have dozed because the next thing I heard was Crystal's voice, and it came to me from a distance. "You hungry?" I opened my eyes to a darkened hogan; the only light was from the glow of burning logs. "You slept. But now must eat."

We made our way to Anna Mae's house. It was full of activity. Women with velvet blouses and strands of turquoise and silver around their necks pulled fistfuls of flour dough from a bowl and patted it between their palms and handed perfectly round pieces off for cooking. Other women sat on the hearth of a stone fireplace and cooked the dough on a wire-mesh grate that straddled a bed of hot ashes. Some of the uncooked discs of bread dough were given to women in the kitchen who stood by large skillets of hot oil and turned the dough cakes into puffy, golden-brown fry bread.

A table in the kitchen held a platter filled with small cakes made of corn meal. Next to the cakes were several varieties of squash and melons, bowls of mashed potatoes, plates of corn-on-the-cob, containers of Jell-O, dozens of grocery store boxes of bakery items, and of course, the ubiquitous fry bread. Crystal handed me a plastic bowl and led the way to the mutton stew. Strung across the front of the kitchen cabinets was a cream-colored tubular object draped like a swag with the knobs of cabinet doors serving as hooks.

"What's that?" I asked.

"Sheep's gut," Crystal said. "Head's over there ... in cardboard box. *Shínálí* uses gut for sausages, an' head's for Sunday's feast."

My appetite for mutton was gone. I set the bowl aside and filled a plate from the smorgasbord of familiar items. People ate in silence; they focused on their food instead of mealtime chitchat. I occupied myself by observing the men and women's faces and behavior. When they did speak with one another, even with no understanding of what they said, I sensed a courtesy, a granting of time for each person to say his mind. People did not go back for seconds, they mounded their plates with food the first time. And when they had taken their fill, they used aluminum foil to cover the uneaten food on the plate—a custom I'd learned was very common. The women, not the men, rarely finished a plate of food. Leftovers were taken home for the next meal.

When I'd eaten, I scraped what was left into the garbage bucket for the sheep, and then surreptitiously looked around to see if anyone had noticed my wastefulness.

"What happens now?" I asked Crystal.

"We wait and rest. Chantin' starts hour before midnight."

"Crystal, I don't understand why Grace is having a ceremony. Does she think this will get rid of the cancer?"

Crystal was slow to answer. "I don't think Mom believes cancer will go away. But, in our ways, she can't stop tryin' … to just think what White doctor says would be givin' up."

I left the heat of the crowded house for fresh air. The sky was a black tapestry with one small crescent tear and millions of pinholes that let through a brilliant light. The distant howl of a lone coyote set the dogs that slept in the sheep pens to barking. As the time approached eleven, interior lights of pickup trucks flashed as men and women crawled out of cab seats where they had slept.

"It's time now," Crystal said and rested her hand on my arm. "Did you bring somethin' to be blessed?" I reached into the passenger side of the Rover and retrieved my double doll. It had come to symbolize the transformation that was occurring in my life. It seemed fitting for the medicine woman to bless the changes.

I'd shown the double doll to Crystal early on in our relationship and told her the story of meeting Nanabah in the canyon north of Gallup. I'd also apologized for the toll time had taken and explained that once the doll had been beautifully adorned with silver beads and, of course, the thunderbird pin. She was fascinated by the magic created by turning the doll upside down, *Diné* and *Bilagáana*. And when we made trips together across the reservation in search of weavings, Crystal often found places that surely must have been where Nanabah lived. She was disturbed by the damage time had taken on the doll—the seams that gave way due to rotted threads, the missing decorations and moth-eaten fabric. As Len and I worked on refurbishing Anna Mae and Roy's home, the women did the same for my double doll: new clothing, handspun yarn for hair, embroidered faces on new material, shiny silver buttons and colorful beads. They did everything necessary to bring the doll back to its original state. "We think doll needs arms," Crystal explained when she returned the anatomically altered double doll. "Can't give hugs without 'em."

Crystal smiled when she saw the item I brought to be blessed. We joined the silent figures that moved ghost-like into the dimly lit hogan. Grace sat regal and godly, nodding as people entered the room. Her purple velvet blouse covered the body paint; her face was still streaked in colors of red, black, and white; and her hair was woven with pine boughs and desert grasses.

"I'm glad you come," she said when I leaned down to kiss her cheek.

To stave off tears that formed and promised to spill over, I moved quickly to my designated place. Crystal and I spoke in hushed tones until she announced it was time to fetch Anna Mae. The hogan began to fill with people. They came in silently and sat on the mattresses. Forty or so people huddled in small groups against the sidewalls talking quietly among themselves—men on the south side of the hogan, women on the north. They spoke to one another in low voices, a monotone cadence of words accentuated with long pregnant pauses. The *hataalii* and her four male assistants assembled in a circle next to the couch. Grace's breathing was deep and labored. They began a low prayerful chant. Once they began, the chanting would continue until dawn.

"Medicine Bundle," Crystal whispered and tilted her chin toward the blanket where the *hataalii* sat, "has sand from Four Sacred Mountains." Buckskin, decorated with beads and small stones, was wrapped around a bundle of objects. People brought small objects and laid them on the medicine woman's blanket, next to the bundle. "For blessin'," Crystal said. "Take your doll."

When I returned, Crystal seemed in a rush to explain as much as possible about what would be happening: "Can't talk once they starts chantin'." Throughout the night the songs would tell the Navajo Creation story. "See medicine bundle ... full of things chants talk 'bout. *Hataalii*

240

takes out each piece, one at a time, and holds up ... then sings of importance. Lessons 'bout life an how to live. *Diné* believes if we follows what chants say we bring self into harmony ... maybe even cured of sickness." I'd read the chants were sung in the old Navajo language, and that no two stories repeated themselves. Becoming a medicine man required one commit to memory a Sing, and that any one *hataalii* can only learn two or three Sings in his or her lifetime. The task was tantamount to committing our Old Testament to memory and reciting it in a chanting form.

A loud drumbeat signaled the start. There was an excitement and tension in the air that kept me alert for the first couple of hours. As the ceremony continued, the heat and the smells within the confined space became overwhelming. Crystal had warned that I could leave only if it were a real emergency; I was sitting on the floor next to Grace, and to get up would be a disturbance. Each chant was supposedly different, but to me, they all sounded alike—the strange language sung with an undulating rhythm, and the constant beating of the drum.

To stay awake, I created a memory game whereby I recalled all the recent times spent with Grace. I thought of our first trip together: Grace's embarrassment when I opened the orange suitcase to find the heavy metate, her smile as she used the prayer sticks to stir the *atolé* for the Amish, her eyes opened wide as Ruth's daughters brought out the delicate and perfectly matched china. I remembered Grace, in all her colorful dress and magnificent jewelry, lovingly guiding the hands of young Rachel through the intricate motions of weaving; the stares and gawks from passersby as she made her way down the Atlantic City boardwalk in full traditional Navajo dress, eating a stick of cotton candy; and her total delight when we toured the nation's capital and she received special treatment as a relative of the Navajo Nation's Vice president. Like peeling away the skins of an onion, my heart opened to the memories.

Midway through the long night, a loud drumbeat sounded. "To use bathroom or catch fresh air," Crystal explained. "Only few minutes." It was a welcome break. I made a beeline to Anna Mae's house and stood in line to use the small bathroom. When I returned to the hogan, my clockwise entry required that I pass in front of Lewis. I could feel him watching me. Images of the young Indian boy sitting on his horse came. Nanabah trivialized the disdain he showed by spitting. I looked Lewis' way, and our eyes met. He, with all of his bullish behaviors, became that boy. Streams of words flooded through my mind: *You're only a girl … We must cleanse you of your filth …You don't belong here … What is your agenda?*

His words, "what is your agenda," came as an affront the day they were spoken; now they crashed around me and forced an internal answer. Early on I tried to convince myself that I was working to help the women, that my actions were altruistic, but in my heart I knew this was wrong. All my efforts surrounding the business were purely for me, my need to prove that I could be successful doing things my way. And every word of caution or admonishment added fuel to that lifelong pursuit to be judged worthy.

There was a time when I faced challenges with a vengeance; I loved the surge of power that came over me when a successful executive asked for help; and I thrived on the game called success—until that rainy day in New York City. I remembered my feet being drenched as a taxicab sped through a nearby puddle, the faulty umbrella that caused the ruin of a new silk suit, the way the water dripped down the back of my neck and my silk blouse clung to my chest as I waited in the boardroom. And I remembered rushing people circling by me as I knelt on the sidewalk and cradled the pigeon with a broken wing.

"I'm gonna fix him up, Missy," the homeless man said and lovingly took the pigeon. And I remembered wondering, *What about me?*

That day brought me to this place, my place for healing. The overly warm hogan became my "somewhere else"; it transformed into the dark, cool cave where the wounded bird was healed. I watched the *hataalii*, chanting all the time, pull a tightly wrapped bundle of sage from a wooden box that sat next to her medicine bundle. She lit the sage stick by the fire and, when it began to smoke, slowly waved it over the treasures people brought for blessing. And then, just as the young boy had done, she passed the smoldering sage over the heads of everyone present.

The chanting continued long into the early morning hours. I don't know if I slept or not, but I experienced a powerful dream-like vision.

I was at a party somewhere; I couldn't tell where. It was like a ballroom in a large hotel. There were lots of people that I knew, going way back to when I was little, but also some people from now. Dad was there, along with a way-out preacher from my tent-revival days—I hadn't thought of him for a long time, the trader who called me Little Lady, the vice president from the stock exchange, and even Lewis. People appeared for a while and then changed into someone else. Everyone, everyone except me, was a man. Janice Gamblin was there too, but she was a man. Len came into the dream—not at first, but later—he kept coming in and then fading away.

At first I was in the ballroom, but it changed to a subway platform in New York City. And I was wearing a silly chiffon thing. It had dozens of brightly colored scarves attached at my waist to make a billowy skirt. I couldn't tell what the top was like, but the skirt, it was like the skirt made me feel important. But then it changed and made me feel very feminine.

I was on the subway platform and all the men made a circle around me; they grabbed at the scarves and tried to rip them away. I was holding my skirt, fighting them off. The men were stripping away everything that was me. My husband was one of the men, but he kept changing. Sometimes he pulled at the scarves with the rest, and then the next minute, he helped me to hold onto them. Then it was over, the tearing away of the scarves. I gave up fighting and was just there, crumpled in the center of the circle.

And then I flew out of the room. At first I was on a blanket that carried me, but then the blanket turned into a large white bird. I was on its back, soaring over the world and looking down. It was beautiful and calm, so very calm—like when I was a child and could fly in my dreams.

Dawn approached and the chanting stopped. People left the ceremony to find a place to be alone with their God. I gathered up my double doll and walked a short distance from the hogan. Streaks of chrome yellows and gold gilded the tops of the mountains and small, wispy clouds randomly turned different shades of saffron, rose and pink. Hulking rock formations, sentinels over time to the ritual of early morning prayers, emerged as the sky lightened. Above it all was Venus, the Morning Star, brighter than ever, heralding the start of another day. Carefully, trying to remember every small detail that Grace had taught me, I pulled out my deerskin pouch and said my prayers. *"Help me to understand and live the message sent to me tonight. Soften my heart against my adversaries so that I may know how to show my love. But most of all, be with Grace."* And I scattered the sacred corn pollen in the four directions and to Father Sky and Mother Earth. It would be many months before the understanding part of my prayer was answered.

Only after the sun crested the mountaintops did I turn and head back to the hogan. The red blanket hung over the doorway of a quiet room. Grace was alone; she laid motionless on the couch, her hair still done up on the top of her head, woven with pine branches, and the painted designs were on her face. She was in a complete state of serenity and peace. I sat on the edge of the couch with my hand cupped over hers and breathed in the cool sweetness of the air. And then Grace motioned for me to lean down so she could whisper to me.

"Today we walked in beauty together," Grace said and closed her eyes.

Last Breath Wishes

By mid-November Grace had entered the Farmington hospital where she could receive the necessary painkillers. It was the day after Christmas when I received the call. "Sharleen, I needs your help. *Shimá's* time is close ... you are only one I can ask 'bout things. Plans must be made ... an none of family will help."

When I'd attended the Blessingway Ceremony, I learned that Navajos did not talk of or prepare for death. Life insurance policies are nonexistent on the reservation. There is a belief that to acknowledge the bad is to give it power and make it happen.

Crystal and I sat beside Grace's bed for four days. After they gave her morphine she would sleep. During those times we went to the mortuary and the florist to make the arrangements no one else wanted to think about. At Grace's request I took my laptop computer and drafted what she called her "Last Breath Wishes."

I, Grace Yazzie, on the 29th day of November 1994, being of sound mind, do hereby bequeath the following belongings to the named individuals:

- *Two acres of farm land west of the school in Red Valley to Naalzheí Redshirt (executed by Crystal Redshirt)*

- *The first name on the grazing permit, Grace Yazzie, changed to Crystal Redshirt. Naalzheí and Little Eagle to be 1ˢᵗ name recipients along with Crystal Redshirt when they come of age*
- *Black GMC truck and gray double cab Ford truck to Crystal Redshirt*
- *All "in and out pawn" jewelry to Crystal Redshirt*
- *Pendleton blankets and all "put away" items to Crystal Redshirt*
- *House at Sheep Ranch, furniture and contents to Crystal Redshirt*
- *Two large looms, one small loom, battens, combs to Crystal Redshirt*
- *All dishes, kitchenware and attic items to Crystal Redshirt*
- *All sheep and five cows belonging to Grace Yazzie to Crystal Redshirt*
- *Permission granted to Anna Mae Hoskie to butcher a goat from time to time*
- *Farm equipment: tractor, water pumps, etc. to Lewis McGuire*
- *All clothing (including blue sweater) to Crystal Redshirt*
- *Ownership of the trailer in Shiprock to Crystal Redshirt*
- *Family ceremonial box and its contents to Lewis McGuire*

I further request that if the $100,000 uranium settlement money comes to Thomas Yazzie, Sharleen Daugherty is named as Trustee.

Signed: _____   *Date: 11/29/94*
          Grace Yazzie

Grace had to ask for the word trustee. She explained that in her culture the men made the decisions, but the women owned the homes, the livestock and any other tangible asset. She wanted to ensure that the money went to the care of Crystal and her two sons. It was strange to me that no items were left to her husband—her grandchildren, her brother, her daughter and her mother were mentioned, but not her husband. The only mention of Thomas came in regard to the possible uranium settlement.

The last lines of Grace's will: *I further request that when the $100,000 uranium settlement money comes to Thomas Yazzie, Sharleen Daugherty is named as Trustee,* were nothing more than wishful thinking—we all knew the money would never come. In my visits with Grace I'd been aware that her material possessions were few, but it took her will to show how few. Material possessions had always been for me a way to judge my success, to show the world, and myself, how accomplished I had become. And yet this woman, in all her beauty and strength, could list her tangible worth on a single sheet of paper.

That afternoon I sat next to Grace's bed. We laughed, and we cried; we shared moments that she and I both knew were close to her last. She slept between periods when she had enough strength to talk, and I held her small, wasted hand.

I'd been through the deathwatch twice before. The first time was with my father—his passing was peaceful. He used his deathbed to preach to others and to me about indiscretions. Mother left in agonizing fear of retribution. Grace would move to the next world as though it was nothing more than another part of her journey.

Grace jolted me from my reflections by touching my hand and asking for a sip of water. And then she motioned for me to come close—she had something to say. Her eyes were different. They held a pleading and fear that was not her demeanor. When I leaned my body toward her, she raised herself from the pillow and spoke in a rasping whisper. "*Adeezhí*, I needs you to be mother to Crystal ... she has only Thomas now."

My first reaction was shock and fear, but my vision of flying out of the hogan during the Blessingway Ceremony had marked a gigantic shift for me. I was no longer shackled by the fear of failure and inadequacy that had attached itself throughout my life. And she called me Sister. Since the adoption Anna Mae frequently referred to me as her daughter, but this was the first time Grace called me her sister. Unlike my father who pushed me away in his dying, Grace was pulling me tightly to her family. The trust she showed me by asking that I protect her most precious possession gave me pause. I didn't really know what it meant to be a mother in the Navajo culture. With my own children I focused on love and acceptance of who they were. Perhaps because I'd spent a lifetime seeking approval, it was important to me that my children not be caught in the same vicious cycle. Grace, in her shy, unassuming way, went through her days full of love, unconditional love that trusted and accepted without regard for circumstances, the kind of love that could only come through *hózhó*: balance and harmony—spiritually, emotionally, physically and mentally.

I was in the early stages of finding *hózhó* within my own life. I didn't know how to help Crystal find it in hers, but I knew this was now my responsibility.

"Yes, *Adeezhí*, of course."

In Beauty it is Finished

PREVIEW FROM

SHE FACES HER ENEMY

The Journey Continues

BOOK 2 IN THE MEMOIR TRILOGY

An Old Woman Weeps

Grace passed the day after I wrote her "Last Breath Wishes." The funeral was set for Sunday, December 4, a day I remember well. I left Durango early the morning of the services and drove to Farmington. The *Bilagáana* or White Man portion of the ceremony was held at a mortuary and much like other funerals I'd attended.

Lewis was there. I knew he would be. "So you come to this too," he remarked tersely. We milled in the lobby before the start of the service. "Haven't you done enough already?"

My legs trembled as I faced him, and I felt a familiar constriction in my throat. Words formed in my mind, words that would cut through Lewis' arrogance and show him that I would not be intimidated. And then the image of Grace Yazzie, her face and chest painted to resemble a deity and pine boughs woven through her hair, replaced the words. I felt the fight drain from my body, replaced by a calm inner strength. By Grace's wish, I was now the one to stand between this man and her adopted daughter, Crystal. And Grace, with her loving, non-confronting manner, had shown me how to do it.

"I loved your sister. Like you, I come to grieve and pay my last respects." Lewis merely turned away.

After the service an odd assortment of vehicles left the mortuary. New and old pickup trucks, regular sedans, my Range Rover, two limousines and a hearse drove in caravan the eighty-some miles to a bluff near Grace's home in Red Rock Valley. When we left the paved highway, we traveled another fifteen-or-so miles on a gravel road, and then turned onto a trail that was nothing more than two ruts across the desert. It took us to the base of a flat-topped mountain. As the hearse laboriously inched its way up the face of the mountain it became evident that many of the vehicles would find it impossible to get to the burial site. The road to the top of the mesa was barely a road at all, and recent rains turned it into a treacherous, slick-clay roadbed that would become more deeply rutted with each vehicle. Only those with high-clearance, 4-wheel drive could make the steep climb. My Range Rover was well suited for these conditions. And so I made many trips up and down the hill, filling my vehicle with mourners and transporting them from the desert below to the burial site.

On top of the mesa, I stepped out of the driver's seat, gulped the cold, fresh air and slowly turned to take in the majesty of the distant mountains. It was as though the entire world had opened around me. The largest and most visible landmass was Sleeping Ute Mountain— shaped like a reclining Indian with a full headdress flowing north, arms folded over the chest, and feet pointing skyward. The Utes have a legend regarding the creation of how this place came to be as it is today. A great Warrior God was hurt, so he lay down to rest and fell into a deep sleep. The blood from his wound turned into living water for all creatures to drink. The massive form loomed over the mesa and was the perfect place for Grace, like the weary warrior, to lie down.

Folding chairs were clustered around a huge mound of dirt and stones left from the digging of the grave. A bitter cold wind blew across the mourners as they huddled together amongst the chairs where Crystal and her sons sat.

I took my place next to Crystal's oldest son, Naalzheí, and to make conversation asked about the hole in the ground. "How did you get it dug? It's huge." It was a standard coffin size in length and width, but was at least ten feet deep. I knew the difficulty in getting a shovel through the hard-packed clay of this country.

"We pay utility company to bring backhoe. Grave has to be deep 'cause of robbers," he replied. "*Hamá sání* will be buried with her favorite jewelry an a basket she wove for her weddin'. We have to make it difficult or grave-robbers can take things."

Naalzheí was only ten, but because of his size and demeanor he appeared several years older. He had the makings of a classic linebacker—a thick neck, a full, hard-packed upper body, and massive legs for support. A quiet, shy child, he seemed to carry a sad resentment hidden below the surface. I had talked with Crystal about this; she explained that the anger was directed toward the father who abandoned the family. His younger brother, Little Eagle, was totally different in appearance and mannerisms. He wore his hair in a long, single braid that reached almost to his waist, had a spark of mischief in his eyes, and was delicate enough in facial features to be mistaken for a girl. Little Eagle was a dancer. Grace had spent many hours making the ceremonial regalia necessary for him to compete at the Indian fairs and powwows.

The grief on the mesa was palpable. A man I'd seen for the first time at the mortuary stood and said several prayers. He was dressed in beaded buckskins, and his hair was plaited in an assortment of small braids that were tied with leather and feathers. He held a gourd rattle that he shook after each prayer—always to the Four Directions and then up high and down low, over Grace's casket. When the prayers were over, Lewis' son, Raymond, stepped forward and played a mournful melody on an Indian flute. He played with such resonance and clarity that surely the Gods must have wept.

The burial service lasted over four hours. There were only two small shovels to cover Grace with her blanket of sacred earth. During the shoveling process an ancient metate, like the one Grace had packed in her suitcase when she traveled with me to Pennsylvania, was unearthed and set aside, creating a perfect headstone for the grave. The metate was seen as a good omen, proof that an ancient woman had inhabited this place. Most of the men shoveled in rotation while the women took reprieve from the bitter cold by climbing into my Rover and other trucks that had made it to the top of the mesa.

On one of my times in the warmth, I shared the seat of my vehicle with the wife of the Vice President of the Navajo Nation. From her I learned that Grace's maternal clan, the Yucca Fruit, produced many respected political leaders of the *Diné*, and that Lewis, when he came back from Korea, took a place of status and worth among his peers. He was quickly elected president of his chapter house and, eventually, a council delegate. I watched Lewis from a distance; it was apparent he was accustomed to being in charge. He held back from the work of shoveling and made it his job to monitor the others. It seemed appropriate that Lewis had changed his name from Hoskie to McGuire; his ways were that of the *bilagáana*.

Just as the mourners needed help up the mountain, they needed help to get down. I was one of the last to arrive at Anna Mae's house. Due to the cold December wind and the lengthy burial ceremony, she and several other elderly women stayed behind to prepare food for the mourners.

The warmth of Anna Mae and Roy's living room was comforting, and the smoke from the wood-burning fireplace smelled of piñon and mesquite. Grandma stood in the center of the room surrounded by at least a dozen elderly women. Bertha was there; our eyes met briefly, but she quickly cast her gaze to the floor. I wondered what went through her mind as I continued to appear at family gatherings—a reminder of her dishonesty. It seemed a lifetime ago that I walked down the dark hallway and stood in front of her empty loom. My thoughts had focused then on her betrayal. Today I saw only the bent body of a woman who'd spent a lifetime in disservice to herself. I moved to where she stood, cupped her frail hand in mine and said, "*ádaa áhólya*." 'Take care of yourself' was the only Navajo phrase I knew that was even remotely appropriate to the circumstances. Bertha acknowledged with *aoó*.

Most of the women were busy. Some patted out dough and cooked the bread on a metal grate in the fireplace, others tended to a pot of mutton stew that simmered on the stove. Anna Mae looked in my direction and, for a brief moment, all language barriers were gone. The sheer grief in her eyes spoke more than words could ever say. This strong, proud woman came to me and allowed me to engulf her in my arms as she wept. We stood there, for what seemed like an eternity, as Grandma clung to me and sobbed. The other women—sisters, cousins, nieces and friends—glanced furtively and tried not to show disrespect by watching Anna Mae cry.

"You probably have no idea the meanin' of what just happened," Crystal whispered and pulled me off to a corner of the room. "In our ways, cryin' is sign of weakness, an' huggin' is not acceptable, 'specially huggin' a *bilagáana*."

"Is this why you said my double doll needed arms?"

"*Shimasáni's* idea. First thing we all noticed 'bout you. You likes to hug."

I finished my meal and was preparing to leave when Lewis approached me. "You come into places where you do not belong." His eyes blazed as he spat the words in my face. "Then you violate our most basic customs."

He was standing too close.

"We have ceremonies to cleanse our spirits when we have come into contact with the *bilagáana*. You show disrespect by huggin' my mother, and you bring shame to all of us by lettin' her cry. Is there nothin' that is sacred to you?"

Lewis' admonishment stung like the deathbed words of my father: *You shame your mother and me with your actions.* Heat rose to my face, and my throat constricted, but I was able to allow a Navajo silence before I spoke. "I'm sorry, *shiánaaí,* that you think I am being disrespectful. I loved your sister and was only comforting *Amá* in her grief."

Lewis' face turned red and he blustered. "You ... you call me brother and, and ... you have no right!"

"Oh, but I do. Ask Anna Mae. It has been over a month since she adopted me as her daughter. That makes me your sister and an aunt to Crystal. Actually, on her deathbed, your sister requested that I be a mother to your daughter, Crystal."

Silence.

"I think I can understand your concern, Lewis, but I have no resentment in my heart for you. And I am trying to learn the *Diné* ways. I know about showing respect for family members and that family priorities always come first. And I know about sharing material possessions if a family member is in need. You now are part of my family, and I will treat you that way." Lewis said nothing. He simply turned and walked out of the house. The hushed room returned to the low buzz of conversation.

Anna Mae was the matriarch; she was ninety-two-years old. Perhaps it was the fact that I was not Indian that enabled her, as she mourned the passing of her favorite daughter, to let her grief show and to cross over that culture line. I'll never know for certain, but looking back, I know that on that day, holding Anna Mae in my arms as she wept, my status and role in the family was changed forever. At future gatherings I was no longer a guest—my presence was assumed.

About the Author

S harleen Daugherty grew up in Albuquerque, New Mexico. She left the Land of Enchantment in 1959 to pursue her education and career as a computer applications consultant. Daugherty held a variety of jobs on the East Coast that ultimately led to owning and managing Business Systems Solutions, Inc. By 1994 Daugherty had sold her computer consulting business, moved to Colorado, and started the Durango Trading Company. In 2005 Daugherty received an MFA in Creative Nonfiction Writing from Goucher College in Towson, Maryland and began to write about her experiences with the Navajo people. Her publications include essays in the anthologies, Voices of New Mexico and Voices of New Mexico, Too; a 2004 Navajo Nation Museum catalog, Men Who Weave; and an article, Navajo Weaving: Alive and Well in the April 5, 1999, edition of Home Furnishings News.

Sharleen currently lives with her husband and two dogs in Silver City, New Mexico. In 2006 she founded a program called *Literacy Alive* with a commitment to promote the love of reading and writing among children and young adults throughout southwestern New Mexico and the Navajo Reservation. This program has published the anthologies, Young Voices of Silver City and Literacy Alive: Young Voices of Silver City, 2014.

Sharleen Daugherty
SharleenDaughertyAuthor@gmail.com
SharleenDaughertyAuthor.com
LiteracyAliveSilverCity.org

CPSIA information can be obtained at www.ICGtesting.com
Printed in the USA
LVOW08*0656270714

396217LV00003B/74/P